Testimonials

'With her trademark charismatic writing style, Helena offers in her book a whole range of practical tips for team leaders, based on the best available science, on how we can communicate with colleagues to promote a productive and positive working environment.'

Ben Bruton
Partner, Winston Strawn LLP

'Helena has done a wonderful job in making the complex science of the brain and how it works understandable and useful for everyday living. What Helena shares in the book helps us understand and answer why. . ..'

Regina Godvin
World Account Manager, Givaudan Flavours and Fragrances Inc.

'Working with Children and Young People on a daily basis I need to understand how their brains work and why they behave the way they do. Helena's book does just that. It's extremely insightful and is a useful tool for me to use to excel in my role.'

Jane Grieve
Children & Young Persons Police Officer, Essex Police

'An easy yet insightful read explaining how to keep learning and stay receptive to new ideas, whilst providing helpful tips for a healthier brain.'

Denise Jagger
Pro Chancellor, University of York & Director Bellway PLC

'Helena has captured the most difficult subject to comprehend and made it possible for everyone who reads her book to understand the brain and use it for everyday life. The book has helped me to transform myself and my business. I can't thank you enough!'

Erick Kervaon
General Manager, Bingham Riverhouse Hotel

'As a psychotherapist I have found this book an invaluable tool as it explains the functioning of the brain in such a clear and concise way. Helena has managed to write about the brain in a style that is easy to understand, and I would recommend this book to anyone who wants to know more about this fascinating subject.'

Tracy Northampton
UKCP/BACP Accredited Psychotherapist

'I can't think of a better time to explore ways in which we maximize our ability and in so doing, take greater control of our destiny. This book can get us there.'

Eileen Redmond-Macken
Private Banking, Investec Bank PLC

'Helena is hugely talented in simplifying our understanding of our most complex organ: the human brain. This book is supported by a multitude of examples from scientific research. It is a must read for anyone who is interested in the psychology of human behaviour and in understanding what influences our perceptions and the way we interact with others. '

Karim Smaira
Founder and CEO, Genpharm Services

'Such a brilliant book, both interesting personally but above all of practical value in business. I applied several of the insights and seen tangible results. For example, we reversed the order of our wine list as a result of the section on anchoring, and wine sales jumped 15% overnight.'

Simon Thomas
CEO, The Hippodrome Casino

'I cannot recommend this fascinating book highly enough! Presented in a clear, logical and accessible way, it has enabled me to understand the most complex organ in my body to new and enlightening depths. It also offers a host of practical ways to apply evidence-based neuroscience to our personal lives in order to enhance our communication and relationships with others, as well as to improve our own mental and physical well-being. I'm already reaping the benefits - read this book and so will you! Rachel Walker

Clinical Scientist, Independent Vascular Diagnostics Ltd

Why We Do What We Do

Why We Do What We Do

Understanding our brain to get the best out of ourselves and others

HELENA BOSCHI

WILEY

This edition first published 2020
© 2020 Helena Boschi

Registered office
John Wiley & Sons Ltd, The Atrium, Southern Gate, Chichester, West Sussex, PO19 8SQ,
United Kingdom

For details of our global editorial offices, for customer services and for information about how to apply
for permission to reuse the copyright material in this book please see our website at www.wiley.com.

Wiley publishes in a variety of print and electronic formats and by print-on-demand. Some
material included with standard print versions of this book may not be included in e-books or in
print-on-demand. If this book refers to media such as a CD or DVD that is not included in the
version you purchased, you may download this material at http://booksupport.wiley.com. For
more information about Wiley products, visit www.wiley.com.

Designations used by companies to distinguish their products are often claimed as trademarks.
All brand names and product names used in this book are trade names, service marks,
trademarks or registered trademarks of their respective owners. The publisher is not associated
with any product or vendor mentioned in this book.

Limit of Liability/Disclaimer of Warranty: While the publisher and author have used their best
efforts in preparing this book, they make no representations or warranties with respect to the
accuracy or completeness of the contents of this book and specifically disclaim any implied
warranties of merchantability or fitness for a particular purpose. It is sold on the understanding
that the publisher is not engaged in rendering professional services and neither the publisher nor
the author shall be liable for damages arising herefrom. If professional advice or other expert
assistance is required, the services of a competent professional should be sought.

Library of Congress Cataloging-in-Publication Data

Names: Boschi, Helena, author.
Title: Why we do what we do : understanding our brain to get the best out of
  ourselves and others / Helena Boschi.
Description: First Edition. | Hoboken : Wiley, 2019. | Includes index. |
  Identifiers: LCCN 2019001150 (print) | LCCN 2019011756 (ebook) | ISBN
  9781119561545 (Adobe PDF) | ISBN 9781119561538 (ePub) | ISBN 9781119561491
  (paperback) | ISBN 9781119561545 (ePDF)
Subjects: LCSH: Self-help techniques. | Brain. | BISAC: SELF-HELP / General.
Classification: LCC BF632 (ebook) | LCC BF632 .B647 2019 (print) | DDC 153—dc23
LC record available at https://lccn.loc.gov/2019001150

Cover Design: Wiley
Cover Image: © nicoolay / iStock.com

Set in 12/14.5 pt KeplarStd Light by SPi Global, Chennai, India

Printed and bound by CPI Group (UK) Ltd, Croydon, CR0 4YY

10 9 8 7 6 5 4 3 2 1

Contents

About the Author

Helena Boschi is a psychologist specialising in applied neuroscience.

Helena is a business practitioner turned practical neuroscientist and has spent many years in listed multinational companies working in sales, marketing, talent management, organisation design and leadership development. She is uniquely placed to bring the world of neuroscience to the business context in a pragmatic and relevant way, using her knowledge of what businesses and business leaders need.

Organisations worldwide now use Helena as a speaker and an educator to help them understand and benefit from neuroscience that explains why we do what we do. She works closely with her clients to shape new thinking and design creative learning initiatives, particularly in the areas of leadership and team development, intercultural communication and organisational change. Helena is particularly passionate about improving physical and psychological wellbeing in a world that is placing increasing demands on our biological and cognitive resources.

Offering a range of compelling messages that are backed by science, grounded in the real world and communicated in a style that engages her audiences, Helena is dedicated to encouraging people to take greater responsibility for the long-term functioning and health of their brain and the brains of those around them. She is a member of the British Psychological Society.

If you would like to contact Helena about speaking or presenting, please email her at: helena@chequeredleopard.com

About Lansons

Lansons is a leading reputation management and public relations consultancy advising companies, organisations and governments across the world.

Organisations with the best reputations outperform rivals in a myriad of tangible ways from recruiting higher quality people to succeeding with smaller marketing budgets to exerting greater influence over governments. We believe that every organisation should consciously manage its reputation, not just in times of crisis.

Formed in 1989, we've won over 80 awards for our work. We lead our industry on gender equality, giving back, employee ownership and being a great place to work.

Our approach is to challenge thinking and innovate, helping clients communicate more effectively. Applying neuroscience to communications is an important part of this. That's why we've supported Dr Helena Boschi in bringing this book to a global audience.

To find out more about Lansons visit www.lansons.com.

Acknowledgements

A huge debt of gratitude goes to the many wonderful people who have encouraged me to write this book and who have always shown so much enthusiasm for and interest in what I do.

First I must thank all the scientists, authors and psychologists who have permitted me to feature their work, as well as those whom I have cited throughout this book. Their work is the reason this book exists. I must, however, issue a cautionary note to the same esteemed community that, in the attempt to provide an easy-to-understand guide to the brain for non-scientists, some of the content may seem over-simplified in places. For this I apologise and hope that the book will be received in the spirit in which it is intended.

I am particularly indebted to Lansons, the reputation management consultancy that has promoted this book and to Clare Parsons and Tony Langham, Lansons' founders, for their continued and positive support. In particular, Suzanne Ellis, Lansons' Director in Communications for Change and Transformation, has shown faith in me and the book from the beginning. Suzanne urged me to write this book and has always been an invaluable source of energy and guidance. During the course of our respective professional engagements and work together, Suzanne and I have increasingly recognised the critical importance of brain health and wellbeing throughout life. Special thanks must go to Emma Read, who has been an invaluable pair of eyes, and Jennifer Ryle for her masterful designs.

Thank you to Annie, Kelly, Caroline and the Wiley team for their professional expertise and insights throughout this process and for working with us all in such a spirit of collaboration. Caroline in particular has given so much of her time to getting this book across the finish line.

I owe a great deal to Denise Jagger, Pro Chancellor, University of York & Director Bellway plc, who has given my work and this book a great deal of her time and who has always been wonderful to work with.

I am also grateful to my fantastic friends, colleagues and clients all over the world, who have inspired me to put what I talk about into writing and who have supported me so much over the years.

Thank you too to Dr Steve Trenoweth for his advice and guidance throughout the whole process. His experience, wisdom and humour are always hugely valued.

Finally, my overwhelming appreciation goes to Stephen, my husband, business partner and best friend. Over the years Stephen has championed me through my PhD, my research and now this book. He has been an unfailing provider of love, encouragement, care and ideas. I really could not have done this without him.

Preface

Why this book?

The human brain today is always on. Technology is everywhere, connecting and consuming us. It has transformed the way we think, communicate and even live. We rely on being plugged in to instant information and real-time feedback. We no longer have to wait for anything: technology has enabled us to have it all now. We can shop, read and watch movies and television programmes whenever we want. We are even able to choose a potential partner simply by swiping right. We are increasingly defined by speedy responses and even faster results. Immediacy is what we all now expect and demand.

The ramifications of this modern world are both good and bad. A world without search engines and direct access to data is unimaginable today: we can automate tasks, coordinate activity, exchange information, direct our own education and read others' opinions at the touch of a button. The downside is that we are subjected to the whims of a fickle, virtual network that can validate and endorse, or demean and destroy. Our identity and success are forged by social opinion and follower numbers, where relationships are tenuous and often temporary.

Humans have an amazing ability to transform their environment. We only need to look back over the last 50 years to see vast differences in the way we live and communicate. But as change has accelerated, so too has our drive to innovate. The problem is that the same *humanness* responsible for all this discovery is simultaneously limited in its ability to cope with the world that we have now fashioned for ourselves.

Despite a world that is speeding up around us, we remain essentially social, emotional, sensual and flawed beings, hampered by a maladaptive biology. Our brain's primary role, which is to keep us alive and functioning, has not yet adjusted well enough to deal with a now-constant bombardment of information. Put simply, we do not have the brainpower to deal with the number of inputs we receive.

And while every advance and latest innovation in technology gives us the illusion of greater efficiency and control over our life, this comes at a cost. Our instinct to survive means that we are naturally prone to interruption – we are attuned to switch our attention to anything that may historically have constituted a threat to life – but incessant data means that we can never switch off. We feel obliged to be responsive and productive, we make rapid decisions, we seek immediate rewards and we deny ourselves the space and time to slow down, breathe deeply and build long-term, meaningful relationships.

Our brain deals with this continuous loop of anticipation, uncertainty and anxiety by releasing chemicals to protect us from any potential threat or danger and to keep us alive. These chemicals place us in a state of alertness, tension and stress, which influences our view of the world and distorts our thinking. And we cannot think clearly when we are focused on survival.

Our modern lifestyle is not helping. We are sitting too much, and exercising and sleeping too little. Because our bodies are not active and mobile, we are witnessing an increase in depression, stress, obesity and degenerative illnesses such as dementia.

And so, as technology frees up effort in one area, we need to work harder to manage the fallout in another.

The good news is that we can all develop strategies and techniques to help us lead happier, healthier and more fulfilling lives. Learning about how our brain functions is an important first step.

Ongoing research in neuroscience provides us with valuable insights into why we do what we do. This book presents some of these insights and offers ideas as to how to apply them to everyday life.

How to read this book

The intention is that this book should strike a balance between knowledge and application by combining scientific research with concrete examples as well as illustrative stories. It is designed to be visual, practical and easy to read.

Each chapter is written as a stand-alone guide to a particular brain area and concludes with five tips for improving brainpower in that area. Additional references to specific studies are also provided for those who would like to explore these in more depth.

It is important to point out that, although the chapters are organised under separate, recognisable headings, it would be too simplistic to suggest that the brain works in a similarly clear-cut way. There are therefore inevitably some areas of overlap among chapters, which reflect the extensive activity and multifaceted nature of our brain.

As neuroscience continues to gain momentum, more studies will undoubtedly be published. In the meantime, I hope that this book will whet your appetite and leave you wanting to find out more.

Remember: it is always valuable to ask 'Why?'

Why do we need to keep our brain in balance?
Why are we emotional rather than rational?
Why do we not remember accurately?
Why can we not multitask?
Why does our brain love (and hate) certain words?
Why do we not see the truth?
Why are we all biased?
Why do we need to reignite our creativity?
Why do most change efforts fail?
Why do we need to manage our stress?
Why do leaders need to learn about the brain?
Why do we need to improve our lifestyle and daily habits?

Chapter overview

Chapter 1 provides a quick look at our brain – how it is structured and how it functions – and the chapter also considers male/female differences and the nature/nurture debate.

Chapter 2 explores our emotional brain; why we have emotions and how our emotions affect our memories.

Chapter 3 looks at how memory works in our brain, the different types of memory we store and how to improve our ability to remember.

Chapter 4 discusses our attentional system, its strengths and limitations, and why focus is essential to learning.

Chapter 5 considers the impact and use of language, the power of certain words and the endurance of storytelling.

Chapter 6 offers insights into visual perception, explaining how our brain 'sees' and why we are susceptible to visual illusions.

Chapter 7 describes some of the biases that we carry within us and discusses why we have developed mental shortcuts to interpret information.

Chapter 8 enters the world of the creative brain and provides some insights into how to reignite the creative spark that we all carry within us.

Chapter 9 discusses the impact of change on our brain, explaining how habits are formed and how we can minimise the pain of change.

Chapter 10 provides information about what stress is doing to us in today's world. It also describes the different symptoms associated with stress, and offers some methods of handling stressful situations.

Chapter 11 looks at leadership and how effective leaders need an understanding of the brain in order to get the best out of the people they lead.

Chapter 12 offers a glimpse into our modern lifestyle and considers how we should protect our brain against daily challenges, with a specific focus on sleep, exercise and food.

'Sitting on our shoulders is the most complicated object in the known universe.'

MICHIO KAKU
Theoretical physicist and futurist (1947–)

chapter one

Our Brain

ABOUT THIS CHAPTER

The brain is the basis of everything we do: how we behave, feel, remember, pay attention, create, change, influence and ultimately live. Learning about how our brain functions is an important starting point to understanding why we do what we do.

Even though it only weighs around one and a half kilograms, our brain is complicated. With the advent of neuroimaging techniques we are now able to see inside the brain and explore its function and structure in greater depth. But despite new advances in neuroscience, neurobiology and neuropsychology, the brain remains the most mysterious, complex and relatively unknown organ in the human body.

This chapter provides an introductory overview of the main structures and functions of the human brain. It explains how our brain helps us respond to the world around us and keeps our system in balance. Some insights are offered into male/female brain differences, whilst also acknowledging the influences of our environment and upbringing.

As we begin to understand more about how our brain works, we become more aware of our own thoughts, responses, behaviours and emotions. We also become better equipped to get the best out of our brainpower in the future.

Part 1: The science explained

The key function of our brain is to keep us alive. This means that our brain needs to be able to anticipate what is safe or harmful in our environment.

In other words, our brain is our *personal prediction machine*. It is constantly scanning and processing the world around us to help us respond appropriately.

Why we need to keep it all in balance

The brain maintains a finely tuned internal balance in order to regulate our heartbeat, breathing, temperature, water, hormonal release and sugar levels. This internal balance is known as *homeostasis,* meaning 'same state'.

Our internal body environment is kept steady and stable despite changes in our external surroundings. This balancing act works on what is called a *negative feedback loop* (see Figure 1.1): when the level of something rises, our brain's control systems reduce that level, and when the level of something falls, our brain's control systems raise that level.

For example, if we are cold, we shiver in order to generate heat, and if we become too hot, we sweat in order to cool down.

Our brain works hard to maintain this balance and to keep our system functioning effectively.

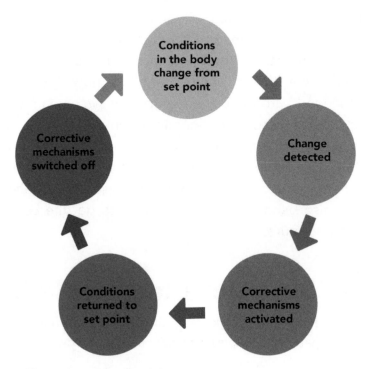

FIGURE 1.1: The negative feedback loop

Our brain, neurons and synapses

Our brain represents just two percent of our total body weight and is made up of approximately 100 billion nerve cells, which are known as *neurons*.

Each neuron can make between 1,000 and 10,000 connections, or *synapses,* with other neurons. Our brain's ability to form new connections, constantly reorganising itself and changing its pattern and shape, is known as *neuroplasticity.* We have two different types of neurons – *sensory* and *motor.*

Sensory neurons carry information from our sensory organs – eyes, ears, nose, tongue and skin – to the brain.

Motor neurons carry messages away from the brain and spinal cord to our muscles.

Our brain has three main parts: *forebrain, midbrain* and *hindbrain.* The midbrain and hindbrain make up the brain stem and connect the forebrain to the spinal cord. The forebrain contains the *cerebrum,* the largest part of the brain, which plays a critical role in processing information.

Our four lobes . . .

The **cerebrum** is divided into four *lobes* (see Figures 1.2 and 1.3). Although these are all interconnected, each lobe is associated with different functions.

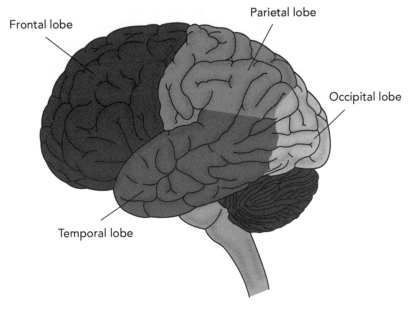

FIGURE 1.2: The lobes of the brain

Frontal lobe	Processes higher cognitive functions and decision-making. This is the centre of our brain's executive functioning and manages complex mental and behavioural responses to the environment.
Temporal lobe	Controls our hearing and processes memories, integrates them with our senses and emotions and regulates our endocrine system, which releases our hormones.
Parietal lobe	Processes information about temperature, taste, touch, movement, reading and spatial orientation.
Occipital lobe	Primarily responsible for vision and the interpretation of information taken in by the eyes.

FIGURE 1.3: Our four lobes

Our lobes work together to enable our brain to operate as a whole and to adapt constantly to keep us functioning. If we lose a sense such as sight, another sense such as hearing gets stronger. The *seeing* part of the brain is then used to process sound.

. . . and two hemispheres

Most mental functions are distributed across the *right* and *left* sides, or *hemispheres,* of our brain. Certain mental processes and tasks are specialised to either one hemisphere or the other (see Figure 1.4). This is known as *lateralisation* of brain function. Scientists believe that this is our brain's way of being more efficient: by avoiding duplication, we optimise our available brainpower.

Our knowledge of the brain's hemispheres can be largely credited to the work of Dr Roger Sperry during the 1960s. Dr Sperry examined the way our brain's hemispheres operate both independently and together and, in 1981, was awarded the Nobel Prize in Physiology or Medicine for his work in this area.

The **left hemisphere** normally directs logical, analytical, mathematical and verbal tasks.

The **right hemisphere** is generally more concerned with music, emotion and tonality, facial recognition, visual imagery and abstract information.

The right hemisphere controls the muscles on the left side of our body, while the left hemisphere controls the muscles on the right side. Damage to one side of the brain, such as that caused by a stroke, affects the opposite side of the body.

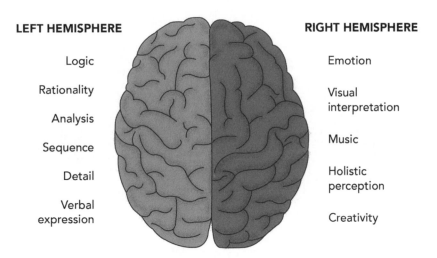

LEFT HEMISPHERE		RIGHT HEMISPHERE
Logic		Emotion
Rationality		Visual interpretation
Analysis		
Sequence		Music
Detail		Holistic perception
Verbal expression		Creativity

FIGURE 1.4: Our two hemispheres and their roles

Connecting the two hemispheres is a network of fibres, called the *corpus callosum*, which enables information to be carried between the hemispheres. The primary function of the corpus callosum is to ensure that our brain functions as one integrated and cohesive unit.

How neurons communicate with each other

All of our neurons pass on information to other neurons. In order to do this, our brain communicates on an electrical as well as a chemical level, involving ions such as sodium, potassium and calcium. Communication between neurons is the core of all our thoughts, emotions and behaviours.

Any new experience stimulates an electrical impulse within a neuron. Electricity cannot travel across a gap or space, called the *synaptic cleft,* so when this impulse reaches the end of the neuron the information has to be relayed by chemicals, known as *neurotransmitters.*

Neurotransmitters are stored in small compartments called *vesicles.* Each vesicle tends to hold one type of neurotransmitter. The neurotransmitters travel in their vesicles to the end of the neuron where they wait to cross over the gap. At the right time, the neurotransmitter is emptied into the gap and travels across to the other neuron. When neurotransmitters travel between neurons, they form a connection with another neuron (see Figure 1.5).

All of this happens with impressive speed and precision.

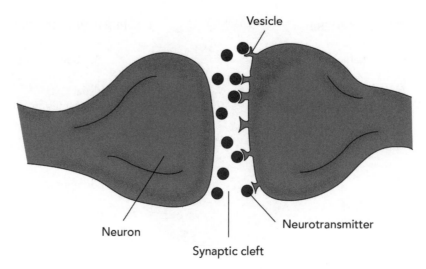

FIGURE 1.5: Neurons and neurotransmitters

Neurotransmitters affect our mood, memory and wellbeing. They are effectively our *chemicals of emotion*.

There are two types of neurotransmitters: *excitatory* and *inhibitory*.

Excitatory neurotransmitters stimulate the brain.

Inhibitory neurotransmitters calm the brain and balance brain stimulation.

The impact of neurotransmitters on our health is the focus of ongoing scientific research. Problems with even minor aspects of their release process from one neuron to another have been linked to many brain disorders and nervous system diseases, including depression, autism, schizophrenia, dementia and epilepsy.

The role and symptoms of deficiency of some of these neurotransmitters are described in Figure 1.6.

Chapter 12, Our Brain and Lifestyle, discusses how certain foods boost the performance of neurotransmitters in our brain.

Our nervous system

The brain controls our nervous system, which regulates how we respond and adjust to the world around us.

Neurotransmitter	Role	Some symptoms of deficiency
Serotonin	Inhibitory neurotransmitter. Plays an important role in regulating mood, happiness, relaxation, appetite, memory, bowel function, learning and hormonal release.	Depressed mood, anxiety, panic attacks, low energy, sleeping problems, feeling tense and irritable, impaired memory and concentration.
Oxytocin	Also known as the *cuddle chemical* or *moral molecule*. Plays a key role in maternal bonding, childbirth, social affiliation and increases romantic attachment and empathy. Makes us more sensitive to social cues around us.	Anxiety, stress, feelings of disconnect with others, depression, loss of appetite, greater sensitivity to pain. Used to accelerate childbirth and improve social engagement in people with autism.
Dopamine	Both an excitatory and inhibitory neurotransmitter. Responsible for movement, memory, pleasurable reward, attention, desire and drive to get things done. Known as our *motivation molecule*. Controls movement and posture.	Memory problems, poor concentration, difficulty initiating or completing tasks, lack of energy, lack of motivation, addictions, cravings, compulsions, a loss of satisfaction and libido. Too little dopamine is implicated in Parkinson's Disease.
Glutamate	Major excitatory neurotransmitter in our brain. Involved in cognition, memory and learning.	Insomnia, problems concentrating, mental exhaustion and depleted energy.
GABA	Inhibitory neurotransmitter. GABA (*gamma*-aminobutyric acid) acts as a natural sedative and tranquilliser and calms nervous activity. Contributes to motor control and vision.	Anxiety disorders, racing thoughts, bipolar disorder, mania, poor impulse control, panic attacks, cold hands and shortness of breath.
Acetylcholine	Widely distributed excitatory neurotransmitter. Major impact on wakefulness, attentiveness and arousal. Needed to turn short-term memories into long-term ones. Released to activate muscles. (Botox is a neurotoxin that blocks the effect of acetylcholine, preventing the facial muscles from moving.)	Low energy levels, memory loss, learning problems, muscle aches, cognitive decline. People with Alzheimer's Disease have altered levels of acetylcholine. Also implicated in Parkinson's Disease.
Noradrenaline	Excitatory neurotransmitter. Triggers changes in the body in response to stress (increased oxygen, heart rate and glucose) to raise our alertness and *fight or flight* capacity. Important for attentiveness, emotions, dreaming and learning.	Depression, loss of alertness, memory problems, lack of energy, focus and motivation.

FIGURE 1.6: Some neurotransmitters and their roles

Function of the nervous system

The nervous system has three main functions (see Figure 1.7):

1. *Sensory*	passing information from our senses to the central nervous system for processing.
2. *Integrating*	using the sensory signals for decision-making or the formation of new memories.
3. *Motor*	activating our muscles and glands.

FIGURE 1.7: Functions of our nervous system

There are two parts to our nervous system (see Figure 1.8):

1. *Central nervous system* (brain and spinal cord).

2. *Peripheral nervous system* (cranial nerves branching from the brain, spinal nerves branching from the spinal cord and rest of the body).

Messages are carried between the central nervous system and the peripheral nervous system to activate the muscles and glands.

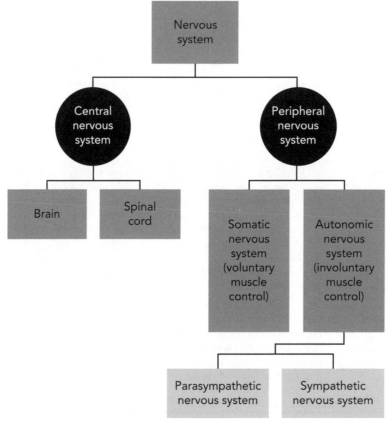

FIGURE 1.8: Our nervous system

Central nervous system (CNS)

The **central nervous system** (CNS) is made up of the brain and the spinal cord and is composed of *grey* and *white matter* (see Figure 1.9). **Grey matter** refers to the neurons, and **white matter** refers to the *axons,* or nerve fibres, that carry impulses between neurons. Axons are white because they are coated with a fatty substance called *myelin,* which gives them their colour. (The role of myelin is discussed later in this chapter.)

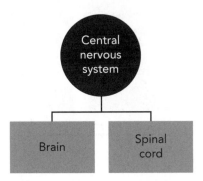

FIGURE 1.9: Our central nervous system

The spinal cord is a single continuous structure running from the brain, through the base of the skull and then down the spinal column.

The CNS controls our responses to the environment. It processes inputs that we receive through our senses and then communicates with the rest of our body by sending messages from the brain through the nerves branching off the spine that make up our peripheral nervous system (PNS).

Whenever we want to move our body, our CNS translates this intention into chemical and electrical messages that provide instructions for our muscles to activate.

If our CNS is injured or affected by disease, we can suffer permanent loss of function or disability.

Peripheral nervous system (PNS)

The **peripheral nervous system** (PNS) works with the CNS to process information from our environment (see Figure 1.10).

The PNS carries information to and from the CNS via our peripheral nerves and regulates our body temperature, blood pressure and thirst. Unlike the CNS, the PNS is not protected by bone. Damage to the CNS can cause damage to the whole body, whereas damage to the PNS is often localised.

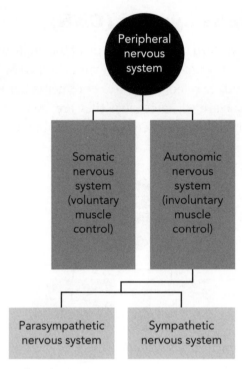

FIGURE 1.10: Our peripheral nervous system

There are two aspects to the peripheral nervous system:

1. The *somatic nervous system* communicates with our senses and is involved in voluntary muscle movements, such as learning ballet or football. **Somatic nerves** come predominantly from the spinal cord and stimulate the contraction of skeletal muscles.
2. By contrast, the *autonomic nervous system* regulates all the involuntary but life-critical activity of the internal organs and hormones – essentially everything internal that we never even think about. **Autonomic nerves** come from both the spinal cord and the brain and help to maintain homeostasis via two systems: the *parasympathetic nervous system* (*rest and digest*) and the *sympathetic nervous system* (*fight or flight*). See Figure 1.11 for more detail.

Parasympathetic nervous system *Rest and digest* This forms the body's response when the body is resting and recovering.		Sympathetic nervous system *Fight or flight* This forms the body's response to acute, short-term stress.
Parasympathetic response	**Area of Body**	**Sympathetic response**
Pupils constrict	Eyes	Pupils dilate
Saliva production increases	Salivary glands	Saliva production reduces
Mucus production increases	Nose	Mucus production reduces
Heart rate slows down	Heart	Heart rate increases
Bronchial muscle contracts	Lungs	Bronchial muscle relaxes
Gastral juices increase	Stomach	Gastral juices reduce
Normal function	Liver	Glucose increases
Urine increases	Kidneys	Urine decreases
Normal function	Adrenal glands	Adrenaline is released

FIGURE 1.11: Our autonomic nervous system

What happens when we activate the autonomic nervous system?

The two parts of the autonomic system (**parasympathetic** and **sympathetic**) are designed to work together in balance: when one part is working, the other stops. Too much activity on one side can lead to ill health.

Although our autonomic nervous system is continually on, functioning day and night, we are not conscious of it working on our behalf.

Our nervous system is vital for our ability to function in every way. It controls all the muscles, tissues and organs in our body. Our brain, spinal cord and peripheral nerves are coated with a protective layer of protein and fatty substances, called a *myelin sheath*. This coating process is known as *myelination*.

Myelin is essential for the proper working of our nervous system. When myelin is damaged, nerve impulses are affected, leading to diseases such as multiple sclerosis. We can promote the health of our myelin sheath by eating a healthy diet, as explained further in Chapter 12, Our Brain and Lifestyle.

Part 2: Impact on our daily life

Do women and men have different brains?

There is considerable debate among researchers as to whether women and men have different brains. Scientists are divided over whether any differences in the brain are the result of our genetic make-up (*nature*) or whether, instead, they are the consequence of the family and culture we are raised in (*nurture*). In fact, a recent study has even suggested that there are no real brain differences between the sexes, and that any brain differences emerge because of the significance we give them.[1] This is a view supported by Professor Gina Rippon who refutes sex-linked brain differences and warns against stereotyping in a world where children are subjected to gender differences from an early age.[2]

Even so, from a biological point of view, men's brains are, on the whole, 10 to 12% bigger than women's brains. But a bigger brain does not necessarily mean a more intelligent brain (see Figure 1.12)! Men's brains tend to be bigger because they control a larger body mass and musculature than those of women. Although all human brains begin as female, there is a release of hormones that then determines the sex of the foetus. Around six weeks after conception, the brain of the male foetus will experience a surge of testosterone, which stimulates growth of the *hypothalamus*, the area of the brain that produces and controls our hormones.

Studies have shown that serotonin is synthesised faster in the male brain than the female brain.[3] This may explain why there are more incidences of depression in women and why women, particularly in times of stress, may be drawn to food rich in tryptophan, an amino acid that enables the production of serotonin, such as chocolate.

The *anterior cingulate cortex*, which regulates thinking and emotion and is involved in detecting errors, is larger in the female brain. Dr Louann Brizendine calls this the 'worry-wort centre'.[4]

The *amygdala* and the *hypothalamus*, which are involved in the body's response to fear and danger, are sensitive to *testosterone* and they both grow larger in young men. This explains why many men are more attracted to competitive sport and why sexual desire can differ in young men and women.

Oxytocin has a different effect on the way men and women process information about other people: it increases bonding and prosocial behaviour in women, and more protective instincts in men.[5]

Although the notion of pain is highly subjective, it does appear that women are more sensitive to pain than men and suffer from pain-related conditions more frequently.[6] Men produce more *endorphins* than women, which could explain men's greater tolerance of pain. Chapter 2, Our Brain and Emotion, discusses endorphins in more detail.

Men's navigational skills and spatial judgement are more effective compared to women's. Men also consistently outperform women on mental rotation tasks unless they suppress their emotions, in which case they perform identically.[7] These differences have been linked to both men's higher levels of testosterone[8] and a larger male parietal lobe.[9]

FIGURE 1.12: Some reported differences between the sexes

One of the biggest differences between male and female brains has been observed in the *hippocampus,* which stores personal memories (explained in more detail in Chapter 3, Our Brain and Memory) and is engaged in processing memories into words. The hormone oestrogen has a direct effect on hippocampal formation and performance. This may explain why women generally excel at remembering words, objects, pictures and faces.

Magnetic resonance imaging (MRI) scans have shown that women have more connections in the corpus callosum, which connects the two hemispheres, integrating information from both sides.[10] However, it is worth mentioning that the role of the corpus callosum has been much debated, with other studies claiming that any male/female differences are spurious or insignificant.

Diffusion tensor imaging (DTI), a water-based imaging technique, has also looked at pathways connecting the different regions of the brain in men and women. The results show that men's brains (illustrated in the top half of Figure 1.13) display front-to-back connectivity *within* the hemispheres, moving between perception and decision-making. Women's brains (illustrated in the bottom half of Figure 1.13) are wired more laterally, between the hemispheres, suggesting greater communication between analysis and intuition.

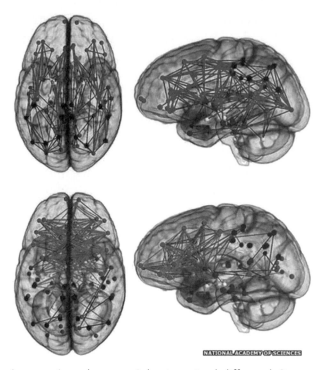

FIGURE 1.13: Are men's and women's brains wired differently?

Credit: Dr Ragini Verma, *Proceedings of the National Academy of Sciences.*[11]

It is nevertheless important to note that these differences emerge only after adolescence, which bolsters the notion that our brains are malleable and adaptable, particularly during childhood.

Male/female differences may therefore develop or be encouraged over time as boys and girls are treated differently within the cultures in which they are raised.

Why are both nature AND nurture important?

We each represent a unique combination and interplay of factors, acquired from early childhood and life experiences, together with our genetic blueprint or inherited tendencies.

And so, even though we may be born with a physiological or psychological predisposition, our upbringing, especially during the early years, plays a critical role in determining whether certain behavioural traits will emerge or remain dormant.

This means that, while male/female biological differences have been observed through various studies, both nature *and* nurture play a combined role in establishing how we develop. Because the brain is a muscle, which like other muscles in our body needs to be kept active, it is strengthened or weakened through reinforcing or reducing certain patterns of brain activity. Throughout our life we can continue to shape our brain by learning a range of skills, embracing new ideas and meeting different people.

What difference does being right- or left-handed make?

Most of us have a dominant hand that we use. We live in a right-handed world, with only around 10% of the total human population being left-handed. There are a number of theories that attempt to explain why this is the case, one of which is that right-handed dominance is an evolutionary adaptation that has been passed down over time.

Culture plays a significant role in determining which hand we use; for example, certain religions do not allow the left hand to be used for eating food or for ceremonial rituals.

Even though the hemispheres control our body diagonally, this does not mean that left-handed people are necessarily more *right-brained* or more creative, or that right-handed people are more *left-brained* or more logical. The complex way in which the hemispheres work together cannot be explained by simply saying that we are governed by either one side or the other.

Most of us may naturally have a preference towards one side and we are influenced by the way we are taught and tested. For example, a large number of education systems cater more for the left hemisphere, focusing on analysis and logic rather than on creativity and the arts.

But in reality, we all benefit from the combined functioning of both hemispheres.

Why do adolescents do what they do?

Over the last 10 to 15 years, research into the teenage brain has gained traction. As mental illness becomes less stygmatised and more socially recognised, scientists are now working hard to understand how and why the brain handles – or struggles to handle – certain transitions throughout life.

The adolescent brain undergoes a significant period of growth and development. The pre-frontal cortex (see Figure 1.14), in particular, is still being remodelled and is not fully formed until around our mid-twenties. This area coordinates our brain and body and our higher-level executive functioning: judgement, personality, impulse control, reasoning, long-term planning, intellect, mood, social skills, conscience and empathy. In other words, we expect teenagers to make important decisions regarding their education and future at a time when they are least equipped to do so.

Although adolescence is an important period of development, research into the adolescent brain is still relatively new. Neuroscientists such as Professor Sarah-Jane Blakemore offer valuable insights into our brain structure and function during this stage of life.[12] Studies show that, as teenagers pursue increased autonomy and develop a greater sense of self, they push against the boundaries around them, heightening their susceptibility to risk-taking and peer pressure. Their quest for independence and social inclusion at a time when their brain is still growing makes them vulnerable to danger and injury, which is a leading cause of death among this age group.[13] For parents and caregivers, it is important to strike the right balance between freedom and safety in order to manage the complex interplay between adolescent neurological changes and a demanding environment.

During our adolescent years, our neural connections grow and any connections that we do not use are pruned to help the brain become more efficient. This is a process called *synaptic pruning*.

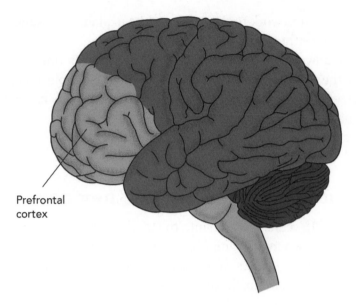

Prefrontal
cortex

FIGURE 1.14: The prefrontal cortex

At the same time as this synaptic pruning takes place, myelination occurs. As explained earlier in this chapter, the process of myelination coats our nerves with a protective fatty substance called myelin, which facilitates the transmission of signals between neurons. As the teenage brain remodels itself, the remaining connections are now able to communicate with each other with more efficiency and speed.

> As a protective measure against the teenage propensity to become distracted or engage in risky behaviour, particularly in front of peers, Ford's MyKey system is designed for parents to limit the speed at which their children drive. The system interfaces with the computer systems on board and places restrictions on drivers. Speed is not the only restriction; car audio can be limited as well.

We mature as our brain improves its ability to integrate and transfer information among its different regions and, as a result, we are able to control our emotions and impulses more consistently.

Part 3: Stories and top tips

Was Einstein's brain different?

The brain of Albert Einstein has been the subject of much debate. Scientists have been intrigued to know whether Einstein had a brain different to the general population.

Seven-and-a-half hours after his death, Einstein's brain was removed by scientists who then studied its structure. They discovered that it had a greater number of connections than the brains of other people of a similar age, suggesting that Einstein had continued to exercise his brain, hence delaying the degeneration that would normally occur during the ageing process.

The main difference in Einstein's brain was in an area of the parietal lobe known as the *inferior parietal region*, used for spatial awareness, mathematical thought and motor imagery. This region was so developed on both sides that his brain was 15% wider than other brains.

As well as enlarged parietal structures, Einstein's brain had a thicker corpus callosum connecting the two hemispheres, particularly in an area called the *splenium,* which facilitates communication among all four of the brain's lobes.[14]

Einstein's genius was therefore likely to have been a result of both a well-functioning brain and constant mental challenges throughout his lifetime.

Should young children head footballs?

There is now evidence to suggest that heading a football can leave younger players with lasting brain damage.[15] The US Soccer Federation has announced its intention to publish guidelines to limit the number of times children between the ages of 11 and 13 can take headers in training, and to ban them altogether for younger children.

Because children's heads are disproportionately large and their brains are not fully formed, there is more movement inside the skull. In addition to this, the brains of children and adolescents have not fully developed the protective myelin that covers neurons and, consequently, may be more vulnerable to head injuries.

The making of Vanessa-Mae

In 2008, a BBC programme called *The Making of Me* explored the nature/nurture debate through examining whether the famous violinist Vanessa-Mae's talent was a result of either her birth or her upbringing.

Vanessa-Mae learned the violin from the age of five and practised daily for four hours. She has sold more than 10 million albums and has performed on stage worldwide with many other renowned artists.

During the programme, Vanessa-Mae underwent a series of tests, including brain scans, heart monitoring and psychometric assessments. She discussed the main influences in her life with geneticists and a psychologist. Throughout these discussions, Vanessa-Mae expressed how she had inherited her talent from her mother. But, at the same time, she accepted that her mother's encouragement to play the violin was a significant influence in honing her musical talent from early childhood.

As Vanessa-Mae claimed during the programme:

'Kids can be born with potential but unless it's encouraged – pushed, even – I don't think it will ever come to fruition.'

The human brain continues to grow and develop throughout our lifespan. Its plasticity means that, whatever the genetic blueprint we are born with, our neural connections and structures are constantly changing to reflect our experiences, choices, environmental influences, even our thoughts and expectations.

Our brain is therefore a reflection of the world we have around us, for better or worse.

Top Tips →
Remember: **BRAIN**

Balance your neurotransmitters in order to regulate your wellbeing and overall mood. Neurotransmitters are essential to our psychological and physical health. Chapter 12, Our Brain and Lifestyle, offers ideas for how to boost neurotransmitter balance through sleep, exercise and food.

Recognise, utilise and celebrate any male/female differences around you. Our evolution has depended on the appropriate dynamic between male and female characteristics. We all have something to offer and can complement each other well.

Activate your brain and challenge it regularly with mental exercises, memory games and new ideas. This will help keep your brain agile. A connected brain is a healthy brain, and if you do not use your brain, you will weaken its connections in those areas. The more you learn, the more connections you will create.

Invest time and effort in practising what you would like to become good at. Becoming an expert at any activity involves a great deal of dedication. There are no shortcuts!

Nourish your brain with the right environment and people around you. Make sure you are surrounded with people who believe in you and want the best for you. How you nurture your brain is as important as the brain you are born with. The influences you give your brain will affect changes to its structure and function throughout your lifetime.

References for Chapter 1

1. Joel, D. et al. (2015). 'Sex beyond the genitalia: The human brain mosaic', *Proceedings of the National Academy of Sciences*, October, 15468–73.
2. Rippon, G. (2019). *The Gendered Brain*. London: Bodley Head.
3. Nishizawa, S. et al. (1997). 'Differences between males and females in rates of serotonin synthesis in human brain', *Proceedings of the National Academy of Sciences*, May, 5308–5313, Karolinska Institutet (2008), 'Sex Differences In The Brain's Serotonin System', *ScienceDaily*, February 2008.
4. Brizendine, L. (2010). *The Female Brain*. London: Transworld Publishers.
5. Gao, S. et al. (2016). 'Oxytocin, the peptide that bonds the sexes also divides them', *Proceedings of the National Academy of Sciences*, June 7650–54.
6. Fillingim, R.B. et al. (2009). 'Sex, gender and pain: A review of recent clinical and experimental findings', *Journal of Pain*, May, 447–85.
7. Fladung, A., & Kiefe, M. (2016). 'Keep calm! Gender differences in mental rotation performance are modulated by habitual expressive suppression', *Psychological Research*, November, 985–96.
8. Pintzkaa, C.W. et al. (2016). 'Changes in spatial cognition and brain activity after a single dose of testosterone in healthy women', *Behavioural Brain Research*, February, 78–90.
9. Koscik, T. et al. (2009). 'Sex differences in parietal lobe morphology: Relationship to mental rotation performance', *Brain Cognition*, November, 451–59.
10. Ardekani, B.A. et al. (2012). 'Sexual dimorphism in the human corpus callosum: An MRI study using the OASIS brain database', *Cerebral Cortex*, August, 2514–20.
11. Verma, R. et al. (2013). 'Sex differences in the structural connectome of the human brain', *Proceedings of the National Academy of Sciences*, January, 823–28.
12. Blakemore, S-J. (2019). *Inventing Ourselves. The Secret World of the Teenage Brain*. London: Transworld Publishers.
13. Johnson, S.B., & Jones, V.C. (2011). 'Adolescent development and risk of injury: Using developmental science to improve interventions', *Injury Prevention*, February, 50–54.
14. Weiwei, M. et al. (2013). 'The corpus callosum of Albert Einstein's brain: Another clue to his high intelligence?' *Brain*, September, 1–8.
15. Di Virgilio, T.G. et al. (2016). 'Evidence for acute electrophysiological and cognitive changes following routine soccer heading', *EBioMedicine*, November, 66–71.

"The best and most beautiful things in the world cannot be seen or even touched. They must be felt with the heart."

HELEN KELLER
World-famous deaf–blind speaker and author (1880–1968)

chapter two

Our Brain and Emotion

Emotions drive our behaviour and shape our responses to what is happening around us. They enable us to take action, make decisions, connect and communicate with other people and build meaningful relationships. Emotions can be short-lived or can last a lifetime.

Emotions have played a valuable role in our survival as a species. Being able to understand emotional displays in others informs us how to adapt our behaviour appropriately.

This chapter explains why our brain is wired to produce a spectrum of emotions, how we read emotions in others, why emotion and memory are closely linked and the impact of emotions on our day-to-day experiences.

Part 1: The science explained

Our brain's emotional circuitry

The emotional circuitry (see Figure 2.1) in our brain is commonly known as the *limbic system,* which is situated predominantly in the temporal lobe. The name comes from *limbus,* the Latin word for 'border', and the word's usage has been attributed to a scientist named Paul Broca, who discovered the area around 150 years ago.

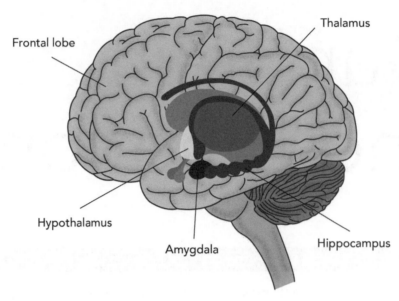

FIGURE 2.1: Our emotional circuitry

The main structures comprising the limbic system surround and interact with the *hypothalamus*; they are the *amygdala*, the *hippocampus* and the *thalamus* (see Figure 2.2). The *prefrontal cortex* is also considered part of the limbic system because, although housed in the frontal lobe, it interacts with the rest of the limbic structures.

Why do we have emotions?

We all know what it is like to experience emotions. Many of us feel a multitude of emotions in a single day. Some emotions help us, while other emotions can make a situation far worse.

Emotions are subjective. Different events may evoke different emotions in us, depending on our background, personality and past experiences. For example, giving a presentation may be an enjoyable experience for some, but a source of intense anxiety for others.

Emotions also help us communicate with other people and recognise how another person is feeling. When we are more aware of our own emotional state, we are often better able to read the emotional state of others.

Equally, our emotions can often affect the way that other people feel; we do not always realise how contagious emotions are.

Limbic system structure	Function
The hypothalamus	Regulates homeostasis (our internal balance) and is one of the most active parts of the brain. The hypothalamus works with the **pituitary gland** to activate our endocrine system or hormonal release in every part of the body. Together these constitute our master gland and drive our responses.
The amygdala (named after the Greek word for *almond* because of its shape)	Activates in response to threats, although in recent years the amygdala has been linked to intense positive emotions as well.[1] The amygdala labels an event emotionally relevant or important based on past experience. It receives information from the thalamus and communicates with the hypothalamus to stimulate our stress hormones, adrenaline and cortisol. When our amygdala is stimulated, it can turn a calm demeanour into aggressive or fearful behaviour. When the amygdala is damaged or destroyed, fear is not registered at all.
The hippocampus (named after the Greek word for *seahorse* because of its shape)	Converts experiences into personal or autobiographical (*episodic*) memories. If our hippocampus is damaged, we cannot build new memories and can only rely on memories from the time before the damage occurred. This is one of the most plastic areas of the brain and the only region where we can grow new neurons.
The thalamus	Receives information from our senses – apart from our sense of smell – to the rest of the brain. Because smell (via our **olfactory bulb**) bypasses our thalamus, it is our strongest sense. The thalamus also regulates sleep, alertness and wakefulness. For example, when we need to sleep, the thalamus shuts off signals from the senses, thereby allowing us to rest.
The frontal lobe	Plays a critical role in our capacity to modulate emotions. This is the newest and most evolved part of the human brain and works together with the rest of the limbic circuitry: the frontal lobe interprets situations and then tells the limbic circuitry to produce the appropriate emotion.

FIGURE 2.2: Limbic system structures and functions

What exactly is emotion?

The word *emotion* is derived from the Latin word *emovere*, meaning 'to disturb'. Emotion therefore represents a change. This change has a cognitive component (the label we give to how we feel – such as *happy* or *sad*) and a physiological component (bodily changes such as increased heart rate or quickness of breath).

An emotion is often followed by an action. If we are sad, we may choose to be alone or find someone to talk to; if we are afraid, we may avoid a dangerous situation or threat; if we are angry, we may confront the source of our anger.

The neuroscientist Dr Joseph LeDoux has influenced much of our understanding about the origins and purpose of emotions.[2] He explains that our emotional responses are hardwired into the brain's circuitry and he believes that emotion can trigger an instinctive reaction without the need for a conscious thought. This means that, even when we think we are being rational, we are in fact being emotional.

Over the years, researchers and theorists have debated the exact dynamic or chronology of the cognitive and physiological elements of emotion. But all agree that emotion involves a change to both our physical and our mental state (see Figure 2.3).

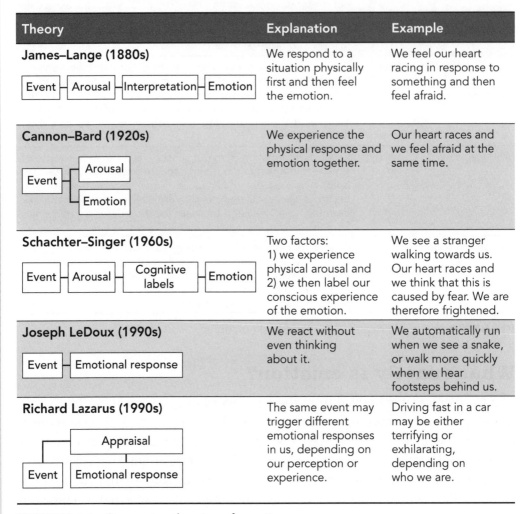

Theory	Explanation	Example
James–Lange (1880s) Event – Arousal – Interpretation – Emotion	We respond to a situation physically first and then feel the emotion.	We feel our heart racing in response to something and then feel afraid.
Cannon–Bard (1920s) Event – Arousal / Emotion	We experience the physical response and emotion together.	Our heart races and we feel afraid at the same time.
Schachter–Singer (1960s) Event – Arousal – Cognitive labels – Emotion	Two factors: 1) we experience physical arousal and 2) we then label our conscious experience of the emotion.	We see a stranger walking towards us. Our heart races and we think that this is caused by fear. We are therefore frightened.
Joseph LeDoux (1990s) Event – Emotional response	We react without even thinking about it.	We automatically run when we see a snake, or walk more quickly when we hear footsteps behind us.
Richard Lazarus (1990s) Event / Appraisal / Emotional response	The same event may trigger different emotional responses in us, depending on our perception or experience.	Driving fast in a car may be either terrifying or exhilarating, depending on who we are.

FIGURE 2.3: Comparing theories of emotion

The importance of endorphins

The word *endorphin* is derived from two words: *endogenous* (meaning 'from within') and *morphine* (a painkiller). The word 'morphine' is name after Morpheus, the ancient Greek god of dreams. An endorphin is therefore essentially an internal painkiller.

Endorphins block the pain receptors in our body, which is why they are also known as *happy chemicals*. When we release endorphins, we experience a feeling of positive wellbeing or euphoria.

Endorphins are produced when we exercise, laugh or are in love – and also when we eat spicy food! We have 20 different types of endorphins, which are all important for the healthy functioning of our body.

As well as blocking our pain receptors, endorphins help to reduce anxiety and depression. They are also a natural relaxant and help us to sleep.

Endorphins also heighten our enjoyment of experiences, normalise blood pressure and enhance our immune system.

How can we read emotions in others?

Our brain is wired to look for *similarities* rather than *differences* in other people so that we can easily identify people who are like ourselves. This tendency may have originated from a survival instinct: we feel safer when we are with people who are just like us, while people who are different may pose a threat to our existence.

Over the last 25 years, neuroscientists have shed light on a system in the brain that enables us to *read* what other people are thinking and feeling.[3] This system is made up of *mirror neurons* or nerve cells that respond equally when we do something ourselves or when we observe someone else performing the same action.

For example, if we are drinking a cup of coffee, specific neurons activate to help us see the cup, move the cup to our mouth, taste the coffee, recognise it as coffee and then decide to continue drinking it, based on whether we like coffee or not. Simply the act of watching someone else drink a cup of coffee activates some of those same neurons – the two brains mimic each other.

First observed in macaque monkeys in the early 1990s by a team of neuroscientists led by Dr Giacomo Rizzolatti at the University of Parma,[4] mirror neurons gained wider recognition in 2000 when Professor V. S. Ramachandran heralded their discovery as doing for psychology what DNA did for biology.[5] Since then, these neural building blocks of behaviour have been an ongoing subject of fascination for scientists.

Our mirror neurons help us to see the world from another person's perspective; we even start to feel how they feel. This is what scientists believe is at the root of *empathy* (literally *'in suffering'*). This is why many of us cry when we see something sad, and it is also why, when someone smiles at us in a genuine way, we find it hard not to smile back.

One of the best examples of how mirror neurons work is when we see someone yawn. We all know that yawning is highly contagious, and scientists believe that it is a primitive expression of empathy.[6] When we see someone else yawn, our mirror neurons activate strongly, making us want to yawn too. When we have an emotionally close relationship with someone yawning, it is even more infectious.

But can mirror neurons help us decode facial expressions in order to understand other people and determine their intentions?

We still have a great deal to learn about the neuroanatomy of social conduct.

Questions have been raised as to whether mirror neurons, whilst eliciting imitation and a paired response (for example, you blink: I blink), can also in fact help us establish underlying meaning.[7] In answer to this, subsequent research does seem to support the role of mirror neurons in enhancing our ability to explain certain aspects of human behaviour.[8]

Empathy: a force for good in the brain?

Empathy has become a fashionable topic in recent years. It has been hailed as a force for good, a driver of pro-social behaviour, a means of understanding the perspective of others in order that we may fine-tune our responses accordingly. But can having empathy also cloud our judgement, lead to skewed decision-making or even paralyse us? And if we feel what someone else feels, are we necessarily best placed to help them if we become caught up in their emotional state?

Paul Bloom, Professor at Yale University, argues that we are more effective when we rely less on empathy and more on reason – when we can decide from a distance.[9] He believes that morality and empathy do not always work together since overidentifying with someone else's pain may not lead to the best outcome. Because our brain's ability to empathise with others is moderated by our own beliefs, opinions and experiences, and is influenced by how much we identify with their race, class, background or even political party, we fall victim to our biases and judgements.

Our brain may drive us to be more supportive of those who are most similar to us and dismissive and cruel to those who are not. Instead, whilst still acknowledging the power of kindness and generosity, Professor Bloom believes that we should employ our frontal lobe regions to exercise greater objectivity and fairness when making decisions. He calls this 'rational compassion'.

We need to read emotional expression

Our face is the main vehicle that we use to express emotion. We have 42 muscles in the face, which enable us to display a huge range of emotional variations.

Our brain is naturally designed to read faces. In fact, we have an area of the brain called the *fusiform face area* (FFA) that is dedicated to reading facial expressions. When we learn to read the emotional messages in someone else's face, we become more aware of how we are feeling ourselves.

Our ability to read emotional expression and connect with people develops from an early age, and interaction with others is critical for our emotional development. We rely heavily on recognising up facial cues to establish an emotional connection with other people. By doing this, we enter into an unspoken reciprocal arrangement whereby we validate each other's words and gestures through both our verbal and non-verbal responses.

Paul Ekman, Professor Emeritus at the University of California, San Francisco, is an expert in facial expressions and gestures.[10] Since the 1970s, Professor Ekman and his colleagues Wallace Friesen and Carroll Izard have been examining emotional expressions around the world to determine if a smile in one country is the same as a smile in another country.

Based on their discovery that everyone reflects happiness and other emotions through the same facial features, Professor Ekman's team has developed the first and only comprehensive tool for objectively measuring facial movement and micro-expressions – the Facial Action Coding System (FACS). This system became well known via the television series *Lie To Me*.

The emotions that are universally recognised around the world are: anger, joy, surprise, disgust, sadness and fear.

The fact that there is consistency across diverse cultures suggests that our basic emotions are indeed instinctive.

More recently, a study has highlighted that there are actually 21 distinct facial expressions of emotion that we use regularly.[11] In addition to the six universally recognised emotions (anger, joy, surprise, disgust, sadness and fear), there are 15 expressions of *compound emotions*, which are constructed by combining different emotion categories, such as happily surprised or disgustedly angry.

The more time we spend with people and really focus on them, the better we are able to detect the range of emotions that register on their face, even if these emotions are signalled as micro-gestures or subtle indications of a feeling. But we cannot guess with 100% accuracy how people are feeling all the time just on facial expressions; we also have to look at other non-verbal cues.

Effective communication therefore depends on our success in reading a range of emotional markers from other people.

The Still-Face Experiment was first demonstrated to colleagues in 1978 by Edward Tronick, Director of the Child Development Unit and Distinguished Professor at the University of Boston.[12]

The experiment has been repeated a number of times and all replicated studies reinforce the premise that young babies need emotional feedback from others and quickly become withdrawn and frustrated if they do not receive it.

Professor Tronick described how an infant after only three minutes of exposure to a non-responsive mother becomes confused, withdrawn and distressed and makes repeated attempts to resume a normal pattern of interaction.

Nowadays, the Still-Face Experiment is used to investigate attachment styles, cultural differences, autism, deaf children, infants with Down's syndrome and the impact of maternal depression.

Why do women tend to be faster than men at identifying emotions?

Researchers have demonstrated that women are faster at processing and differentiating between emotional expressions than men.[13] The male brain, it seems, has to work harder to evaluate emotion in others.

A study using magnetic resonance imaging (MRI) divided participants into three groups:[14]

1. Women
2. Men
3. Men with Asperger's syndrome (a disorder that impairs the ability to understand others)

All three groups were shown faces with different expressions and asked to decide whether those faces looked trustworthy, approachable or intelligent.

Their responses were timed, and as they gave their answers, their brains were scanned to see which areas of the brain were activated.

Both groups of men (those with and without Asperger's syndrome) experienced greater blood flow to the part of the brain responsible for social function, suggesting that they had to work harder than the women to read the facial expressions.

Those with Asperger's syndrome showed the greatest brain activity, suggesting that they had to work the hardest.

Evolutionary psychologists suggest that males and females are wired differently because of distinct social roles that have evolved over time: men are able to detach from emotion and stay calm in a crisis, whereas women need to be able to detect emotion in order to respond to younger family members and nurture people around them.

Scientists have also examined the effect of *testosterone* on emotional sensitivity. Testosterone is a hormone that makes us more logical, rational, goal-oriented and more prone to aggressive behaviour. Men have higher levels of testosterone than women.

Simon Baron-Cohen, Professor of Developmental Psychopathology at the University of Cambridge, explains how sex differences in emotional connection may be perceived. He suggests that the male brain is more systemising than empathising (S>E) and the female brain is more empathising than systemising (E>S).[15]

According to Professor Baron-Cohen, men are better at working out how systems operate, such as repairing an engine (systemising), while women are better at working out others' feelings (empathising).

Professor Baron-Cohen also believes that an *extreme male brain* is one that is very good at systemising but very poor at empathising, and this may be connected to the condition known as autism – a condition that tends to affect more men than women.

Testosterone also suppresses the effects of *oxytocin,* a neurotransmitter that helps us form bonds of trust with others. It seems that even small amounts of testosterone can prevent us from identifying emotions and even alter the connections between regions of the brain involved in emotional processing.[16]

However, the issue of sex differences in an emotional context is still quite controversial: many social scientists argue that any distinction we see is largely the result of stereotyping and the expectations placed on male and female roles in society.

Why is our brain designed for fear?

Much of our brain is devoted to the human fear response. Fear has effectively kept us alive as a species. If we were fearless, we would not have learned to avoid danger.

Fear has an immediate and dramatic effect on our physical state: our heart rate increases, breathing quickens and stress hormones are released. We learn to be frightened quickly and early in our lives – and the effects of fear can often be enduring. For this reason, fear continues to be one of our most researched emotions.

The regions of the brain that govern our fear responses and memories are the amygdala and the hippocampus, two brain structures that were mentioned earlier in this chapter. They work together to stimulate our response to threat and prepare our body accordingly.

When we experience any threat or danger, the amygdala helps us to store this information so that we avoid the threat or danger in the future. The hippocampus remembers the context or location of the threat. Both the hippocampus and the amygdala activate as a warning signal when we find ourselves in a new situation that has similarities to a past event.

Why do psychopaths not feel fear?

The term *psychopath* (literally, 'suffering of the mind') was first used in 1900 to describe people who appeared outwardly normal but who exhibited a lack of morality or conscience. In 1930 the term was changed to *sociopath* (meaning 'suffering of society') to indicate the harm that these people could inflict on others. Nowadays, both terms are often used interchangeably and generally describe the same personality traits.

The closest mental condition to psychopathy is *antisocial personality disorder,* which is described in the fourth edition of the *Diagnostic and Statistical Manual of Mental Disorders* (DSM IV), a reference guide used by psychologists and psychiatrists to categorise and diagnose mental illness. The current approach to defining psychopathy and its related terminology is based on a checklist of criteria, the most commonly used of which is the *Psychopathy Checklist Revised* (PCL-R) developed by Robert Hare, Professor Emeritus at the University of British Columbia.

The PCL-R describes psychopaths as showing emotional detachment and a lack of empathy. A number of studies have demonstrated psychopaths' inability to detect expressions of fear in the faces of other people.[17]

Brain imaging has also linked abnormalities in psychopaths' amygdalae with their inability to process fear, but not anger.[18] The fact that the amygdala is activated whenever we feel threatened suggests that psychopaths do not feel a sense of danger – which may lead to increased risk-taking. This is supported in a 2016 analysis of studies dating back to 1806, all of which highlight how psychopathic individuals do not detect threats.[19]

Hallmarks of a psychopath

According to Professor Hare, signs of psychopathy include: superficial charm and emotional responsiveness, a grandiose estimation of self, the need for stimulation and impulsiveness, pathological lying, cunning and manipulativeness, lack of remorse or guilt, callousness and lack of empathy, a parasitic lifestyle, poor behavioural controls, early behaviour problems, lack of realistic long-term goals, irresponsibility, short-term relationships.[20]

Psychopaths will display insincere charm in order to manipulate people quickly. They use deception and mimicry, often adapting their views and reactions to whomever they are dealing with.

Professor Hare also warns that anyone can be taken in by a psychopath.

From a neurobiological perspective, the brains of psychopaths do not register empathy for pain in the same way as for most other people. One of the key areas of the brain linked to pain perception (the *insula*) is triggered in psychopaths when they consider their own pain, but fails to activate when other people are in pain. Individuals who are rated as highly psychopathic have even shown an increased response in the area of the brain associated with pleasure when asked to imagine pain in others.[21]

Part 2: Impact on our daily life

Why do emotions influence our decision-making?

Emotion and decision-making are deeply intertwined in the brain and are not separate or opposing processes. In fact, many of our decisions are instant and based almost entirely on emotion.

The research of neuroscientist Professor Antonio Damasio has been instrumental in helping us understand how emotions influence our behaviour – in particular, our decision-making.[22]

Professor Damasio studied people with damage to the brain's emotional circuitry. In addition to finding that such people could not feel emotions, he also uncovered that they are unable to make decisions. These people could describe, in rational terms, the actions that they knew they should be taking, but could not settle on any decision, even a simple one, such as what to eat.

Emotions are therefore a key component of our decision-making process. They enable us to weigh up options, rule out wrong choices and come to what we hope will lead to a positive outcome.

We rationalise – but we are not rational!

When we make a decision, we are always looking for a way to satisfy a basic human urge to be happy. This is why many of our decisions are unconscious attempts at minimising the impact of negative feelings such as guilt or fear, while heightening the effect of positive feelings such as happiness and love.

This dynamic interrelationship between emotions and decisions means that we often make a quick decision based on an emotion. We then associate a new emotion with the decision we have just made.

But the strong influence exerted by our emotions over our thought processes means that our decisions are susceptible to error. And because many of our decisions are fast and instinctive, we often do not realise the full impact of this emotional interference.

To illustrate this point, Nobel Prize winner and Professor Emeritus at Princeton University, Daniel Kahneman, describes the brain as operating two contrasting systems (see Figure 2.4):[23]

System 1
Fast, intuitive, automatic and emotional – but also prone to mistakes and biases.

System 2
Slower, more logical and rational – and it counterbalances System 1.

FIGURE 2.4: Daniel Kahneman's Systems 1 and 2

Professor Kahneman explains that most of us would like to think that we are engaging our System 2 more often than we actually do. However, System 2 is often slow and lazy to activate – and it sometimes even supplies evidence to support System 1's rapid conclusions.

Example of System 1 thinking:

The following test, devised by Professor Shane Frederick of the Yale School of Management, illustrates how quickly we are drawn to the wrong answer:

If it takes 5 machines 5 minutes to make 5 widgets, how many minutes does it take 100 machines to make 100 widgets?

Intuitively we reach for the wrong answer (100 instead of 5 minutes in this case) and do not slow down to think and make the correct calculation.

In other words, we make a decision quickly and then justify it afterwards. We think we are being rational when we are actually just rationalising what has already been decided!

Why do fear and anger colour our judgement?

Fear feeds off uncertainty. We worry when we do not know something, and then we often expect the worst. We may turn to anger to give us the confidence to act and take risks.

The problem with anger is that it can also make us oversimplify a situation and become more polarised and judgemental in our thinking.

In 2003, a study was conducted by Professor Jennifer Lerner at Harvard about the impact of emotions on decision-making. The study compared two groups:[24]

Group 1 was asked to read a news story about anthrax mail-threats (designed to instil fear)

Group 2 was asked to read an account of celebrations by some people in Middle Eastern nations related to the 9/11 attacks (designed to elicit anger)

Those in Group 2 (who were made to feel angry) voted for tougher penalties to be imposed than those in Group 1 (who were made to feel fear).

Another study has demonstrated that just by looking at angry facial expressions we are more likely to stereotype and condemn others.[25]

Of course this has important implications for our interactions with others. The emotional expressions that we wear ourselves, and those we read on the faces of those around us, seep into the judgements and assumptions we make on a daily basis.

By slowing down our thinking we may be able to stall our early responses and come to a more considered and balanced view. And even if our first response is correct, we still always benefit from a period of reflection or a second opinion.

Why are emotional memories so vivid?

When we have an emotional experience, the amygdala is involved in how this experience is stored and then remembered. The amygdala labels the memory as emotionally significant, and heightens both our visual perception and our sensory response to it.[26] The amygdala therefore increases the intensity of the memory – rather like increasing its brightness and volume in our brain.

But how we experience something is not always how we remember it. Even though an emotional memory may be more vivid than our other memories, we do not recall an exact replica of our experience.

The amygdala's role is to give us the big-picture view but not much else. From an evolutionary point of view, thinking about the detail may have slowed us down in the past and cost us our life. So the amygdala leaves the peripheral detail out – and we often fill this detail in ourselves later.

So while the intensity of the memory may give us confidence about what we have remembered, this confidence is not matched by accuracy or detail in our recall. We are even adamant that we have remembered details that did not actually happen! This is covered in more detail in Chapter 3, Our Brain and Memory.

Emotional memories also often have a physical element. When we store an emotional memory, the amygdala and hippocampus work together to stimulate the production of *adrenaline* and *cortisol* to produce a physical response. The hippocampus then stores the memory for future reference, as a fusion of the physiological and emotional experience.

This is why when we recall emotional memories, we may also reactivate the same original physiological response. Because we can remember emotional memories so strongly, any disturbing memories we have stored may resurface and affect daily life, as in *post-traumatic stress*. Research is ongoing in this field to help people cope with such memories in order to resume normal living.

What is our gut feel?

Much of what we do every day takes place below the level of conscious thought. For example, we do not think about how we walk, nor do we stop to think about how we eat or use our cutlery.

Performing some tasks automatically means that we are freeing up other parts of our brain to take on a new cognitive challenge. This is discussed in more detail in Chapter 4, Our Brain and Attention.

When our cognitive processes fall below the level of consciousness, we no longer think about them and they become second nature. They also become part of our System 1 thinking and form our *gut feel*.

We use our gut as a reference point for a great deal in our lives. We feel that we can trust it as our own personal database. And we rarely question it – instead we reinforce what we believe to be true and relevant. As a result, the world we observe around us is often a reflection of the world we carry within ourselves. In other words, we see things as *we* are, not as *they* are. This is explained in more detail in Chapter 6, Our Brain and Visual Perception.

Whenever we have a new experience, we look for ways to strengthen our existing memories. When the memory has a strong emotional element, we fortify both the memory and its associated emotion every time we recall the memory.

Because, from an early age, we are constantly storing experiences, we do not always remember each experience. Rather we are left with their emotional residue, such as our likes and dislikes, often without knowing their root causes.

As Maya Angelou said:

'I've learned that people will forget what you said, people will forget what you did, but people will never forget how you made them feel.'

Emotional intelligence: thinking about feeling

Emotional intelligence (EQ or EI) is a term first used by Professors Peter Salovey and John Mayer in 1990 to describe the ability to manage emotions and then to use this ability to guide behaviour.

Six years later, the psychologist Dr Daniel Goleman gave the concept widespread appeal in his book *Emotional Intelligence*, in which he divided emotional intelligence into four quadrants (see Figure 2.5) to highlight the key areas of focus.[27]

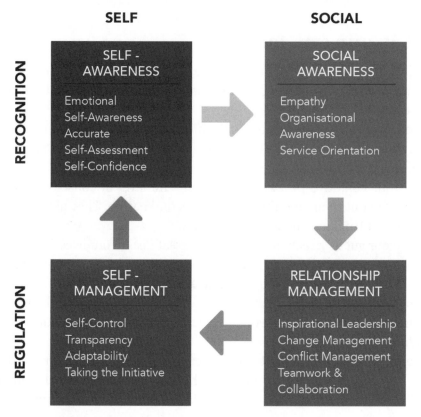

FIGURE 2.5: Daniel Goleman's model of emotional intelligence

The thinking behind Dr Goleman's model is that if we understand our own and others' behaviour, we can communicate more effectively and appropriately in any situation. But much of the time we tend not to wait for our emotions to pass to allow reason to intervene and lead us and, instead, allow them to override our thoughts, which can exacerbate an already tense or difficult situation.

Emotional intelligence therefore encourages us to mobilise our System 2 thinking and evaluate our feelings, rather than acting on them immediately.

Over the years, emotional intelligence has been cited as a hallmark for success in any domain and at any age. The topic is now being taught in schools, and some companies are using emotional intelligence criteria to hire and reward their people. When we observe and evaluate our emotions, we strengthen our ability to regulate our responses appropriately.

With technology dominating much of our social interaction today, we are at risk of misreading and misunderstanding each other. Email communication or electronic messaging may even create a psychological numbing, or emotional detachment, leading to a dwindling ability to empathise, connect and communicate in a genuine manner.

We therefore need to dedicate significantly more time and effort to thinking about our emotions and those of the people around us.

Part 3: Stories and top tips

We are fooled by our emotions

We may be more aware of why we should monitor and how we feel in order to provide considered and appropriate responses, but we are still fooled by our emotions. We judge others based on how they look, we trust people without knowing much about them, we become anxious at a sudden noise that we cannot immediately identify and we make decisions without considering hard evidence. And we do not always get it right. Our emotions can lead us to make the wrong predictions and errors of judgment. This is explained more in Chapter 7, Our Brain and Biases.

For example, after the September 11 tragedy in the United States, in which nearly 3,000 died, many people took to their cars to escape New York even though road travel has always carried a higher fatality risk than air travel. Emotion overrode logic, and the higher numbers on the roads inevitably led to many more deaths. Professors Wolfgang Gaissmaier and Gerd Gigerenzer at the Max Planck Institute for Human Development in Berlin estimated that there were an additional 1,595 Americans killed in car accidents during the year after the attacks.[28]

A dream that stirred a nation

Words are a powerful emotional vehicle. On 28 August 1963 at the Lincoln Memorial, Washington D.C., Dr Martin Luther King spoke straight to the hearts of his audience.

The 'I have a dream' speech, delivered with confidence, presence and conviction, appealed to a basic need in people to belong and to reject isolation and the 'dark and desolate valley of segregation'.

By reaching people on an emotional level, Martin Luther King delivered an oration that stirred a nation and inspired hope with its promise of a better future. His words are still remembered today, having been passed down from generation to generation.

A display of affection that touched a child

In October 2013, Carlos, a six-year-old Colombian orphan, wandered on to the stage at the Vatican where Pope Francis was giving a speech about families. Carlos hugged the Pope's legs, sat in his chair and even played with the crucifix around the Pope's neck.

Even though this was a highly irregular incident, the Pope's response was one of empathy, tolerance and sensitivity. Displaying immense compassion, he seemed to understand the response the little boy needed; he patted Carlos on the head affectionately, as if he were his own child.

The dark side of emotion

The degree to which politicians successfully rouse and rile the public is expounded in Adam Curtis's 2016 film *HyperNormalisation*. Curtis takes us on a four-decade journey through political machinations that he claims have blinded us to what is normal – and his premise is that we can no longer see what is really there.

Voting behaviour is in itself an act of emotion and something that political scientists refer to as the 'voting paradox'.[29] This describes how the effort of voting is never matched equally by reward: each individual separately has no influence on the election outcome, but we still vote because it is an expression of feeling. Political debate feeds our emotions and

'Politics of fear are very strong in persuading audiences who don't have much information to vote with their gut feeling, which is where rational discussions don't find a space.'

Ruth Wodak
Emeritus Distinguished Professor at Lancaster University

divides our opinions. Drew Westen's book *The Political Brain* describes voters as thinking with their 'guts'.[30]

The 2016 campaign for the United Kingdom to leave or remain in the European Union is an example of what is now being termed in the media as 'emotional politics'. During the campaign, politicians on both sides were accused of influencing and directing voters' behaviour with scaremongering tactics rather than reasoned facts.

Sayeeda Warsi, the former chair of the Conservative Party, resigned amid accusations that the *Leave* campaigners were resorting to messages of 'hate and xenophobia'.

Leave supporters were incited to anger through references to immigration, loss of sovereignty and the drain on the National Health Service. The *Remain* campaign issued threats relating to uncertainty, insecurity and instability. On both sides, emotion held sway over rational thought.

And the emotion did not stop after voting had taken place. For some, the fear and anger that coloured the electorate's initial decision-making later turned to grief and regret. The aftermath even spawned new terms like 'Bregret' and 'Bregrexit'.

The 2016 American presidential election played to similar emotions. The arguments put forward by both presidential candidates seemed to be deliberate attempts to incite fear and, in particular, *anger*: anger against the other party, anger against the other candidate, anger against another country, anger against other people.

The impact of medication on our mood

Medication is part of modern life. Most of us have taken painkillers or antibiotics at some stage and we turn to prescription drugs to treat a range of illnesses, from diabetes to depression. The question is: are we fully aware of the effects of medication on our brain?

Over the years, headlines have featured the impact of medication, such as L-dopa being linked to increased impulsivity or addiction,[31] sleeping pills leading to irrational outbursts or even acts of violence[32] and anti-asthma medicine being linked to the development of ADHD symptoms.[33]

Professor Beatrice Golomb,[34] at the University of California, San Diego has been investigating the impact of statins and other medications on mood and behaviour. In some cases she has found that medications have an opposite effect to what is expected, such as anti-depressant medication leading to increased rage and aggression.

Other studies have found that lowering cholesterol in primates[35] and flies[36] has been shown to increase aggressive behaviour, and, more recently, research involving giving statins to fish[37] has been associated with decreased levels of serotonin and more violent behaviour.

Pain researcher Dr Dominik Mischkowski, at the University of Ohio, has conducted research into paracetamol (acetaminophen in the United States) and has found that it can reduce positive empathy (empathy for other people's pleasure).[38]

Paracetamol features on WHO's List of Essential Medicines and is widely used to treat physical pain in the same areas of the brain that are also involved in social pain. These areas enable us to empathise with others.

There is no doubt that medication has brought a wide range of benefits and a prolonged lifespan, and in fact many of the side effects are specified clearly. But it is also important that we become more aware of how any drug can affect the entire human system and not just the condition it is intended for. As we learn more about the brain and body, we will be able to make better choices about how we live.

Positive emotions make us strong

After suffering burnout in 2011, Ruby Wax enrolled on a Master's Degree at Oxford University in mindfulness-based cognitive therapy. Her book *Sane New World* discusses the need to live in the present and feel more positive and focused.[39]

Positive emotions change our brain's structure and function, enabling us to derive more pleasure from our experiences. When we savour a moment, whether through tasting something or listening to birdsong or laughter, we expand our brain's ability to appreciate and enjoy our experiences and surroundings. And importantly, we offset the scourge of our negativity bias, a topic which is explored in more detail in Chapter 7, Our Brain and Biases.

Positive emotions strengthen our system and enable it to flourish. Studies[40] have shown how psychological resilience and our ability to bounce back from adverse events are greatly improved when we consciously develop strategies to cultivate optimism, curiosity and openness.

Top Tips
Remember: **EVOKE**

Engage people by taking time to read the emotion in their faces. This will activate your mirror neurons, enabling you to connect with people on a deeper level. Give people visual feedback and facial cues to show them that you are listening and paying attention. Keep your mobile telephone out of sight: it is an unnecessary distraction and will detract from your ability to read the emotional expression of others.

Vocalise your emotions in order to manage communication with others. Learn to articulate how you feel and whether your immediate response is appropriate. Recognise and identify the source of your emotional triggers. Assess the emotional temperature of a conversation and try to defuse any tension through your own language and behaviour.

Overrule your gut System 1 response by slowing down to think and assess what is happening. Our decision-making is fallible, emotional and easily influenced. By applying some logical systems of evaluation and using System 2 thinking, you will be able to judge situations more accurately and calmly.

Know how and why you may be influenced by the opinions, views and criticisms of others. Notice how often you find yourself being carried along by other people's fear and anger without even realising or questioning it.

Encourage different opinions and find people who do not always agree with you to be both a second pair of eyes and a second brain on an important decision you need to take. An opposing perspective or a challenging view helps us to become more considered and rational in our thinking.

References for Chapter 2

1. Bonnet, L. et al. (2015). 'The role of the amygdala in the perception of positive emotions: An "intensity detector"', *Behavioural Neuroscience*, 7 July. https://doi.org/10.3389/fnbeh.2015.00178

2. LeDoux, J. (1999). *The Emotional Brain: The Mysterious Underpinnings of Emotional Life*. New York: Simon & Schuster.

3. Rizzolatti, G., & Craighero, L. (2004). 'The mirror-neuron system', *Annual Review of Neuroscience*, March, 169–92.

4. Rizzolatti, G. et al. (1994). 'Premotor cortex and the recognition of motor actions', *Cognitive Brain Research*, March, 1131–141.

5. Ramachandran, V.S. (2000). 'Mirror Neurons and imitation learning as the driving force behind "the great leap forward" in human evolution'. Edge.org.

6. Platek, S.M. et al. (2010). 'Yawn, yawn, yawn, yawn; yawn, yawn, yawn! The social, evolutionary and neuroscientific facets of contagious yawning', *Frontiers of Neurology and Neuroscience*, March, 107–12.

7. Hickok, G. (2014). *The Myth of Mirror Neurons: The Real Neuroscience of Communication and Cognition*, New York: WW Norton & Co. Inc.

8. Glenberg, A.M. (2015). 'Big myth or major miss? reviewed work: The myth of mirror neurons: The real neuroscience of communication and cognition by gregory hickok', *The American Journal of Psychology*, Winter, 533–39.

9. Bloom, P. (2016). *Against Empathy. The Case for Rational Compassion*. London: Vintage.

10. Ekman, P., & Friesen, W.V. (2015). *Unmasking the Face: A Guide to Recognizing Emotions from Facial Clues*. Cambridge, MA: Malor Books.

11. Du, S. et al. (2014). 'Compound facial expressions of emotion', *Proceedings of the National Academy of Sciences USA*, April, 1454–62.

12. Tronick, E. et al. (1978). 'Infants' responses to entrapment between contradictory messages in face-to-face interaction', *Journal of the American Academy of Child and Adolescent Psychiatry*, Winter, 1–13.

13. University of Montreal. (2009). 'Women outperform men when identifying emotions', *Science Daily*, 21 October. www.sciencedaily.com/releases/2009/10/091021125133.htm

14. Hall, J. et al. (2012). 'Social cognition, the male brain and the autism spectrum', *PLOS ONE*, December, 60. doi.org/10.1371/journal.pone.0049033

15. Baron-Cohen, S. (2003). *The Essential Difference*. London: Penguin Books.

16. Bos, P.A. et al. (2016). 'Testosterone reduces functional connectivity during the "Reading the Mind in the Eyes" test', *Psychoneuroendocrinology*, March, 194–201.

17. Hastings, M.E. et al. (2008). 'Psychopathy and identification of facial expressions of emotion', *Personality and Individual Differences*, May, 1474–83.

18. Marsh, A. (2013). 'What can we learn about emotion by studying psychopathy?' *Frontiers in Human Neuroscience*, April, 193–213.

19. Hoppenbrouwers, S.S. et al. (2016). 'Parsing fear: A reassessment of the evidence for fear deficits in psychopathy', *Psychological Bulletin*, June, 573–600.

20. Hare, R. (2016). 'This charming psychopath: How to spot social predators before they attack', *Psychology Today*, June. www.psychologytoday.com/articles/199401/charming-psychopath

21. Decety, J. et al. (2013). 'An fMRI study of affective perspective taking in individuals with psychopathy: Imagining another in pain does not evoke empathy', *Frontiers in Human Neuroscience*, September, 61.
22. Damasio, A. (2005). *Descartes' Error: Emotion, Reason and the Human Brain*. New York: HarperCollins.
23. Kahneman, D. (2012). *Thinking Fast and Slow*. London: Penguin Books.
24. Lerner, J. et al. (2003). 'Effects of fear and anger on perceived risks of terrorism: A national field experiment', *Psychological Science*, March, 144–50.
25. Bodhausen, G.V. et al. (1994). 'Negative affect and social judgement: The differential impact of anger and sadness', *European Journal of Social Psychology*, January, 45–62.
26. Todd, R.M. et al. (2013). 'Shared neural substrates of emotionally enhanced perceptual and mnemonic vividness', *Frontiers in Human Neuroscience*, 6 May. Prepublished online 22 March. doi.org/10.3389/fnbeh.2013.00040
27. Goleman, D. (1998). *Emotional Intelligence*. London: Bloomsbury.
28. Gaissmaier, W., & Gigerenzer, G. (2012). '9/11, Act II: A fine-grained analysis of regional variations in traffic fatalities in the aftermath of the terrorist attacks', *Psychological Science*, 1449–54.
29. Klor, E.F., & Winter, E. (2007). 'The welfare effects of public opinion polls', *International Journal of Game Theory*, February, 379–94.
30. Westen, D. (2008). *The Political Brain: The Role of Emotion in Deciding the Fate of the Nation*. New York: Public Affairs.
31. Carvalho M. et al. (2017). 'Effect of levodopa on reward and impulsivity in a rat model of parkinson's disease', *Frontiers of Behavioural Neuroscience*. 1–13. https://doi.org/10.3389/fnbeh.2017.00145
32. Paradis C. et al. (2012). 'Two cases of zolpidem-associated homicide', *The Primary Care Companion for CNS Disorders*, August. https://doi:10.4088/PCC.12br01363
33. Islam F.A., & Choudhry, Z. (2017). 'What role does asthma medication have in ADHD or depression?' *Current Psychiatry*, June. 50–51.
34. Golomb B. et al. (2015). 'Statin effects on aggression: Results from the UCSD statin study, a randomized control trial', *PLOS One*. July. https://doi.org/10.1371/journal.pone.0124451
35. Kaplan, J.R. et al. (1994). 'Demonstration of an association among dietary cholesterol, central serotonergic activity, and social behavior in monkeys', *Psychosomatic Medicine*. November–December, 479–84.
36. Dierick, H., & Greenspan, R. (2007). 'Serotonin and neuropeptide F have opposite modulatory effects on fly aggression', *Nature Genetics*, 678–682.
37. Aguiar A., & Giaquinto, P.C. (2018). 'Low cholesterol is not always good: Low cholesterol levels are associated with decreased serotonin and increased aggression in fish', *Biology Open*, December. https://doi: 10.1242/bio.030981
38. Mischkowski, D. et al. (2019). 'A social analgesic? Acetaminophen (paracetamol) reduces positive empathy', *Frontiers in Psychology*, March. https://doi.org/10.3389/fpsyg.2019.005
39. Wax, R. (2013). *Sane New World: Taming the Mind*. London: Hodder & Stoughton.
40. Tugade, M.M., & Fredrickson, B.L. (2004). 'Resilient individuals use positive emotions to bounce back from negative emotional experiences', *Journal of Personality and Social Psychology*. February, 320–33.

"Memory is a great artist. For every man and for every woman it makes the recollection of his or her life a work of art and an unfaithful record."

ANDRÉ MAUROIS
Author (1885–1967)

chapter three

Our Brain and Memory

Our memory serves an important protective function in our life. It provides us with a reference guide that helps us respond quickly to events and experiences.

Our memory is effectively our brain's data-storage unit and filing system. We access this stored data to help us interpret and compare new information that we take in via our senses.

For this reason, memory is a critical resource for us, and without it we would be lost. Our collection of memories effectively makes us who we are.

But memories for the same events do vary from person to person – we all choose to remember different aspects of our life's experiences.

This chapter explains how memory works in our brain, the different types of memory that we create, where these memories are stored, why memory is not always a reliable reference point and how we can improve our capacity to remember.

Part 1: The science explained

How do we research memory?

Memory is very complex and personal – and it is not an easy topic to research. Studies using a laboratory setting have been criticised on the grounds of low ecological validity, meaning that they cannot always be applied to a real-world environment. In addition to this, the questions used by researchers to prompt participants' memories can affect recall ability and accuracy, which is explained in more detail later in this chapter.

Over the years, however, scientists have been able to build a picture of how and where memory works in our brain (see Figure 3.1). As well as the various studies that have been conducted, valuable insights have been obtained through incidents of brain trauma or brain damage.

Every new discovery brings us closer to a better understanding of our memory function.

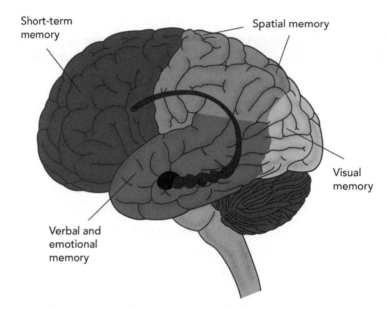

Short-term memory

Spatial memory

Visual memory

Verbal and emotional memory

FIGURE 3.1: Different types of memory in our brain

How does memory work in our brain?

As we grow and mature, the neurons in our brain communicate and connect. Our memories are formed and then consolidated when certain connections are strengthened.

We are constantly connecting the new information that we receive through our senses with the details that we have already stored.

Memory is therefore both *reconstructive* and *constructive*: when we remember something we may add or delete detail to create a new version of our experience.

And every time we access that same memory, we alter it slightly, so that over time it becomes markedly different to what actually happened in the first place.

This is why our memories are never an exact replica of the event in question. Because we each attribute varying levels of emotional significance to the experiences we share with others, our memories of the same experience may differ.

The psychologist Professor Daniel Kahneman describes our two selves as the *experiencing self* and the *remembering self*.[1]

The **experiencing self** operates in the present – in the *now* – with each moment lasting about three seconds.

The **remembering self** represents how we *think* about the experience and what we remember from it.

The last moments of an experience can colour how we choose to remember the whole event. So even if our general experience has been pleasurable, an unpleasant occurrence towards the end will affect how we then remember it overall.

As Professor Kahneman explains, the remembering self is heavily influenced by our protective negativity bias: we are hardwired to hold on to negative rather than positive experiences. Chapter 7, Our Brain and Biases, explores this in more detail.

How do we form memories?

When we receive information into our memory through our senses, we need to store it. This storage process is called *encoding* (see Figure 3.2) and it involves changing any incoming information into various formats.

There are three main formats:

Type of Encoding	What It Means	Example
Visual (Picture)	We see something	*We see a person's name written down*
Accoustic/auditory (Sound)	We hear something and repeat it back	*We try to pronounce a person's name*
Semantic (Meaning)	We try to understand the context or meaning	*We think about where a person's name is from or what it means*

FIGURE 3.2: How we encode information

The way that we encode and store this information affects later *retrieval*.

If we make an effort to encode the same information through a number of different channels, we increase our chances of remembering it later.

For example, if we need to remember a person's name, we can see it written down (*visual*).

If we see it and then repeat it (*visual and acoustic*), we have a better chance of remembering it.

If we see it, repeat it (*visual and acoustic*) and then find out what the name means or where it comes from (*semantic*), we significantly increase the likelihood of remembering the name.

Different types of memory

There are three basic memory types as shown in Figure 3.3. There has been considerable research into the relationship and differences between short-term and long-term memory.

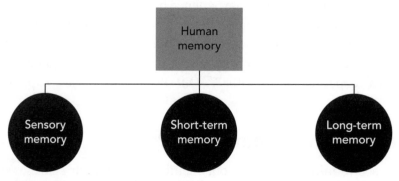

FIGURE 3.3: Different types of memory

Sensory memory

Sensory memory is the shortest element of memory and is a critical first step in storing information in short-term memory. The problem with sensory memory is that we forget much of what we see within less than a second. This rapid process of forgetting is known as *decay*.

Of all the senses, smell is probably the one most likely to result in longer-lasting memories. The *olfactory bulb* transmits olfactory (relating to smell) information from the nose directly to the *limbic circuitry (hippocampus* and *amygdala),* which is central to memory consolidation (see Figure 3.4).

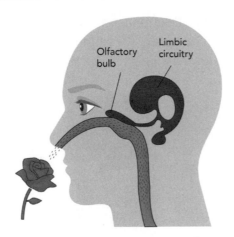

FIGURE 3.4: Smell is closely associated with emotional memory

Short-term memory

Short-term memory (STM) refers to information held in our current consciousness and is very brief, lasting only a few (0–30) seconds.

Traditional theory has suggested that most adults can store between five and nine items in their short-term memory because of limited capacity. Seven is the number that is often quoted as our limit for storing single items.[2] We can observe this when we try to remember a list of words or numbers.

When we group or *chunk* words or numbers together, we have a greater chance of remembering them, compared to trying to remember an ungrouped or unchunked list of words or numbers. For example, we are more likely to remember chunked words like *night and day, don't look now* and *job well done* than a random list of words, such as *night, look, job, and, done, day, now, well.*

We store and retrieve short-term memory sequentially. This means that we will tend to recall words in the same sequence in which we encoded them.

If we do not actively pay attention to storing new information, we will lose it quickly. However, we can increase the duration of short-term memories by rehearsing and repeating any new information that we receive (see Figure 3.5).

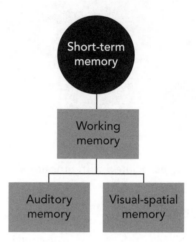

FIGURE 3.5: Short-term memory

Working memory is part of STM and is the process whereby we continually focus on material for longer than STM alone will allow. Working memory plays an important role in concentration and following instructions. It activates an area of the frontal lobe, the **prefrontal cortex**, which is an energy-intensive part of the brain.

We hold information in our working memory so that we can quickly compare it to other information. Our working memory is particularly switched on by novel or unfamiliar information. In other words, our brain is naturally attracted to what is new!

There are two types of working memory: *auditory memory* (records what we hear) and *visual–spatial memory* (records what we see). Chunking in working memory helps us learn words and figures more easily.

Long-term memory (LTM)

In contrast to short-term memory, the capacity of our LTM is thought to be unlimited. Information stored in it can last a lifetime.

We store and retrieve long-term memory by association with previously stored information.

There are two main types of LTM: *declarative* and *non-declarative* (see Figure 3.6).

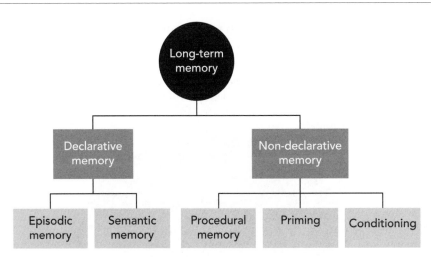

FIGURE 3.6: Long-term memory

The two tables below (Figures 3.7a and 3.7b) explain the differences between **declarative** and **non-declarative** long-term memory.

Declarative/Explicit Memory	
Memory that you know that you can tell to other people and that you can consciously recall.	
Episodic Memory	*Personal events or experiences, such as getting married or visiting Paris for a holiday.*
Semantic Memory*	*General knowledge, such as Paris is the capital of France.*

* Semantic memory is generally derived from episodic memory and may have had a personal association but, over time, sensitivity for certain events is reduced and it becomes generalised as factual knowledge.

FIGURE 3.7a: Declarative memory

Non-Declarative/Implicit Memory	
Memory of what we can do or tasks we perform, often without thinking.	
Procedural Memory	*Knowing how to ride a bicycle, drive a car, tie a shoelace or play a musical instrument. Typically acquired through repetition and practice.*
Priming	*Being influenced in a certain way by being exposed to another factor (behaviour, smell, temperature or language).*
Conditioning	*Responding to a light, sound or smell based on a previous experience (such as salivating when we see/smell our favourite food).*

FIGURE 3.7b: Non-declarative memory

Different aspects of memory involve different reward systems in the brain as shown in Figure 3.8.

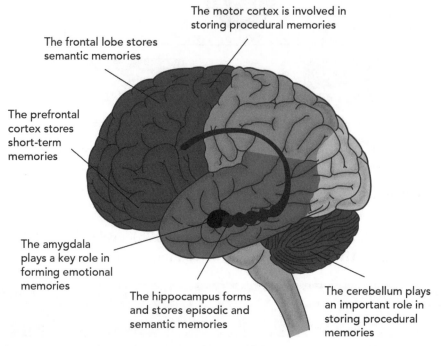

The motor cortex is involved in storing procedural memories

The frontal lobe stores semantic memories

The prefrontal cortex stores short-term memories

The amygdala plays a key role in forming emotional memories

The hippocampus forms and stores episodic and semantic memories

The cerebellum plays an important role in storing procedural memories

FIGURE 3.8: Memory types and brain structures

One of the best-known studies of memory has provided valuable insights into how memory is stored.[3]

An epilepsy patient who was referred to as H.M. had his hippocampus removed and was subsequently unable to form new personal and episodic memories. At the time, this outcome indicated that the hippocampus alone was involved in the formation of these memories. Later studies have since confirmed that the hippocampus is not the only structure implicated in memory formation; other surrounding structures, such as the amygdala, also play a key role in the construction of emotional and personal memories.

Even so, damage to the hippocampus does affect our ability to form lasting episodic memories. Alzheimer's Disease, which reduces hippocampal volume, is also characterised by episodic memory impairment.

By contrast, procedural memories do not appear to involve the hippocampus at all and are encoded and stored by the areas of the brain involved in motor control. This has been observed in cases of amnesia that result in loss of memory related to personal events, but which do not affect the ability to play the piano, for example.

Part 2: Impact on our daily life

Why do we remember what we remember?

There are several effects on memory:

Primacy/ Recency effect	We remember information that occurs first and last better than information that comes in the middle.
Von Restorff effect	We remember something that is noticeably different or new. This switches on our working memory. For example, we may not be aware of driving past sheep grazing in a field, but we would certainly remember it if we passed a bright pink sheep!
Frequency effect	The more we repeat something, the better we will remember it.
Associations/ Mnemonics	When we associate or attach information to other information that we already know it becomes easier to remember. *Mnemonics* are memory devices that help us remember a list of facts or people's names. The word *mnemonic* is derived from the Ancient Greek word meaning 'relating to memory'. A mnemonic can take the form of a song, rhyme, acronym or image that is associated with the facts you want to remember.

For example, we can remember the colours of the rainbow like this:

- *Richard of York Gave Battle In Vain*

- *Red, Yellow, Green, Blue, Indigo, Violet*

The five tips at the end of each chapter in this book take the form of an acronym mnemonic to help you remember them.
Visual imagery mnemonics (linking a word to vivid or unusual pictures) have also been found to be a successful technique.
For example, when trying to remember people's names, we can use pictures as an encoding device, such as Katherine (a cat wearing a ring) or Michael (a microphone calling someone).

Types of amnesia

There are two main types of amnesia (see Figure 3.9), both of which may be caused by head injury, trauma or brain damage.

Retrograde amnesia	An inability to retrieve memories of the past, before the onset of the amnesia.
Anterograde amnesia	An inability to form new long-term declarative memories after the onset of the amnesia. However, non-declarative memories, such as procedural memories, may remain intact. This is explained in the stories section towards the end of this chapter. The amnesia featured in movies such as '50 First Dates' is usually anterograde amnesia.

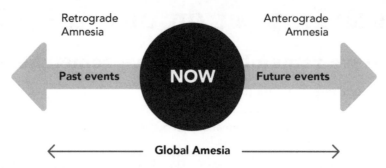

FIGURE 3.9: Two types of amnesia

A total loss of memory is known as *global amnesia. Transient global amnesia* may last for a few minutes or may last for hours.

Our loss of very early childhood memories, known as *infantile amnesia,* has been explained by scientists as being due to our primary brain development and the rapid creation of many new neurons blocking access to old memories.

What memories are most memorable?

Emotional memories are often remembered with an intensity that is not matched by other types of memories.

Memories that leave us with a strong and lasting impression are often referred to as *flashbulb memories.*

Emotional memories were described in 1890 by William James as:[4]

'. . . so exciting emotionally as almost to leave a scar upon the cerebral tissues.'

The concept of flashbulb memories was first put forward in 1977 by psychologists Roger Brown and James Kulik, who described them as so emotionally important to us that they are captured as vividly and completely as a photograph.[5]

However, there has been an ongoing debate about how flashbulb memories are encoded in the brain. When strong emotion and memory collide, the amygdala is activated and influences the way the hippocampus registers the information, as discussed in Chapter 2, Our Brain and Emotion.

The problem with the amygdala's involvement is that it enhances the emotional elements of the memory but does so at the expense of peripheral detail. So even though we think we have remembered something clearly, much of the detail is often missing.

In January 1986, the day after the space shuttle *Challenger* had exploded just 73 seconds into its flight, leading to the deaths of its seven crew members, Ulric Neisser, Professor of Cognitive Psychology at Emory in the United States, asked his students to record what they were doing when they heard the news, whom were they with and where they were.[6]

Two-and-a-half years later, Professor Neisser asked the same students the same questions. When the two sets of answers were compared there were very few similarities. Even though people were very clear about what they said they saw and remembered, their later memories were not true representations of what actually happened.

And so we can never be sure that someone else has remembered the same event in the same way as we have remembered it.

What affects our memory?

A number of factors can interfere with our ability to remember (see Figure 3.10). Because the brain is so adaptive, it changes for the better or worse by virtue of the lives we lead.

Factor	Effect on memory
Sleep	Daily habits, such as exercise and sleep, can improve or worsen our memory. Lack of sleep can adversely affect the ability of our brain to strengthen our synaptic connections and boost our ability to remember. Research has also shown that a nap lasting just six minutes is sufficient to enhance memory function.
Food	Certain foods can help our memory function better. Foods that sustain a healthy heart will sustain a healthy brain. Oily fish (salmon, tuna, sardines, herring) are good sources of docosahexaenoic acid (DHA), a type of omega-3 fatty acid. Dark berries, such as blackberries, blueberries and cherries, are a rich source of anthocyanins, as are other flavonoids that may boost memory function. Walnuts and green tea improve working memory and reduce cognitive impairments. Vitamins B6 and B12 may also slow shrinkage in the hippocampus.
Exercise	A passive lifestyle is detrimental to brain health over time. Sitting for more than 20 minutes at a time increases our risk of diabetes and heart problems;[7] it can also cause our brain to atrophy or shrink. Exercise improves oxygenated blood flow to the brain and stimulates the growth and connectivity of neurons in the hippocampus. In particular, taking exercise enables neurons to release a protein called brain-derived neurotrophic factor (BDNF), which directly benefits our ability to learn and remember. A study has shown that monkeys taking regular exercise learn tasks twice as quickly as monkeys that are sedentary.[8]
Stress	When we are stressed, anxious or depressed, we lose connections between neurons, thereby making memory formation and retrieval more difficult. When we are exposed to stressful situations over time, certain regions of our brain start to reduce in size, including our prefrontal cortex (needed for working memory) and our limbic regions (needed for emotional and episodic memory).[9] Stress also makes us more vulnerable to depression or addiction.
Smoking	Smoking impairs the blood supply to the brain and may also lead to lapses in memory. Studies show that smokers have problems with memory, compared with non-smokers.[10] Smoking may also cause certain proteins to accumulate in our brain, which then interfere with brain function and information processing.
Alcohol	It does not take much alcohol, consumed on a regular basis, to affect our memory function. Alcohol can prohibit blood flow to the brain and cause nerve damage. Recent research has shown that even two and a half drinks every day may accelerate memory loss by six years in middle-aged men.[11] No differences were observed between beer and wine: they have the same effects on cognitive function.

FIGURE 3.10: Factors affecting memory

Is the Internet making us stupid?

We have access to unlimited information via the Internet. However, this *Google effect* has a downside because the availability of information means that the brain does not need to remember all the information we are exposed to. For example, we now forget details that in the past we would have memorised, and we no longer bother to commit to memory what we can look up or store instead. In effect, we are using our technological devices to store our long-term memories for us.

This phenomenon of forgetfulness is known as *digital amnesia*. A recent study claims that 90% of us cannot even remember our children's or partner's telephone numbers.[12]

We seem to be losing the ability to reflect, deliberate and associate – all skills that our memory needs to encode and store for later retrieval. The steady stream of visual input from our electronic devices requires immediate responses, and our thinking skills are now being sacrificed in favour of endless and superficial short-term scanning and sifting. Researchers in Germany have found that people browsing the Web will spend less than ten seconds on each page.[13]

In his book *The Shallows*, Nicholas Carr describes a world of speed and superficiality that is breeding ignorance and changing the way we think and remember.[14]

Memory requires concentration and attention, and it is clear that the more we are bombarded with different distractions, the less we remember.

Our recently acquired ability to shift quickly from one thing to another has come at the cost of other higher-level cognitive processes such as problem solving, creativity, reflection and critical thinking. This view is supported by Professor Patricia Greenfield, a developmental psychologist at the University of California, Los Angeles, whose research has analysed the impact of the Internet on the way students learn.[15]

Among the studies that Professor Greenfield refers to is one involving students who were given access to the Internet during class, compared with another set of students who were not given access. The Internet group did not process and remember the lecture as well as the students who did not have access to the Internet.

As Professor Greenfield states:

'The developing human mind still needs a balanced media diet.'

But it is not all bad news. Technological devices, such as video games, have increased our spatial awareness, our ability to attention-shift rapidly and our hand-to-eye coordination. And because our brain is so plastic, it has started to adapt in order to cope with our digital world.

Technology is therefore changing the structure of our brain and the way that we process and remember information. But as some connections are strengthened in our brain, so others weaken.

Our increasing reliance on satellite navigation (Satnav/GPS) is, for instance, affecting our innate ability to navigate and orientate. When technology fails us we find that we are left with a diminished ability to think for ourselves. People who regularly use Satnav/GPS report that they no longer pay attention to their surroundings and find it harder to remember where they have been, compared to those use maps.[16]

The impact of technology on our cognitive abilities is being hypothesised and debated globally. What is clear is that our world is changing exponentially around us, and we need to consider carefully how we manage this transformation.

In 2016, Stephen Hawking warned of the threat of rapid technological advances that may well supersede human ability.

The creation of powerful artificial intelligence will be:

'. . . either the best or the worst thing ever to happen to humanity.'

Stephen Hawking speaking at the opening of the Leverhulme Centre for the Future of Intelligence (LCFI) at Cambridge University in 2016.

Use it or lose it

All memories grow weaker over time. In 1885, Herman Ebbinghaus called this the *Forgetting Curve* (see Figure 3.11).[17]

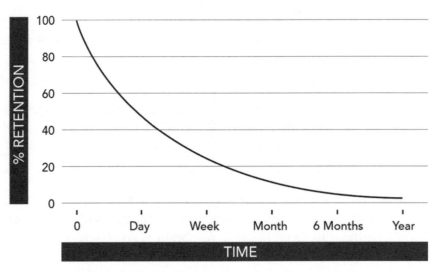

FIGURE 3.11: Ebbinghaus's Forgetting Curve

The more we revisit and recall memories, the more likely we are to retain them. And our memories strengthen with frequency of recall. If we make a deliberate effort to retrieve a memory at spaced intervals, we will have a better chance of holding on to it (see Figure 3.12).

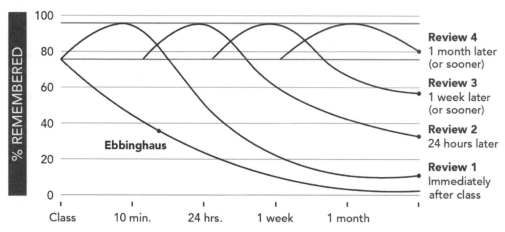

FIGURE 3.12: Overcoming the Forgetting Curve

When we remember something for a one-off purpose, such as an exam, and then do not retrieve it later, we often forget it as quickly as within a month. When we actively retrieve a memory, we then recreate and reinforce it.

Our brain also finds ways of linking memories together; for example, sleep can be a very helpful time to consolidate information we need to remember. If we try to encode a memory just as we are going to sleep, we have a better chance of remembering it later.

Lost and false memories

When we cannot remember something that we know we should know, it can feel very frustrating. This is called a *lost memory*. When we look for a route through to the memory via various associations or connections with the memory, it can often trigger the memory for easier retrieval.

Relaxation can prompt a lost memory to resurface. This can have both positive and negative consequences, as discussed in Chapter 10, Our Brain and Stress. While we often welcome the return of a memory that has proved elusive and hard to retrieve, the reappearance of certain repressed memories (for example, from childhood) may also cause anxiety. Accessing relaxed or meditative states in those with past trauma therefore needs to be handled carefully.

Sometimes our brain quickly stores the wrong information, creating a *false memory*. This may occur because it is easier for our brain to hold on to inaccurate or misleading data than to spend time analysing what we have heard. And because we remember it, we may then store it as truth. We are more likely to do this when fact and fiction are merged to form one story and we are unable to untangle the two.[18]

A false memory may also form if the memory is distorted by subtle cues that steer us in the wrong direction. As a consequence, we believe that we have clearly remembered something that never happened, which is discussed in Part 3.

Daniel Schacter, Professor of Psychology at Harvard University, divides memory errors into seven 'sins',[19] as listed in Figure 3.13.

How do we improve our memory?

Our memories are a precious resource. We rely on our memories when dealing with incoming information or learning anything new. In fact, the same brain regions are activated when we are imagining the future as well as when we are remembering a past experience. Memories glue our shared experiences and are our building blocks for the future. Our collective memories as a species have helped us to survive. Without our memories we would not be able to connect fully with the world around us. Improving and strengthening our ability to remember require active and constant effort. If we do not make a point of recalling and reviewing our memories, they will be lost to us as part of their natural decay. We also need to protect our memories from a poor lifestyle and harmful influences.

The way we encode information in the first place is also key to its later retrieval: the more elaborative the encoding the greater the chance of remembering. And while acknowledging that some memory techniques can be time-consuming and cognitively demanding, it is also worth pointing out that our brain works through making constant associations, and we can increase these associations in different ways. We just need to keep our brains active.

As the neuroscientist Dr David Eagleman says:

'Almost any silly suggestion can work. Drive home via a different route, brush your teeth with your opposite hand . . . the more senses you involve the better.'

1. Transience	Memory weakens and worsens over time (see Ebbinghaus' *forgetting curve*).
	Transience can be caused by a number of factors: decay (as explained earlier in the chapter), ageing or damage to the brain. Transience is also affected by interference of old memories that stop us remembering new information (*proactive interference*) or new memories that stop us remembering old information (*retroactive interference*).
2. Absent-mindedness	We forget where we have put something, such as keys or glasses. This tends to occur as a result of poor encoding, often when we are paying attention to something else, or when we are carrying out a routine task that does not require concentration.
	As Chapter 4, Our Brain and Attention, explains, our attentional system is limited and easily distracted. When our attention is focused elsewhere, we will be more prone to absent-mindedness.
3. Blocking	Words, such as people's names, are sometimes evasive and are sitting somewhere in the brain. This is the cause of the *tip of the tongue* phenomenon, which can be very frustrating.
	Blocking seems to worsen with age, partly because there is more to remember across a longer time span, and partly because neural transmission slows down as we get older.
4. Misattribution	This is linked to false memories. We make associations or connections that did not happen.
	Sometimes we link events we did experience with information that we have merely imagined. Psychologists refer to this as an error of 'memory binding'. This is the sin associated with eye-witness testimony and its effects are illustrated in the film 'My Cousin Vinny'.
5. Suggestibility	Memory is suggestible and questions or prior information may affect the way we remember (see the work of Loftus and Palmer referred to earlier in the chapter).
	Suggestibility can make us vulnerable to coercive questioning or undue pressure from others, which then lead to false memories and confessions. It can also result in people claiming to remember events when they were two years old or even younger (most of us can only remember from the age of five).
6. Bias	Current knowledge and beliefs distort memory of the past. This subject is looked at in more detail in Chapter 7, Our Brain and Biases.
	Memory of pain, for example, is affected by any current pain we are experiencing; we may also remember past relationships differently, depending on our present situation; or we may feel that our past predictions were accurate, based on the outcome.
7. Persistence	Memories resurface of traumatic events. These memories have a strong emotional component and can haunt us throughout our life.
	Our state of mind at the time affects the kinds of memories we recall: when we are in a happy mood we are more likely to retrieve positive rather than negative experiences, and the opposite happens when we are feeling sad.
	When it comes to dealing with traumatic events, it is important that persistent memories are not avoided or suppressed, which may create a rebound effect, but instead are worked through carefully, which may help to lessen their impact in the long term.

FIGURE 3.13: Daniel Schacter's Seven Sins of Memory

A well-cited study by Dr Elizabeth Loftus and John Palmer highlights how the simple use of a verb can influence the recalled accounts of different eyewitnesses.[20]

In their experiment, participants watched a film in which two cars crashed into each other.

Participants were then randomly allocated to one of five groups and asked to answer some questions about the film. Each group had one particular question that differed slightly in its wording between the groups, such as:

'About how fast were the cars going when they **collided** with each other?'

'About how fast were the cars going when they **contacted** each other?'

'About how fast were the cars going when they **smashed** into each other?'

'About how fast were the cars going when they **bumped** into each other?'

'About how fast were the cars going when they **hit** each other?'

Those who were asked the question with the word *smashed* gave a higher speed estimate (40.8 mph) compared with *collided* (39.3), *bumped* (38.1), *hit* (34.0) and *contacted* (31.8). This study illustrates how language can have a distorting effect on memory and our estimates of speed.

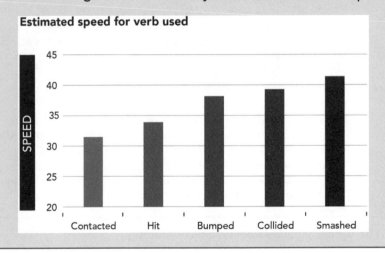

Estimated speed for verb used

Part 3: Stories and top tips

We do not remember accurately

Our memory for an event is affected and distorted by information we receive after the event has happened. This information is known as *after-the-fact information* and sometimes provides irrelevant detail that subsequently becomes incorporated into the earlier memory of the event.

This phenomenon has been observed in studies where people exposed to certain interview techniques go on to develop false memories based on the language and behaviour used by the interviewers. People even say they remember doing something that never actually happened. This is why eyewitness testimony, a key part of criminal investigation, is often unreliable.

A recent report, *Identifying the Culprit: Assessing Eyewitness Identification* (2014), is likely to challenge the validity and use of eyewitness testimony in the United States, particularly in the wake of wrongful convictions that have later been overturned using DNA evidence.[21]

A memory of 10 seconds and still a brilliant musician

In 1985, British conductor and musician Clive Wearing suffered one of the severest recorded cases of *anterograde amnesia* after a brain infection, herpes encephalitis. He was left with a memory span of between 7 and 30 seconds. However, his musical ability and much of his musical memory remained unaffected. Today he is still able to play the piano and read music.[22]

German neurologists have been fascinated by the similar case of a professional cellist who suffered herpes encephalitis in 2005, lost his memory of simple detail but could still play his cello.[23]

Herpes encephalitis affects the temporal lobe, which houses our *episodic memory* (memory that is based on our past experiences and is therefore personal to us), whereas *procedural memory* (such as the memory of how to play music) remains intact because it is stored elsewhere in our brain.

For example, Clive Wearing plays the piano, but does not remember that he can play, nor can he recognise his piano until he is told about it. He can, however, retrieve memories from his childhood and he remembers his wife, whom he knows he loves. Every time he sees his wife, he greets her with delight because he believes he has not seen her for a long time, even though she may have just left the room. Because he has no memory, he feels like he has just woken up from a coma.

As Clive Wearing's wife, Deborah, explains, her husband's memory lasts for only a blink of an eye, with every new blink revealing a new view of the world:

'When the music stops he falls back into this abyss. He doesn't know anything about his life. He doesn't know anything that's happened to him ever in his life.'

How does Alzheimer's Disease affect long-term memory?

Alzheimer's Disease (AD) was first described in 1906 by Dr. Alois Alzheimer, a German neurologist, who examined a woman's brain tissue under a microscope after her death. AD begins by affecting short-term memory. Because symptoms are gradual and are sometimes confused with ageing they are not always reported quickly. The person may just seem forgetful. But AD may be more successfully diagnosed, treated and controlled if these symptoms are recognised early.

Because short-term memory is essential for encoding information for long-term memory, over time people start to suffer from amnesia. They may not be able to store information or retrieve it. AD usually affects *episodic memory* (personal memories) first, then *semantic memory* (memory of words and general knowledge) and finally *procedural memory* (how to perform tasks or skills). This is highlighted in Figure 3.14.

In the early stages of AD, two proteins, *tau* and *beta-amyloid,* are involved. The tau protein, which normally supplies nutrients to the neurons, becomes tangled; nutrients are shut off, killing the neuron. Beta-amyloid forms deposits known as plaques, which impair communication between neurons.

The neurons eventually die and the hippocampus, in particular, starts to shrink, eroding the memories that have been stored and making the formation of new long-term memories impossible. This is why people suffering from AD lose a sense of who they are and how their life has been constructed.

Alzheimer's Disease is now the most common form of dementia, which is the umbrella term for a group of symptoms affecting cognitive tasks

As the actress Carey Mulligan, the Alzheimer's Society's first Global Dementia Friends Ambassador, says:

'It's so important that everyone living with the condition is treated with the respect and dignity that they deserve. At the moment, there's not nearly enough awareness about what dementia is and as a society we all have a duty to change that.'

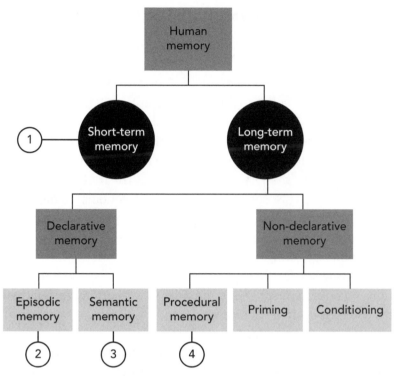

FIGURE 3.14: Order in which Alzheimer's Disease affects memory

such as memory and reasoning. According to the World Health Organization, 47.5 million people around the world are now living with dementia. Awareness and an early diagnosis are critical to addressing this growing problem.

Does time of day affect our memory?

Researchers in Japan have recently proved that time of day affects our memory recall.[24] As Chapter 12, Our Brain and Lifestyle, explains, we follow an internal circadian clock that drives our biological and behavioural rhythms every 24 hours.

This clock is responsible for regulating our sleep-wake cycles and scientists have also suspected that it affects our ability to form memories.

The experiment, designed to test the memories of mice at various intervals, by comparing a healthy group with a group whose circadian system had been disrupted, showed that their internal clock had an impact on their memory recall.

It is not clear what evolutionary purpose that this would have served, but scientists are now investigating the significance of these findings on our neural pathways linked to learning and memory.

The brain of the London black cab driver

As Chapter 1, Our Brain, explains, our brain is plastic and can change over the course of our life.

In 2011, Eleanor Maguire, Professor of Cognitive Neuroscience at University College London and her colleague, Dr Katherine Woollett, published a five-year study involving a group of 79 trainee black cab drivers.[25]

In order to earn their licence, black cab drivers need to pass a series of tests known as 'The Knowledge'. They spend three to four years driving around London on mopeds, committing the city's 25,000 streets, 320 routes and around 20,000 landmarks (museums, parks, churches, theatres and schools) to memory.

During the study, the 79 trainees were given memory tests and their brains were scanned using magnetic resonance imaging (MRI). The results were compared to a group of 39 non-drivers.

The trainees that successfully qualified as black cab drivers showed an enlarged hippocampus on both hemispheres, compared to when they started their training. The growth could be seen particularly at the back, which is important for spatial navigation. The same changes could not be seen in those who did not qualify or in the non-driver group.

As Professor Maguire said:

'The human brain remains "plastic", even in adult life, allowing it to adapt when we learn new tasks.'

Top Tips
Remember: **STORE**

Sleep! This is so important for our memory function. Chapter 12, Our Brain and Lifestyle, discusses the optimum hours of sleep per age group. If you are suffering from lack of sleep, short naps of between 10 and 30 minutes during the day have been found to boost and restore brainpower.

Test your brain with challenging cognitive exercises such as cryptic crosswords or memory games. Beat the Forgetting Curve by practising your recall and making associations. The best way to remember anything is to teach it to someone else!

Organise words or concepts with systems or devices, such as mnemonics that chunk information into a memorable format. Use different types of mnemonics to vary the way you encode information. The act of creating a mnemonic will help you remember the information.

Regulate your diet and include salmon, mackerel, tuna and other fish that are rich in heart-healthy omega-3 fatty acids, which are important for the normal functioning of neurons. Green tea, walnuts and vitamins E, D, B6 and B12 are also good for enhancing memory.

Exercise! The hippocampus, where we store personal memories, is able to grow new neurons through physical exercise and can even regenerate itself throughout our life (known as *neurogenesis*). Exercise also protects neurons from damage by increasing oxygen-rich blood flow to the brain.

References for Chapter 3

1. Kahneman, D. (2012). *Thinking Fast and Slow*. London: Penguin Books.
2. Miller, G.A. (1955). 'The magical number seven, plus or minus two: Some limits on our capacity for processing information', *Psychological Review*, May, 45–62.
3. Squire, L. (2009). 'The legacy of patient H.M. for neuroscience', *Neuron*, January, 6–9.
4. James, W. (1890). *The Principles of Psychology*. New York: Cosimo Inc.
5. Brown, R., & Kulik, J. (1977). 'Flashbulb memories', *Cognition*, March, 73–99.
6. Neisser, U., & Harsch, N. (1992). *Phantom Flashbulbs: False Recollections of Hearing the News about Challenger. Affect and Accuracy in Recall: Studies of 'Flashbulb' Memories*. New York: Cambridge University Press, 9–31.
7. Wilmott, E. et al. (2012). 'Sitting for protracted periods increases risk of diabetes, heart disease and death', *Science Daily*, October. www.sciencedaily.com/releases/2012/10/121015090048.htm
8. Rhya, I.J. et al. (2010). 'Effects of aerobic exercise training on cognitive function and cortical vascularity in monkeys', *Neuroscience*, June, 1249–48.
9. Ansell, E.B. et al. (2012). 'Cumulative adversity and smaller gray matter volume in medial prefrontal, anterior cingulate, and insula regions', *Biological Psychiatry*, July, 57–64.
10. Heffernan, T. et al. (2016). 'The impact of active and passive smoking upon health and neurocognitive function', *Frontiers Media*. doi.org/10.3389/978-2-88919-977-8
11. Sabia, S. et al. (2014). 'Alcohol consumption and cognitive decline in early old age', *Neurology*, January, 332–39.
12. Wimber, M. et al. (2015). 'Retrieval induces adaptive forgetting of competing memories via cortical pattern suppression', *Nature Neuroscience*, February, 582–89.
13. Weinreich, H. et al. (2006). 'Off the beaten tracks: Exploring three aspects of Web navigation', in *Proceedings of the 15th International Conference on the World Wide Web*, Edinburgh, 133–42.
14. Carr, N. (2011). *The Shallows: How the Internet is Changing the Way We Think, Read and Remember*. New York: Norton and Company Inc.
15. Greenfield, P.M. (2009). 'Technology and informal education: What is taught, what is learned', *Science*, January, 69–71.
16. McKinlay, R. (2016). 'Technology: Use or lose our navigation skills', *Nature*, March, 573–75.
17. Ebbinghaus, E. (1885). *Memory: A Contribution to Experimental Psychology*. Translated by H.A. Ruger and C.E. Bussenius (1913); originally published New York: Teachers College, Columbia University.
18. Rapp, D. (2016). 'The consequences of reading inaccurate information', *Current Directions in Psychological Science*, August, 281–85.
19. Schacter, D.L. (2002). *The Seven Sins of Memory: How the Mind Forgets and Remembers*. New York: Mariner Books.
20. Loftus, E.F., & Palmer, J.C. (1974). 'Reconstruction of automobile destruction: An example of the interaction between language and memory', *Journal of Verbal Learning and Verbal Behavior*, October, 585–89.
21. National Research Council. (2014). *Identifying the Culprit: Assessing Eyewitness Identification*. Washington, D.C.: National Academies Press.

22. Wearing, D. (2011). *Forever Today: A Memoir of Love and Amnesia.* London: Transworld Books.

23. Finke, C. et al. (2012). 'Preservation of musical memory in an amnesic professional cellist', *Current Biology*, 591–92.

24. Hasegawa, S. et al. (2019). 'Hippocampal clock regulates memory retrieval via Dopamine and PKA-induced GluA1 phosphorylation', *Nature Communications,* December. https://doi.org/10.1038/s41467-019-13554-y

25. Woollett, K., & Maguire, E.A. (2001). *Acquiring "the Knowledge" of London's Layout Drives Structural Brain Changes*, Current Biology, December, 2109–14.

Concentrate all your thoughts upon the work at hand. The sun's rays do not burn until brought to focus.

ALEXANDER GRAHAM BELL
Scientist, inventor, engineer and innovator (1847–1922)

chapter four

Our Brain and Attention

ABOUT THIS CHAPTER

We have an excellent capacity to focus and concentrate. From an early age, our attention directs us to what is important and relevant to us.

But our brain is constantly being bombarded with different sensory information and does not have the capacity to deal with all the inputs it receives. Our attentional system is the mechanism by which we select what we want to concentrate on and discard everything else.

We all need a better understanding of the strengths and limitations of our attentional system so that we can get the best out of it. Distractions interrupt our ability to focus and can even be fatal. We have to learn to pay attention to the right things at the right time.

This chapter provides an explanation of how we pay attention, and why we need to improve our capacity to concentrate.

Part 1: The science explained

How do we pay attention?

A huge amount of information comes in through our eyes. In fact, 90% of the information we absorb is visual.

Because we do not have the brainpower to manage at a conscious level all the information we receive, we have to filter and select what to pay attention to on a continual basis. We are constantly including and excluding information: we keep information that we are interested in and ignore or delete anything that is anomalous or of no concern to us.

There are two ways in which our attention is caught. The first is called *bottom-up processing*, which is stimulus-driven, and the second is *top-down processing*, which is goal-driven.[1] The differences between these two types of processing are explained in Figure 4.1.

Bottom-up Processing	Top-down Processing
Sensory information enters the brain.	Attention is directed to something based on our expectations, previous experience or context.
The brain pieces it together to make sense of it.	This information is combined with data already stored and interpreted accordingly.
The processing is carried out in one direction (from the retina to the visual cortex), is data-driven and takes place in real time.	We use pattern recognition to make sense of the information. This is explained in more detail in Chapter 6, Our Brain and Visual Perception.
Example: Imagine we are having a conversation with someone and then suddenly we hear a loud bang. This bang will divert our attention away from the conversation.	*Example:* When we read, we use the whole text to make sense of the letters and words. Our knowledge of the context or meaning helps us fill in any gaps. This is why we do not need to see the whole word or the word spelled correctly in order to understand it.

FIGURE 4.1: Two types of processing

Once we have decided to hold on to information, we then use our store of memories and knowledge and our beliefs to interpret and make sense of it, and then look for further supporting evidence. This is explained in more detail in Chapter 3, Our Brain and Memory.

For years it has been thought that our attentional system works like a spotlight: when we pay attention to something, we shine the spotlight on it. And when we need to shift attention, we effectively move the spotlight to something else, leaving everything else in the dark.

In 1984, the geneticist Francis Crick,[2] proposed that our attentional system was controlled by the *thalamus*, the structure he called the 'gate-keeper' that interacts with the *prefrontal cortex* in receiving sensory information, and then selects what to send on to other regions of the brain.

More recently, Dr Michael Halassa, a neuroscientist at the McGovern Institute for Brain Research at the Massachusetts Institute of Technology, has found a circuitry of neurons that connect the pre-frontal cortex with another group of structures called the *basal ganglia,* which are associated with motor control, habit-learning and decision-making.[3] The basal ganglia intercept incoming information before it reaches the thalamus and visual cortex.

This suggests that, instead of our attentional system being a means of *focusing on* something, it may instead be a system that *filters out* what is unnecessary or irrelevant and explains how we are able to tune out noisy distractions.

The involvement of the basal ganglia also suggests that attention and action are connected, with one guiding the other. This means that our actions influence how we see the world, and vice versa.

Our view of the world – and our interactions with it – therefore affect how we direct our attention and filter new incoming information. We seek and process details that correspond with what we expect, and we reject any evidence that contradicts it.

We do not see what we do not expect to see

Our brain's filtering system means that we may be discarding information that is important, or we may fail to see what we are not expecting to see. We can even miss what is right in front of our nose!

Even when we are concentrating hard, we can still fail to spot signs that would be obvious if we were actually looking for them.

We also lack positive evidence for our lack of attention. In other words, we do not know what we have failed to see, and we only become aware of these misses after they have been pointed out to us. The good news is that our brain may have a way to mitigate against our risk of missing something the first time. It seems that our brain is designed to stay open to new inputs periodically in order to avoid being too focused on one thing for a certain amount of time. In fact, our brain will shift focus four times in one second as a way of re-evaluating what it is paying attention to.[4]

How do we know what to focus on?

Our brain's filtering system is known as the *reticular activating system* (RAS), which is a network of neurons and neural fibres running through our brain stem (see Figure 4.2). Nearly all the information entering the brain via our senses is filtered through the RAS. The only sense that goes directly to our emotional centres is our sense of smell.

The RAS is always on, bringing relevant information to our attention.

Imagine walking through a busy airport full of noise. Our RAS will respond immediately if our name is called over the public address system. It will help filter out everything else and help us hear only our name above all the other noise.

Our RAS makes sure that we focus on what is important to us.

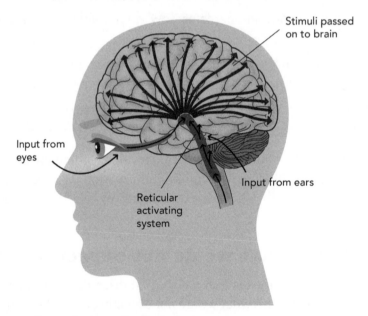

FIGURE 4.2: Our reticular activating system

Examples of how our RAS works are below:

When we buy a new car, we start seeing the same car everywhere.
A pregnant woman will become aware of other pregnant women around her.
The cry of our baby will wake us up immediately.
When we are thinking of going on holiday, we will see more travel agents or holiday commercials around us.

Even though the world around us may not alter, our RAS will help us pick out the specific details that we want and need at the time.

Our autopilot makes us lazy thinkers

Conscious thinking requires effort. It uses our brain's cognitive and physical resources. For this reason, conscious thinking is a considerably inefficient process (see Figure 4.3).

In order to free up its resources, our brain makes many of our conscious cognitive processes automatic. With practice and repetition, these cognitive processes fall below the level of conscious attention. In other words, we do not need to think about them any more. This is what we call *autopilot*, or automacity.

We often develop bad habits without being aware of them because they are below our conscious radar.
Because conscious thinking requires effort and discipline, we often defer to what feels easier and we stop challenging our view of the world.
We accept information too easily because it seems to be right.
We can be impatient and seek instant gratification.

FIGURE 4.3: The pitfalls of automaticity

We regularly defer to this autopilot because it feels fast and effortless. And we love being able to repeat familiar patterns of behaviour because they are predictable. As was discussed in Chapter 2, Our Brain and Emotion, Professor Daniel Kahneman calls this fast route to behaviour *System 1 thinking*.[5]

For example, consider the way that, after years of being a motorist, we no longer have to think about every movement, manoeuvre and signal that we make. We would find it difficult to describe every single thing we do when we drive, especially along a familiar route.

With practice, our automatic performance in any task becomes more efficient until it becomes hardwired into the physical structure of our brain. This is how habits are formed: a new task demands mental exertion, but as we practise over time, the mental activity that is needed decreases. This is known as *cognitive ease*.

But while automatic processes free our brain up to take on new and additional challenges, they can also be problematic.

In order to challenge or override something that we have made automatic in our brain, we effectively need to rewire our brain with a new habit. We can find this very difficult, which is why we may resist change or taking on something new or different: it all feels like too much hard work. This is discussed in more detail in Chapter 9, Our Brain and Change.

Part 2: Impact on our daily life

Why do experts miss what is right in front of them?

Experts can perform certain tasks effortlessly. When we become an expert at anything, our brain adapts and changes to reflect that expertise.

An experiment was conducted recently by Dr Trafton Drew at Harvard Medical School with 24 expert radiologists.[6] These radiologists were asked to look at computerised axial tomography (CAT) chest scans and search only for any cancerous nodules or abnormalities that could identify lung cancer. Without their knowledge, in the last scan, Dr Drew inserted an image of a gorilla 48 times larger than the average nodule, circled in the picture below.

Over 80% of the radiologists claimed that they had not seen the gorilla, even though an eye-tracking monitor showed that half the group who said they did not see the gorilla had looked straight at it.

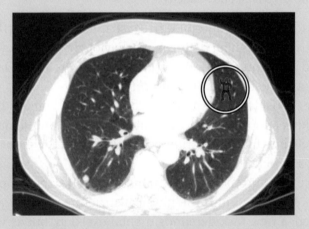

Dr Drew commented:

'Part of the reason that radiologists are so good at what they do is that they are very good at narrowly focusing their attention on these lung nodules. And the cost of that is that they're subject to missing other things, even really obvious large things like a gorilla.'

Credit: Dr Trafton Drew, *Psychological Science*, 2013.

But expertise can come at a cost. It involves a trade-off in our brain: as we strengthen certain connections, we may weaken others.

And so, when we specialise in a particular area of knowledge, we reduce our field of focus and centre only on this domain. In doing so, we tend not to incorporate information outside this specialism. In other words, our attentional spotlight narrows down our perspective and our view becomes increasingly concentrated and constricted.

When our attention is diverted and we do not notice the appearance of an object that is unexpected, it is known as *inattentional blindness*.

Dr Drew's study has important implications for the way we are given instructions, or where we choose to focus our attention: we will tend to see only what we are told or expect to see, and we may miss something else. Attention, it seems, is a zero-sum game: in order to think about or focus on something, we stop thinking about or focusing on something else. We cannot direct our attention at two things at the same time.

Focus is critical to improvement . . .

Our brain's connections strengthen when we decide to pay attention to something. When we practise a technique or a habit every day, we reshape our brain. This applies to whatever we choose to focus on: the more we do it, the more our brain adapts to help us.

Professors Christopher Chabris and Daniel Simons have conducted one of the most well-known studies in psychology.[7] Participants were asked to watch a short video in which six people (three in white shirts and three in black shirts) pass basketballs around, and then count the number of passes made by the people in white shirts.

During the game, a 'gorilla' strolls into the middle of the game and beats its chest. Over half the people watching the video fail to see the gorilla, even though it is in full view for several seconds.

In fact, participants were astounded when, having been told about the gorilla, they looked again at the video and saw it!

In 2004, as a result of this and other experiments, the two professors shared the Ig Nobel Prize in Psychology, awarded for 'achievements that first make people laugh, and then make them think'.

. . . but focus can also make us blind

Another aspect of our attentional system, which is closely linked to inattentional blindness, is a phenomenon called *change blindness,* which happens when we fail to spot unexpected changes in our visual world (see Figure 4.4). Once these changes are pointed out or subsequently noticed, they seem obvious.

Our susceptibility to change blindness is why magicians are so successful. When magicians distract our attention in one direction, we miss what they are doing elsewhere.

During change blindness, the visual system is working and processing inputs as normal, but because there are often too many inputs, a bottleneck occurs in our brain, and we miss what should appear to be obvious once we know it is there.

Change blindness provides an explanation of why . . .
Traffic accidents happen.
Continuity errors in movies go unnoticed.
Eyewitness testimony is often considered unreliable.
Drivers looking for other cars on the road may not be aware of cyclists or motorcyclists.
Baggage screeners at airports find it easier to focus on looking just for single items, such as explosives or knives, rather than trying to detect many items at once.

FIGURE 4.4: Consequences of change blindness

No one can multitask

Many women believe they can multitask, perhaps because of their ability to shift more easily between brain hemispheres than men, as explained in Chapter 1, Our Brain.

However, none of us truly have the ability to multitask. We do not have the brainpower to pay attention to two things at the same time. Imagine, for example, trying to read a book while writing a letter!

We may be able to process information from at least two non-competing stimuli at the same time. So we can look at someone, listen and nod our head. Or we can wash the dishes and listen to music.

But trying to use the same cognitive processes together is a physiological impossibility. For example, if we try to count numbers and say the alphabet simultaneously, we quickly realise that it is unfeasible.

Trying to multitask effectively splits our brain. When we quickly withdraw our attention from one task to focus on another, the brain is effectively blank for a split second. This is called a *post-refractory pause* and, over time, the sum of these small losses of attention may be dramatic.

Even one moment of inattention can have significant consequences.

Trying to multitask hurts our brain

Since the 1980s, scientists have been repeating that performance suffers when people try to multitask. We are prone to more errors, we have difficulty retaining information, our focus is impaired and we become more stressed.

In fact, people who try to multitask regularly are much worse at filtering irrelevant information and cannot even switch between tasks, compared to those who tackle one thing at a time.[8]

But we live in a world where our cognitive resources are under constant pressure. According to a report by the McKinsey Global Institute, we spend an average of 13 hours a week dealing with emails.[9] And the more quickly we answer our emails, especially when they pop up when we are in the middle of doing something else, the more productive we feel.

But this constant shifting between tasks is stressful and mentally exhausting. It also increases production of the stress hormone cortisol, which in the long term can even shrink our brain, as discussed further in Chapter 10, Our Brain and Stress.

Why does multitasking make us feel good?

However, while trying to multitask actually makes us less productive, it makes us feel good![10] This may explain why we still try to do it even though it affects our performance. When we feel that we are achieving a great deal – even though we may not actually be as efficient as we would like to think we are – it gives us a sense of emotional fulfilment.

The thrill of our email inbox or Facebook page releases *dopamine,* the neurotransmitter mentioned in Chapter 1, Our Brain. Dopamine helps to regulate our movement, direct our attention and activate the reward centres in our brain.

Dopamine is released in a region of the brain known as the *nucleus accumbens,* which registers pleasure. Recreational drugs and alcohol bring about a particularly intense surge of dopamine in this region. And because dopamine also plays a role in learning and memory, it ensures that the brain not only likes something, but also stores it as a pleasurable experience in our memory.

When we repeat a behaviour that makes us happy, the nucleus accumbens and the *prefrontal cortex* (the area of the brain involved in attention, planning and execution) work together to make us seek it even more. This is what we call *addiction.*

Our world of constant distraction is feeding a neural addiction in our brain. The more we try to multitask, the more we want to multitask, despite the fact that we are not being as effective as we think. We may feel good, but we are also paying a cognitive price.

Scientists are now claiming that over half the developed world is addicted to something, and, in particular, this addiction is to technology-driven behaviours, a subject that is explored in Adam Alter's book *Irresistible.*[11] Alter cites stories and examples of how games are crafted to entice and entertain, how a near-win holds more appeal than an actual victory, and how gamers will spend more time on a mission to kill rather than save a life. And, ironically, the people who are designing these games generally limit their own children's usage of technology.

Why is distraction so dangerous?

Our addiction to technology and often obsessive checking of our email or social media sites are creating a myriad of problems that range from minor errors to potentially fatal consequences.

When we are distracted, we pay less attention and we are more likely to make mistakes. We need to give our attentional system all the help it needs. Because we cannot predict what we will miss or notice in our visual field, we need to limit any distraction.

But distractions are everywhere.

The use of technology, such as satellite navigation systems or talking on the telephone while driving, steals our attention away from the road, and both activities constitute a potentially hazardous situation.

In some Australian, German and Dutch towns, *in-road* traffic lights for pedestrians approaching a road crossing are now positioned on the ground because people are constantly looking down at their phones.

We cannot give up the technology to which we have become accustomed, but at the same time we do need to recognise the impact of endless distraction and lack of attention on the way we are now living.

We take mental shortcuts to deal with information

Because we can only process a limited amount of information at once without being overloaded, we take mental shortcuts to speed up our decision-making. These mental shortcuts are known as *heuristics* and they help us act or make decisions with minimal effort.

But while heuristics can give us the illusion that we are thinking quickly and efficiently, they can also introduce errors and bias. By deferring to our heuristics, we will often rely on what has worked well in the past. The problem is that past experiences, however successful they were at the time, are not always helpful or appropriate for dealing with future challenges.

And we are often unable to see beyond our successes in order to interpret new information accurately. As a result, we may not consider different possibilities or listen to opposing viewpoints. This is explained in more detail in Chapter 7, Our Brain and Biases.

Why do we like our comfort zone?

We like to operate best in places we know, and we are able to navigate a familiar place with greater efficiency. This is called our *comfort zone*.

As change speeds up and uncertainty looms everywhere, our need for comfort becomes stronger than ever. And since many of us are creatures of habit and routine, we stick to what we know: we follow the same route to work, we have our favourite places to stand, sit and shop, and we even take the same holidays. We know what we like and we like what we know.

Our comfort zone is so comfortable that leaving it can feel uncomfortable – or even painful. And when we try to move into unknown territory we often find ourselves rushing back towards what is familiar. Even certain criminals prefer to operate close to their homes, with serious offences usually being committed between just one and two miles from where the offender lives.

The advantage of our comfort zone is that it helps us to stay calm and it reduces our anxiety, which is a healthy strategy when we are living in a fast-moving and rapidly changing world.

However, personal growth and learning are dependent on our openness to new experiences and challenges. The more we learn to deal with the discomfort of change, the more we will expand our comfort zone and thereby increase our overall resilience.

Part 3: Stories and top tips

Attention-related accidents are on the rise

Reports of road accidents caused by drivers failing to pay attention are on the increase. In the United Kingdom, driver distraction (listening to music, using mobile phones or satellite navigation systems), rather than speed, is now the main cause of road accidents, and groups are lobbying for legislation to address driver concentration.

The US government now has a website (www.enddd.org/distraction-gov) to help educate the public about the dangers of distracted driving. One simple example is that sending or receiving a text message will divert a driver's eyes from the road for almost five seconds. If we are driving at 55 miles per hour, in those five seconds we are not looking at the road for the entire length of a football field.

The 2016 tragedy in Newbury – a town in the United Kingdom – when a mother and her three children were killed after a lorry driver crashed into them at 50 miles per hour, was linked to driver distraction. The dashcam footage shows that the driver was so focused on his mobile phone that he did not notice any of the traffic in front of him.

The march of the machine

Human fallibility and susceptibility to error and blindness mean that computers are now starting to replace humans in cognitive tasks. For example, computer search patterns (such as Google Flu Trends and Google Dengue Trends) are now more accurate than doctors' predictions, and algorithms rather than human-made models are being used to inform decision-making.

In South Korea, scientists have developed technology on a smartphone that will diagnose diseases such as cancer and diabetes with 100% accuracy.[12] This technology is designed to detect biological signals such as biomolecules via the touchscreen. The hope is that this technology will revolutionise medical diagnoses around the world.

In January 2017, the *Financial Times* announced the April launch of Babylon, an app built by 100 artificial-intelligence researchers based in London, which can provide a medical diagnosis and treatment via a smartphone.

Babylon is a repository of amassed data, and will be the first robot to be certified clinically by the UK's Medicines and Healthcare Products Regulatory

Agency to provide medical diagnoses – with 92% accuracy or ten times greater precision than a doctor.

This may be good news for patients. Medical errors and misdiagnoses have been the subject of considerable scrutiny in recent years. Medical leaders across the world are voicing their concerns about the state of healthcare and mounting pressures on doctors, both of which lead to flawed thought processes. About 1,000 people a month in the United Kingdom die through medical error; this is also reported as being the third-leading cause of death in the United States.[13]

Haematologist-oncologist Jerome Groopman has detailed in the first book of its kind how doctors miss vital signs when making diagnoses.[14] Dr Groopman explains how physicians frequently make snap judgements within as little as 18 seconds about a patient's illness and course of treatment. In order to compensate for their inability to see all the vital signs and symptoms that they need to see, medical professionals are increasingly using a thorough checklist system.

But checklists may not be able to stop the march of technology and the shifting confidence of those patients who may be more reassured by mechanical accuracy than by the human touch with all of its foibles.

Is our attention span shrinking?

Opinion is divided as to whether the average human attention span is shrinking. Some researchers claim that it has shortened considerably from twelve seconds in 2000 to eight seconds in 2015 – blaming the internet and social media.[15] On the other hand, there are those who believe that research in this area is spurious and who state that there is no such thing as an 'average attention span' and even if there was, it would be difficult to measure.[16]

However, there now seems to be evidence from a Danish study[17] that confirms that our collective attention span has indeed reduced. And the reason? The huge increase in publicly available information.

This study used data sources such as Twitter, Google, Wikipedia and Reddit, and examined three aspects of collective attention: the length of time a topic lasted in public discussions (such as over Twitter), the volume of discussion on the topic, and the speed of switching away from the topic in favour of something new. Collective interactions over several years were compared. Results showed that peaks and falls of interest have become steeper over time. The greater the volume of content, the shorter the collective attention.

This trend is set to continue as news channels, websites, advertising and algorithms compete for our attention. Our tendency to switch rapidly to the next item is exacerbated by a strong novelty bias (explained more in Chapter 7, Our Brain and Biases), and we are increasingly susceptible to short, catchy and possibly superficial – or even inaccurate – reporting.

Our attention span is unlikely to improve in the future. We live in an age of copious and constant rapid-fire communication that is placing more pressure than ever on our attentional resources. And so perhaps we need to be re-thinking the way we generate, consume and share information instead.

The relationship between attention and learning

When we learn to pay attention to detail, we increase our intelligence and accuracy in performing tasks. We also build stronger relationships with other people because we are better able to detect common interests and opportunities for collaboration.

In 2015, a study published by the London School of Economics found an improvement in exam results among pupils in schools that had banned mobile phones.[18] The researchers stated that the reduced distraction caused by the removal of phones led to better results and increased productivity.

In 2018, President Emmanuel Macron's government passed a law in France stating that all smartphones and tablets were to be banned in schools for children between 3 and 15 years of age. Schools for older children can choose to adopt this law. Across the world, there is increasing concern about the amount of time children spend on their phones, but France is one of the first countries to address the issue.

Ontario, Canada, has restricted the use of mobile phones in classrooms to enable pupils to focus more on their school work. Some schools in the United Kingdom have now banned mobile phones altogether.

One school in England has recently brought about a complete change in pupils' behaviour since banning mobile phones. Pupils are forbidden to use their phones during the day, with detentions imposed on anyone found with a handset between 8:15am and 5:45pm. These rules are supported by the pupils' parents.

The head teacher behind this initiative claims that the removal of this distraction has meant that more time is spent by the pupils conversing and debating with each other, instead of worrying about social media. The school still uses tablets and laptops for teaching, but pupils themselves have said that the experience has freed them from the pressures of social media, leaving them better able to concentrate on their studies and on building relationships with each other.

We can all benefit from learning to pay better attention.

As the author and Zen teacher Ezra Bayda says:

'When you really pay attention, everyone is your teacher.'

Top Tips
Remember: **AWARE**

Acknowledge that you cannot multitask, particularly in a situation that could jeopardise your safety. Remember that a car is potentially a lethal weapon! A few seconds of inattention could have permanent and deadly consequences. Focus on one thing at a time.

Work at changing your routine and leaving your comfort zone on a regular basis. Learn something new, such as a new language, musical instrument or sport. People who regularly seek out fresh experiences tend to be more creative and emotionally resilient than those who remain stuck in their comfort zone.

Accept challenges to your thinking. Question the heuristics or mental shortcuts that you are using. Even if you have an expertise or specialism, you may not have all the right answers. Welcome other viewpoints, even if they contradict what you think you know.

Remove all possible distractions in meetings. Computers and telephones should be kept out of sight so that you are able to concentrate fully on what people are saying. You will take in far more information about people if you pay full attention to them.

Expand your view of the world. Learn to look around you and take the time to pick up details about your environment and other people. Think about everything you are taking in through your senses.

References for Chapter 4

1. Connor, C.E. et al. (2004). 'Visual attention: Bottom-up versus top-down', *Current Biology* October, 850–52. https://doi.org/10.1016/j.cub.2004.09.041

2. Crick, F. (1984). 'Function of the thalamic reticular complex: The searchlight hypothesis', *Proceedings of the National Academy of Sciences*, July, 4586–90. https://doi.org/10.1073/pnas.81.14.4586

3. Nakajima, M. (2019). 'Prefrontal cortex regulates sensory filtering through a basal ganglia to thalamus pathway', *Neuron*, August. https://doi.org/10.1016/j.neuron.2019.05.026

4. Fiebelkorn, I.C., & Kastner, S. (2019). 'A rhythmic theory of attention', *Trends in Cognitive Sciences*, December, 87–101. https://doi.org/10.1016/j.tics.2018.11.009

5. Kahneman, D. (2012). *Thinking Fast and Slow*. London: Penguin Books.

6. Drew, G. et al. (2013). 'The invisible gorilla strikes again: Sustained inattentional blindness in expert observers', *Psychological Science*, July, 1848–53.

7. Chabris, C., & Simons, D. (2011). *The Invisible Gorilla: And Other Ways Our Intuition Deceives Us*. New York: HarperCollins.

8. Ophir, E. et al. (2009). 'Cognitive control in media multitaskers', *Proceedings of the National Academy of Sciences*, 15583–87.

9. Chui, M. et al. (2012). 'The social economy: Unlocking value and productivity', McKinsey Global Institute, July. www.mckinsey.com

10. Wang, Z., & Tchernev, J.M. (2012). 'The "myth" of media multitasking: Reciprocal dynamics of media multitasking, personal needs, and gratifications', *Journal of Communication*, April, 493–513.

11. Alter, A. (2017). *Irresistible: The Rise of Addictive Technology and the Business of Keeping Us Hooked*. New York: Bodley Head.

12. Yeon W. et al. (2011). 'A touchscreen as a biomolecule detection platform', *Angewandte Chemie International Edition*, November, 748–51.

13. Makary, M.A., & Daniel, M. (2016). 'Medical error – the third leading cause of death in the US', *BMJ*, May. doi.org/10.1136/bmji2139

14. Groopman, J. (2007). *How Doctors Think*. New York: Houghton Mifflin Company.

15. McSpadden, K. (2015). 'You now have a shorter attention span than a goldfish' *Time*, May.

16. Maybin, S. (2017). 'Busting the attention span myth', *BBC World Service More or Less*.

17. Lorenz-Spreen, P. et al. (2019). 'Accelerating dynamics of collective attention', *Nature Communications*. doi:10.1038/s41467-019-09311-w

18. Beland, L.P., & Murphy, R. (2015). 'Communication: Technology, distraction & student performance', *Centre for Economic Performance*, May, 61–76.

'Without language one cannot talk to people and understand them; one cannot understand their hopes and aspirations, grasp their history, appreciate their poetry or savour their songs.'

NELSON MANDELA
Anti-apartheid revolutionary, politician and philanthropist
(1918–2013)

Our Brain and Language

ABOUT THIS CHAPTER

Language is one of our most significant evolutionary adaptations. Our ability to communicate using language is fundamental to our success as humans. Through our use of words, nuance and tonality, we are able to convey different meanings and levels of intensity in a way that is not possible for animals.

For the last 150 years, scientists have been studying the way we formulate and interpret language. Our extensive linguistic ability has enabled us to develop ideas, transform societies and incite others to action.

This chapter looks at language – both written and spoken – and how it works in our brain. Research is continuing in this area and there is much about our language systems and pathways that we are still discovering today.

Part 1: The science explained

Where is language processed in our brain?

When we hear a word, our brain determines whether it recognises the word and its meaning. Scientists have used brain imaging to localise where in the brain we hear sounds and then where we process language (see Figure 5.1).

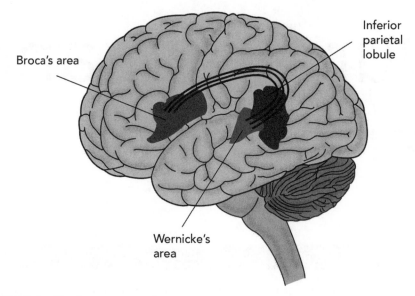

FIGURE 5.1: Our language pathways

Three scientists in particular provided our first significant insights into how we process language:

1) Paul Broca

In 1861, Paul Broca, a French neurologist, discovered a region of the brain associated with the production of spoken language. He found that damage to this area resulted in speech deficiencies.

Broca had been working with a patient who was known as 'Tan' because this was the only syllable the patient could utter. After Tan died, Broca conducted a post-mortem and found damage to an area of Tan's brain associated with speech production.

This area is now referred to as *Broca's area* and it is where we *construct* language.

Broca's work in the world of brain science and understanding was pioneering. Since then, research into brain problems has continued to provide valuable insights into how language works in our brain.

2) Carl Wernicke

Ten years after Broca, German neurologist Carl Wernicke found that Broca's area was not the only place in the brain where damage could cause a language deficit to occur.

Wernicke identified a language problem in which certain patients were able to speak but were not able to comprehend language. By examining the brains of patients suffering from this language problem, Wernicke revealed damage at a junction of the parietal, temporal and occipital lobes. This region of the brain is now known as *Wernicke's area* and is associated with the *understanding* of spoken and written language.

3) Norman Geschwind

In the 1960s, Norman Geschwind discovered that the *inferior parietal lobule* (IPL) of our brain also plays an important role in processing language. The neurons in the IPL can take stimuli from all our senses (this is called *multimodal*) and help our brain understand the construction, sound and meaning of spoken and written words.

The IPL is one of the last structures of the human brain to have developed over the course of human evolution and it exists only in a basic form in other primates. The IPL also matures later in children, which may explain why we cannot begin to read and write until we are about five years old.

The legacy of these three scientists is that we are now able to link certain language impairments with specific brain regions, and we can see how brain recovery can result in neural restructuring where brain pathways are repaired.

Language: a left-brained thing?

Scientific evidence suggests that we use both hemispheres of the brain to enable us to communicate.

In most people, it does seem that the left hemisphere is dominant for language, while the right hemisphere is involved in understanding simple words, metaphors, poetic metres and intonation.

But when the left hemisphere is damaged, the right hemisphere will step up and undertake a greater role in processing language. This has been observed in young children who have suffered from epilepsy and who undergo an operation called an *hemispherectomy*, in which a large section of the affected hemisphere is removed. After the left hemisphere has been removed in these cases, the right hemisphere has assumed responsibility for language functions almost perfectly.

The capacity of the right hemisphere to take on many of the main functions of language has important implications for those with damage to their left hemisphere. It also proves that our brain, although bilaterally organised, works as one unit.

How is language affected by injury or brain trauma?

Communication problems after brain injury are very common. A language disorder that affects both production and comprehension of language is known as *aphasia* (or in a less severe form as *dysphasia*).

The most common types of aphasia are shown Figure 5.2. These are only general labels for aphasia because, depending on the areas of the brain affected, and the severity of the injury, people may experience more than one kind of communication problem.

Global Aphasia	Patients cannot read or write, and their speech is very limited, speaking and understanding only a little.
Broca's Aphasia	Patients' ability to express language in the form of speech and writing is severely reduced. They speak mostly in nouns and produce a few words in non-fluent sentences. Example: 'Dog. . .walk. . .food. . .forget.'
Wernicke's Aphasia	Patients may not be able to read or write. They can speak fluently in nonsense without realising that this is happening. Example: 'Train and better teacher football headaches and finishing. Very good London.'
Anomic Aphasia	Patients understand speech and can read, but cannot speak or write easily.

FIGURE 5.2: Types of aphasia

There are many different successful ways of treating aphasia, depending on the type and cause. Speech and language therapy is the main treatment and, over time, this does help to alleviate symptoms.

Language is complex

Because language is complex, scientists have struggled to explain how it actually works in the brain. Recent research now suggests that language activates more of the brain than previously thought,[1] and involves multiple, interconnected brain regions, including the *right hemisphere* and the *parietal lobe*. The *occipital lobe* also plays a language-related role with people who are born blind. (Chapter 1, Our Brain, discusses these brain regions in more detail.)

The dynamic interaction of these brain regions mean that we can contextualise words, asses tonality, infer meaning or intention and make predictions. It seems that language is therefore a result of a sophisticated series of connections that extend across our whole brain.

Intonation affects meaning

Intonation – the tone of our voice – is one of the methods by which we communicate. Functional magnetic resonance imaging (fMRI) has provided valuable insights into how our brain separates speech into words and intonation.[2]

Most words are interpreted in the left temporal lobe for processing, while the intonation is channelled to the right side of the brain, a region more stimulated by music.

The emotion contained in the speaker's tone can ignite an emotional response in the listener that is remembered long after the actual message has been delivered.

Our intonation affects the meaning of the words we use.

Think about the following sentence:

'I didn't say he should stroke the dog.'

By emphasising different words through our intonation, we automatically change its meaning, as shown below.

Emphasis	Meaning
'**I** didn't say he should stroke the dog.'	Someone else said it.
'I **didn't** say he should stroke the dog.'	I am denying it.
'I didn't **say** he should stroke the dog.'	I implied it, pointed it out or wrote it down.
'I didn't say **he** should stroke the dog.'	Someone else should stroke the dog.
'I didn't say he **should** stroke the dog.'	It is not an obligation.
'I didn't say he should **stroke** the dog.'	He should just look at the dog.
'I didn't say he should stroke the **dog**.'	I meant that he should stroke the cat.

Different words light up different parts of our brain

Recent research is providing additional insight into language as a complex set of activities in our brain that may not be localised only in one or two areas.

A recent study has shown that, for the first time, scientists have been able to map different groups of words to different parts of the brain in order to examine how we represent meaning, or *semantics*.[3]

Using an fMRI scanner to monitor blood flow, scientists asked participants to listen to two hours of storytelling with over 10,000 English words involved. The results showed that our brain groups words together depending on what their significance is to us. For example, the same region in the temporal lobe – associated with emotion – lights up with words such as 'wife', 'house', 'pregnant' and 'family'.

Similarly, illustrative and vivid words that enable our brain to conjure up images (such as 'red rose' or 'blue sky') are reflected in activity in the occipital lobe, the area of the brain associated with processing visual information.

This research is a valuable starting point in explaining how information is stored across our brain. Clinical professionals may be able to use this semantic map to treat language disorders, and we may also gain greater insight into the neurological impact of messages in the public domain.

Our brain is organised for communication

Whether words are spoken or demonstrated with sign language, the brain treats them the same, and the same neural regions are activated by both.[4]

Our brain interprets signing as language and not as gestures, which would be associated more with games such as charades. In fact, research shows that signing and charades activate different brain areas, even when some of the hand gestures are similar.

> Researchers showed 29 deaf signers using American Sign Language (ASL) and 64 hearing native-English speakers pictures of objects such as a cup or a parrot and asked the subjects to either sign or speak the word.
>
> At the same time, they measured brain activity and blood flow using a positron emission tomography (PET) scanner.
>
> In both groups, Broca's and Wernicke's areas were equally active.

Our brain *sees* words

The brain converts words into visual associations almost immediately.

As explained in Chapter 6, Our Brain and Visual Perception, we have an area in the brain called the *fusiform face area* (FFA) that recognises faces quickly. We also have a *visual word form area* (VWFA) that helps us read words quickly; this helps us see the whole word at once rather than analysing its component parts.[5]

When we are skilled at reading, we do not need to process the sounds in each letter. Instead our brain recognises words quickly as part of a pattern.

> In 2013, Taiwanese-born entrepreneur ShaoLan Hsueh gave a TED talk on how to read Chinese. The following year, she published a book entitled *Chineasy: The New Way to Read Chinese.*[6]
>
> Motivated to teach her English-speaking children to read Mandarin, ShaoLan's aim was to create a pictorial connection to Chinese words through their associated images.
>
> Armed with her understanding of Chinese characters (she is the daughter of a calligrapher), ShaoLan commissioned the graphic artist Noma Bar to create a simple and visual system of symbols.

Part 2: Impact on our daily life

Why nouns make us respond more quickly than verbs

When we learn to read as children, we learn nouns before verbs. We are more able to form a mental image of nouns than of most verbs, which is why nouns tend to be easier to learn. And, as adults, we respond more quickly to nouns than other words.[7]

Advertising often uses adjectives as nouns such as:

'Rightmove. Find your **happy**.'

'Show us your Heinz.'

Where there is **happy** there has to be Heinz.'

'Olay. Your best **beautiful**.'

When we use one part of speech as another (a term known as *antimeria*, from the Greek *anti* meaning 'opposite' and *méros* meaning 'part'), such as using a verb as a noun, it helps attract more attention and for that reason is a clever advertising ploy.

We see words as shapes

As mentioned earlier in this chapter, our *visual word form area* (VWFA) enables us to read a word as a whole and become familiar with *word shapes*.

This is why road signs are increasingly using upper and lower case together, rather than upper case only, because we can see the pattern of the word, register it quickly and then respond quickly.

Compare this road sign:

to this one:

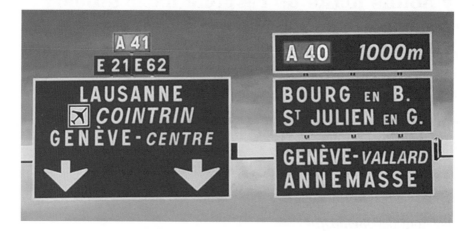

Understanding how our brain reads words also has important implications for how we teach children to read, particularly those who struggle with traditional methods. For example, children may find it easier to see the whole word as a visual object instead of having to learn it phonetically.

Can an understanding of language help stroke patients?

Strokes often affect people's ability to speak or perceive language. If a stroke has affected the right side of the brain, the patient may be unable to detect emotional intonation, whereas damage to the left side of the brain could affect their ability to comprehend certain words.

Knowledge of how language is processed in the healthy brain may therefore help scientists to develop more effective solutions for stroke patients to regain their mastery of language construction and comprehension.

What do our emails say about us?

Researchers are examining the language we use in emails. Thousands of emails have been analysed from participants who also completed personality questionnaires assessing levels of extrovertism or neurosis.[8] The more neurotic the participants, the greater their use of exclamation and quotation marks and the more erratic their use of commas and adverbs.

We now rely heavily on email for the majority of our communication even when we would often be better served by face-to-face contact. As discussed in Chapter 4, Our Brain and Attention, we are spending an average of 13 hours a week sorting out our inbox.[9]

When we overuse email, we do not promote proper dialogue or problem-solving and, worse, we risk misinterpretation.

In 2001, the Chief Executive of a US healthcare software development company, with 3,100 employees worldwide, sent an email to his 400 managers.

An excerpt from his email is shown on the following page:

> 'We are getting less than 40 hours of work from a large number of our K.C.-based EMPLOYEES. The parking lot is sparsely used at 8 a.m.; likewise at 5 p.m. As managers you either do not know what your EMPLOYEES are doing; or you do not CARE. In either case, you have a problem and you will fix it or I will replace you. NEVER in my career have I allowed a team which worked for me to think they had a 40-hour job. I have allowed YOU to create a culture which is permitting this. NO LONGER.
>
> I am tabling the promotions until I am convinced that the ones being promoted are the solution, not the problem. If you are the problem, pack your bags.
>
> I think this parental type action SUCKS. However, what you are doing, as managers, with this company makes me SICK. It makes me sick to have to write this directive.
>
> I am giving you two weeks to fix this. My measurement will be the parking lot: it should be substantially full at 7:30 AM and 6:30 PM. The pizza man should show up at 7:30 PM to feed the starving teams working late. The lot should be half full on Saturday mornings. We have a lot of work to do. If you do not have enough to keep your teams busy, let me know immediately.
>
> You have the responsibility for our EMPLOYEES. I will hold you accountable. You have allowed this to get to this state. You have two weeks. Tick, tock.'

This email was posted on Yahoo, and in three days the valuation of the company, which had been $1.5 billion on 20 March, plummeted by 22%.

An analyst with Goldman Sachs was reported as saying:

'It did raise two real questions for investors. One: Has anything potentially changed at [the company] to cause such a seemingly violent reaction? And two: Is this a CEO that investors are comfortable with?'

The power of words

The language we use has a powerful effect on our brain. A Spanish study has shown how the brain's region for taste and smell (*olfactory cortex*) lit up when shown the words 'garlic', 'cinnamon' and 'jasmine'.[10] Words can therefore stimulate our brain to conjure up a real sensory experience.

Another study in France used words describing motions such as 'grasp' and 'kick' and observed an increase in activity in the motor cortex, which coordinates the body's movements.[11] More specifically, when the movement was arm-related (such as 'grasp'), one area of the motor cortex responded, and when the movement concerned the leg (such as 'kick'), a different part was triggered.

It therefore seems that our brain cannot tell the difference between reading an experience and actually living through it; the brain behaves in exactly the same way in both cases.

OUR NAME

Our attentional system switches on when we hear what is relevant to us. And we love the sound of our name being used. Hearing our name validates us and affirms our identity.

As Dale Carnegie said:

'Remember that a person's name is to that person the sweetest and most important sound in any language.'

INSTANT

Some words actually spur us on to act. If we read or hear 'instant', 'immediate' and 'fast', our brain's reward centre is activated. We now live in a world of instant gratification. We have become used to getting real-time information and feedback. We want everything now! For example, we can see and upload photographs as soon as we have taken them, and then gauge people's responses immediately. When we cannot have something we want quickly, we become impatient and anxious.

And so, when we use language that denotes speed and immediacy in our conversations with others, we reduce any uncertainty that they may feel and we activate their brain's reward circuit.

NEW

Our brain loves being stimulated, and nothing stimulates it is more than novelty. For this reason, we love being told what is 'new'. Our brain reacts to 'new' information that is relevant to us, and even more so when it is unexpected or even grammatically wrong. When we see or hear old or known information, we do not notice it in the same way and may even miss some of the detail.[12]

But we have to strike the right balance between novelty and familiarity. Our impulse for having what is new drives most industries today, and the language of novelty often constitutes the sales message.

As Steve Jobs famously said (talking about Apple products):

'A lot of times people don't know what they want until you show it to them.'

Despite our attraction to the 'new', we nevertheless gravitate towards familiarity because it feels safe and secure. When something represents a significant departure from the old, it can represent too much of a challenge. So even though we have a strong novelty bias, we also like to be reassured and reminded of what we are used to.

BECAUSE

The word 'because' is powerful since our brain just needs a reason – and often any reason will do! The word 'because' informs us and helps us to make connections in our brain.

You need this product ***because*** . . ..

We always use this product ***because*** . . ..

I like this one better than that one ***because*** . . ..

We are more likely to accept unpopular or unfavourable decisions when we are given a reason. We often just need to know *why*. We only have to imagine how we feel when we are sitting on a train and it suddenly stops for no apparent reason. Our anxiety levels build the longer we are left waiting for an explanation.

YOU/YOUR

When we combine 'you'/'your' with 'because', the effect is very powerful.

Buy this product today ***because*** it will really help ***your*** business.

Go and buy a big car ***because your*** family is growing.

Do you want to know why **you** are always late?

It's **because you** need a new watch.

TOGETHER

Because we need to belong to a social group, the word 'together' carries a great deal of weight. So when we hear 'together', our brain's reward centre is activated and we feel more positive about what we are doing.

A recent study examined the impact of the word 'together' on the work of two groups.[13] Both groups started a task together and were then divided to work separately.

Group 1 were told that they were working on the task 'together', even though they had now been allocated a separate room.

Group 2 were just given the task.

The results showed that Group 1 worked for 48% longer, solved more problems correctly and enjoyed the work more than Group 2.

The word 'together' made all the difference.

The danger with NO . . .

Because we are naturally programmed to be negative and look for threats to our survival, we are easily influenced by words that sound negative.

Our brain responds in the same way, both when we express negative words ourselves and when we spend time with people who constantly use negative language.

Brain imaging studies have shown that if we see the word 'no', even for just a second, the same hormones and neurotransmitters that are produced in stressful situations are immediately released. These chemical releases interrupt our normal brain function, affecting the way that we think and communicate.

And it is not just the word 'no'. Any words with a negative association will have a harmful impact on us and can worsen our symptoms if we are feeling depressed or anxious. Language can therefore carry the *nocebo* (meaning 'I will harm' in Latin) effect and psychologically prepares and primes the brain for pain. This has important implications for how we use our words, which is explained in more detail later in this chapter in the section about feedback.

The research of Baruch Krauss, Associate Professor of Paediatrics at Harvard Medical School, focuses on anxiety and pain relief in children undergoing medical procedures.[14] Professor Krauss uses language with children that engages them and diverts their attention away from the pain and towards a motor activity such as colouring. He also examines the way children later recall and speak about their experience. By encouraging children to concentrate on a fun task, he finds that this is what they remember from the experience.

. . . and the importance of YES

It is not easy or straightforward to convert the brain from a negative to a positive state using just positive words. When we have been influenced negatively, we then have to work much harder to generate positive thoughts. In other words, negative information has a more profoundly lasting effect on us and is *cognitively stickier* than positive information.[15] We observe this phenomenon when consumer confidence, eroded by an economic downturn, remains resistant to emergent signals of recovery.

Positive words and thoughts stimulate the motivational centres of the brain into action and they make us more resilient to challenges. Our brain needs a constant diet of positive language and emotion if it is to build durable personal resources and coping mechanisms.[16] By generating positive language about ourselves and others, we decrease the impact of negative emotions and actively lay the cornerstone for a healthy, happy brain.

When to use BUT

The use of the word 'but' can kill communication and the flow of ideas and suggestions. We often start a sentence with it and we do not even realise how much we use it! The problem with the word 'but' is that it is a negation word; it cancels everything that precedes it:

'I appreciate what you are saying, **but** . . ..'

'That is a great proposal, **but** . . ..'

'You have done a great job, **but** . . ..'

When we hear 'but', we forget or ignore anything that has been said before it, even if the preceding words have been positive. We sometimes try to reduce the impact of 'but' by using 'however' – which is just a longer way of saying 'but'!

Some people are even advised to say the word 'and' instead of 'but'. This does not work either because 'and' is often still heard as a 'but', particularly if it is used too much. The way that we often arrange our sentences in two halves – a positive, followed by a negative statement – means that our brain is still hooking on to the negative.

However, 'but' can be used in a positive way. Because 'but' effectively invalidates what goes before, it can be used as a refocusing technique. For example, when we need to deliver bad news, we can apply 'but' to soften the blow, particularly when used in conjunction with the word 'because':

'We cannot do this **because** . . .,

. . . **but** what we can do is . . .'

Here *but* is used to minimise the preceding negative and to emphasise the positive alternative.

Be careful of DON'T

Although many words we use are *seen* by our brain, the word 'don't' is not one of them! We say to people:

'**Don't** look behind you.'

'I **don't** want you to be upset about this.'

'Please **don't** hesitate to contact me.'

We say to small children:

'**Don't** touch that.'

'**Don't** knock that over.'

'**Don't** spill that drink.'

And then we are surprised when we witness the very behaviour we think we have tried to prevent!

When we are told not to think about something, our brain immediately conjures up the very image or behaviour associated with the word that we can see. If we would like people to do something for us, we therefore need to reinforce what we *want* to see, and not what we *do not* want to see!

Why do some words annoy or repel us?

There are some words and phrases that we all find annoying. Lucy Kellaway, the former *Financial Times* journalist, presents annual *corporate guff awards* for terrible use of language in business. These include such terms as 'chief manifesto specialist', 'life-performance solutions', 'through the lens of humanity', 'right culture' and 'values-driven organisation'. Kellaway's dictionary of business jargon, or *guffipedia,* contains an extensive list of words and phrases that many of us will be familiar with!

These *guff* words of corporate nonsense mostly make us feel irritated and prompt us to switch off: our brain does not appreciate the simple made complex.

There are also some words that actually make us shudder, and even evoke an extreme visceral response, when we hear them. This phenomenon is known as *word aversion.*

Professor Mark Lieberman at the University of Pennsylvania explains that our aversive reaction to these words is not based on misuse, overuse or grammatical error.[17] Our distaste is based on the fact that these words actually feel disgusting. Among the words that Professor Lieberman lists as causing offence are 'cornucopia', 'hardscrabble', 'pugilist' and 'wedge'. Other words that provoke a negative reaction are 'crevice', 'slacks', 'luggage' and 'phlegm'.

But it seems that the most repellent word of all is 'moist'. Understanding word aversion may help us guard against the words that we should not under any circumstances use in promotional or marketing literature.

Neuroscientist Dr David Eagleman suggests that the word-aversion phenomenon may be similar to *synaesthesia,* where our senses conjoin and certain sounds or words are associated with images or emotions.[18]

This subject is covered in more detail in Chapter 8, Our Brain and Creativity.

Does feedback work?

Feedback is one of the most debated processes in the business world.

When we give feedback to other people we are effectively telling them what we think about their performance or behaviour.

We normally give feedback for three reasons: 1) to praise people for a job well done, 2) to improve their performance in the future and 3) to change their behaviour.

The question is: does feedback actually work?

In 2019, Marcus Buckingham and Ashely Goodall published an article in the *Harvard Business Review* about feedback,[19] debunking the three reasons why feedback is considered a force for good in most businesses: 1) other people can see our weakness better than we can, 2) we all need to learn and 3) performance can be assessed and described. Instead, we should accept that we are not always good at evaluating other people objectively; we all learn and develop differently and excellence cannot be achieved by examining failure.

Many businesses follow a well-trodden path for performance appraisal every year whereby managers give feedback to their employees. The format that is most frequently used for this process is called the *feedback sandwich.*

So how we do we make a feedback sandwich?

The bread on the outside of the sandwich constitutes positive or neutral feedback. The filling in the middle is composed of advice for further development; this filling is often heard as the negative or main message.

The problem with the feedback sandwich is that our brain's natural negativity bias interferes with the whole process. The *positive* messages on both sides of the *development* segment are filtered out and the developmental *filling* is quickly turned into criticism. A feeling of being censured or even attacked is therefore what the employee is left with.

John, I think you have worked really hard this year. Well done for meeting your objectives.

In terms of your development, I have heard that some of your colleagues find you quite difficult. So we will need to think about how we can address that. Perhaps there are some training courses you can attend.

But overall you have won us a great deal of new business which is excellent.

We are now so conditioned by the traditional appraisal discussion that, when we hear the positive words at the outset, we brace ourselves for what is coming next! Even the word 'feedback' carries negative connotations. The brain will prepare the body for a threat response and so, when we tell someone we are about to give them feedback, we may as well be warning them that we are about to punch them in the face!

The *nocebo* effect of language has been mentioned earlier in the chapter. In the medical world, where patients, forewarned that a procedure 'will only hurt a little', report higher levels of pain.[20] Negative expectations can therefore cause an adverse neurobiological reaction.[21]

In the business environment, the effect is the same. Imaging studies show that when we focus people on what they are not doing well, the same stress response activates.[22]

Positive words do not constitute a threat to our survival and so the brain barely registers them, particularly when they are placed next to negative words that do feel threatening to the brain. And so, by combining both positive and negative messages, the feedback sandwich as one standalone process cannot possibly work.

Rather than motivate employees to do a better job, the feedback sandwich often deters and even crushes effort. The process is worsened by the fact that appraisal discussions often take place only on an annual basis, so managers effectively avoid difficult discussions throughout the year and then open the floodgates, expecting employees to cope with a tsunami of comments all at once.

The praise and criticism messages should therefore be separated, with each message given regularly and appropriately.

Three separate feedback conversations

1) Give praise – and be specific

Praise should be used to acknowledge good effort or successful achievement. This should happen every time the employee does something praiseworthy, not be reserved for a formal setting or an annual review. When we give praise immediately after an event, we are more likely to see that behaviour or action being repeated and reinforced in the future. It is important to remember that praise must be specific. 'Good job!' is not as effective as 'You did a great job answering that person's questions'.

Teachers could say to their pupils:

> 'Your story is very good. I particularly like the way you gave real examples and brought it to life.'
>
> Managers could say to their employees:
>
> 'You have worked really hard on this project. I especially appreciated how you coached the new team members and worked closely with them to bring them up to speed.'

2) Help someone to improve – and focus on the future, not the past

When we are in a position whereby we can influence someone else's performance of a task, we need to consider how to structure our support of their efforts. Any conversation must be carefully timed so that the person can direct their attention on future endeavour. For example, if we are trying to encourage someone to be better at giving presentations – and in particular, organising visual information – we need to tell them what they should be doing *just before* their next presentation. In a sense, we are feeding *forward*, not *back*.

This conversation could sound like:

> 'Sarah, I know you are preparing for the meeting next Tuesday. I have a few suggestions that may help with the way you set out your points and illustrations. Shall we go through them together on Monday?'

Because the conversation is directing effort towards a future activity, the person on the receiving end does not feel criticised but rather can focus on improvement. This is much more effective than telling them what they did not do well just after an event, which can often be demotivating.

3) Change an aspect of their behaviour – and be clear and factual

When we are asking someone to change an aspect of how they behave, we need to be calm, clear, factual and specific. Generalisations such as 'You always do this' or

'You never do that' are not helpful and simply result in the other person becoming defensive. We need to refer to the exact action or behaviour and when it happened. It is also important that the person acknowledges what has happened before you proceed with the conversation.

> 'Peter, I noticed you interrupted Sam three times at last Tuesday's meeting. What was your reason for this?'

The explanation that is then given by Peter also serves as an acceptance that this situation occurred.

We should then explain the impact of that particular act or behaviour:

> 'Because you interrupted him he was unable to give us a full briefing. As a result, we need more time to go through it all together again.'

The impact can be attached to the leader, the team or even the business. It is then important to ask the person to help find a solution or way forward:

> 'How do you suggest we handle the next meeting?' and then agree on a new action together.
>
> 'So what we will do is . . ..'

The difference between this approach and the feedback sandwich is that the messages are not mixed and the conversation here is focused on one incident and one specific outcome. The person is left with a clear message about what needs to happen next, rather than feeling personally attacked by mass generalisations.

Importantly, when this approach is used to address small incidents or episodes at the time when they occur, it reduces the need for a bigger discussion, which many managers avoid anyway.

Part 3: Stories and top tips

Language inspires us

We are all aware of the inspiring effect of words. Throughout history, words have been used to mobilise and ignite nations.

As mentioned in Chapter 2, Our Brain and Emotion, even years later, we can quote Martin Luther King's 'I have a dream'. And we can still appreciate Winston Churchill's 'This was their finest hour'.

Throughout history, words have communicated aspiration, hope, change and endeavour; they have reflected and reinforced belief, and unified people behind them.

Today, we can see how politicians and their aides use language to reach the masses. For example, Frank Luntz, a political consultant in the United States, understands the power of language and has advised Republicans for years on their messaging strategy. In the 1990s, Luntz suggested the reframing of 'global warming' to 'climate change' because it sounded less frightening.

In a party memo (reported in 2003) Luntz stated:

'A compelling story, even if factually inaccurate, can be more emotionally compelling than a dry recitation of the truth.'

As Chapter 2, Our Brain and Emotion, has already explained, when emotion is injected into our language, it can radically mobilise mass effort. This can be seen clearly in Donald Trump's use of language in the run-up to the 2016 US presidential election on the following page.

Trump's language is not complex and his sentences are short and impactful. He draws people in ('Look') and he uses simple techniques such as repetition and exaggeration. The net effect is that people are swept along on a wave of rhetoric.

Similar techniques can be observed in Trump's inauguration speech, which at 15 minutes was also one of the shortest in history. His opening was punchy and explicit:

'We will face challenges. We will confront hardships, but we will get the job done.'

Television interview between Donald Trump and Jimmy Kimmel, December 2015

'But, Jimmy, the problem – I mean, *look*, I'm for it. But *look*, we have people coming into our country that are *looking* to do tremendous harm. You *look* at the two – look at Paris. *Look* at what happened in Paris. I mean, these people, they did not come from Sweden, okay? *Look* at what happened in Paris. *Look* at what happened last week in California, with, you know, 14 people dead. Other people going to die, they're so badly injured. And what I wanna do is find out what it – you know, you can't solve a problem until you find out what's the root cause. And I wanna find out, what is the problem, what's going on.'

Trump's words then painted a dark and depressing picture of a United States filled with gangs, drugs, crime, poverty and unemployment, and featuring graphic allusions to 'rusted-out factories scattered like tombstones' and 'American carnage'. His language throughout was unconventional, evocative and dramatic, stirring strong emotions and polarising people all over the world.

Language sells

As Chapter 7, Our Brain and Biases, will explain in more detail, language can have a powerful influencing effect on our behaviour. Advertising plays to this and often uses emotional messaging to sell the benefits of products or services. For example, an explanation of how a car will improve our lifestyle is a more successful sales message than a list of the various features of that car.

Emotional statements sell.

We only have to consider Harley-Davidson's sales message:

'What we sell is the ability for a 43-year-old accountant to dress in black leather, ride through small towns and have people be afraid of him.'

Advertisers understand the power of language and the words that will get people to buy. Apple's language appeals cleverly to two demographics at opposing ends of the technology spectrum: bookworms and digital natives.

> **'MacBook. The most interesting book in the world.'**

Promotional messages avoid the language of price and expense, which are negatively loaded, and focus instead on adventure and lifestyle:

Language is therefore used to sell products, reposition brands and influence our behaviour in ways that we often do not realise or question.

> **'The new Mercedes SLK is as wild as you want it to be. With a retractable hard top, a 302 hp supercharged engine and undeniable style, the SLK will take you anywhere you go.'**

As will be explained in Chapter 7, Our Brain and Biases, the *framing effect* is potent.

For example, we are more likely to buy meat that is 90% lean than 10% fat; £50 a month sounds much more manageable than £600 a year.

We are also susceptible to language that helps us avoid a loss rather than make a gain. Consider the two statements below. Which one is more likely to persuade you to act?

'**You are losing** money by not replacing the boiler in your home.'

'**You will save** money by replacing the boiler in your home.'

We like feeling that we have found a good deal, which is why Buy One Get One Free (BOGOF) offers are highly effective. These deals are so seductive that we often end up buying what we do not need or did not even want in the first place!

Headlines harness and hold attention

News of the recent coronavirus has reverberated around the world. Mass media have directed global attention to the crisis with headlines designed to make individuals and organisations respond quickly.

'Britain ready for the worst' (UK), 'Corona Chaos' (Australia), 'First NZ Coronavirus Case PANDEMONIUM' (New Zealand), 'Alerte Jaune' (France)

Recent headlines have featured words like 'Deadly', 'Panic', 'Threat', 'Killer' and 'Crisis'.

As Chapter 6, Our Brain and Visual Perception, explains (see the section about the two different *Wall Street Journal* headlines), headlines manipulate our emotions, direct our attention and leave an impression before a word of the actual article has been read. Acting as a priming effect, headlines determine how we will read the body of the text and the key message we take away. (The priming effect is discussed in more detail in Chapter 7, Our Brain and Biases.)

The problem is that headlines can also be misleading. They feed pre-existing biases and trigger associated memories, however skewed and unreliable, to colour our interpretation and make it all the subjective. Headlines stop us processing the main article objectively and so once we have read information in a way that makes sense to us, we then find it difficult to correct any initial false impressions.

Compare:

'Dallas police officer charged with manslaughter in fatal shooting of unarmed man in his own apartment' (CNN, September 9, 2018)

With:

'Police officer charged in shooting death of unarmed neighbor' (Fox News, US, September. 10, 2018)

The two stories are the same, but each has been presented with a different spin to move our thinking in a certain direction, targeting our existing beliefs about the police.

Ullrich Ecker, a psychologist and cognitive neuroscientist at the University of Western Australia, has demonstrated that misleading headlines affect the way we remember and make judgements based on what we then read.[23]

Participants were given the same articles to read where the only difference was the headline. For example, one headline said, 'GM foods are safe', but another stated 'GM foods may pose long-term health risks'. The headline was enough to affect their memory and judgement of the article. Another group was given a headline and accompanying photographs of faces, followed by an article about a crime. The headline affected the impressions formed of the faces, even when the person referred to in the headline was not the person in the photograph.

The more emotional salient the opening statement, the more later logical reasoning is impaired. For example, our fear of the coronavirus and our worry about an unknown infection – and our brain does not react well to anything it cannot predict – have been exacerbated by the proliferation of dramatic headlines announcing the latest fatality numbers. Our urge to know what is happening in the world around us sends us reaching for answers in the news, but we become caught up in media's *cognitive warfare* where emotive headlines compete with statistics. And headlines usually win.

Stories switch on our brain

Stories engage us and fascinate us. They inspire us and give us hope. Through stories, we connect with people and identify with their challenges and struggles. And, more importantly, we remember them.

Studies on the neurobiology of storytelling have considered the impact of personal stories on brain function. When we hear a story, the same area of the brain lights up as if we were actually telling the story ourselves.[24]

> We remember stories over statistics. Professor Jennifer Aake at Stanford's Graduate School of Business refers to a study in which students were asked to give a one-minute presentation to their fellow students.
>
> Only one of the presentations contained a story, while all the other presentations included statistics.
>
> The researcher then asked the students to note down on paper what they remembered.
>
> 5% of the students remembered a statistic.
>
> 63% of the students remembered the story.

When we hear stories that engage us emotionally, we produce more *oxytocin*, the neurotransmitter released when we build trust or invest in loving relationships.[25] The effect of this is that our memories of these stories are more enduring.

The influence of storytelling on the creative arts such as writing and movie-making may be observed in Joseph Campbell's *The Hero with a Thousand Faces*.[26] Campbell's work details how all storytelling is largely built around the principles of the *hero myth*, with which we all engage. The hero, sometimes reluctantly, is persuaded to accept a mission, overcomes adversity often with the help of loyal companions and in the end succeeds. This theme runs through many of the movies and stories that we enjoy today. Consider the adventures of Simba in *The Lion King*, Luke Skywalker in *Star Wars* and Dorothy in *The Wizard of Oz*. Their stories all follow a similar format.

Nelson Mandela (the South African anti-apartheid revolutionary political leader and President between 1994–1999) was born in 1918 in South Africa. He joined the African National Congress, working against the ruling National Party's apartheid policies.

In 1962, he was brought to trial on the basis of trying to overthrow the South African Government. He was sentenced to life in prison.

In 1990, Mandela was released from prison and restarted his work to end apartheid. In 1993, he was awarded the Nobel Peace Prize and in 1994, he became the first black president of South Africa.

Nelson Mandela overcame hardship and fought for what he believed in. He became an inspirational role model all over the world. His story will be told for years to come.

In Nelson Mandela's words:

'I learned that courage was not the absence of fear, but the triumph over it. The brave man is not he who does not feel afraid, but he who conquers that fear.'

Top Tips
Remember: **SPEAK**

Simplify your language and make it visual and memorable. Avoid jargon where possible. Think about the people you are talking to and be aware that the language of your business or specialism may not mean much to others. Use words that the brain can digest easily and visualise quickly.

Practise reframing your messages in order to make them more effective. Think carefully about your words, the context in which you are positioning them and where you are putting particular emphasis. Be aware of the impact of your language on other people. Our words have the ability to create or destroy in seconds.

Engage people on a personal level by telling a story. We especially love stories that trigger emotional responses. Try to begin your presentations with a personal story to hook your audience. Remember that stories ignite the brain.

Avoid using negatively charged words or words that elicit distaste in others. The strength of word aversion, combined with our natural negativity bias, mean that we need to work harder at using positive and supportive language.

Kick-start and stimulate the senses where possible. Sensory words can bring your language to life and engage other people in your message. The more senses you activate in others, the more they will remember your message.

References for Chapter 5

1. Hagoort, P., & Indefrey, P. (2019). 'The neurobiology of language beyond single-word processing', *Science*, October, 55–58. doi: 10.1126/science.aax0289
2. Scott, S.K., & Wise, R.J. (2003). 'Functional imaging and language: A critical guide to methodology and analysis', *Speech Communication*, August, 7–21.
3. Huth, A.G. et al. (2016). 'Natural speech reveals the semantic maps that tile human cerebral cortex', *Nature*, April, 453–58.
4. Emmorey, K. et al. (2007). 'The neural correlates of sign versus word production', *Neuroimage*, May, 202–08.
5. Glezer, L.S. et al. (2009). 'Evidence for highly selective neuronal tuning to whole words in the "Visual Word Form Area"', *Neuron*, April, 199–204.
6. Hsueh, S. (2014). *Chineasy: The New Way to Read Chinese*. London: Thames and Hudson.
7. Rodriquez-Fornells, A. et al. (2010). 'Nouns and verbs are learned in different parts of the brain', *Neuroimage*, February, 156. www.sciencedaily.com/releases/2010/02/100225084640.htm
8. Oberlander, J. & Gill, A. (2004). 'Language generation and personality: Two dimensions, two stages, two hemispheres?' in *Papers from the AAAI Spring Symposium on Architectures for Modeling Emotion: Cross-Disciplinary Foundations*, Spring, 104–11.
9. Chui, M. et al. (2012). 'The social economy: Unlocking value and productivity', *McKinsey Global Institute*. www.mckinsey.com
10. Gonzalez. J. et al. (2006). 'Reading cinnamon activates olfactory brain regions', *NeuroImage*, August, 906–12.
11. Boulenger, V. et al. (2009). 'Grasping ideas with the motor system: Semantic somatotopy in idiom comprehension', *Cerebral Cortex*, August, 1905–14.
12. Hagoort, P & Indefrey, P. (2019). 'The neurobiology of language beyond single-word processing'. *Science*, October, 55-58. doi: 10.1126/science.aax0289
13. Carr, P. & Walton, G. (2014). 'Cues of working together fuel intrinsic motivation', *Journal of Experimental Psychology*, July, 169–84.
14. Krauss, B. et al. (2016). 'Managing procedural anxiety in children', *New England Journal of Medicine*, April. doi: 10.1056/NEJMvcm1411127
15. Ledgerwood, A., & Boydstun, A.E. (2013). 'Sticky prospects: Loss frames are cognitively stickier than gain frames', *Journal of Experimental Psychology*, March, 1–10.
16. Garland, E.L. et al. (2010). 'Upward spirals of positive emotions counter downward spirals of negativity: Insights from the broaden-and-build theory and affective neuroscience on the treatment of emotion dysfunctions and deficits in psychopathology', *Clinical Psychological Review*, November, 849–64.
17. Lieberman, M. (2012). 'Literary moist aversion'. https://languagelog.ldc.upenn.edu
18. Thibodeau, P.H. (2016). 'A moist crevice for word aversion: In semantics not sounds', *PLOS ONE*, April, 157. doi.org/10.1371/journal.pone.0153686
19. Buckingham, M., & Goodall, A. (2019). 'The feedback fallacy', *Harvard Business Review*, March–April, 92–101.
20. Krauss, B.S. (2015). '"This may hurt": Predictions in procedural disclosure may do harm' *BMJ* (Clinical research ed.), February. doi:10.1136/bmj.h649

21. Bingel U. et al. (2011). 'The effect of treatment expectation on drug efficacy: Imaging the analgesic benefit of the opioid remifentanil', *Science Translational Medicine*, February. doi:10.1126/scitranslmed.3001244
22. Boyatzis, R. et al. (2019). *Feedback Is Not Coaching: Coaching with Compassion Invites Learning and Change*. Boston: Harvard University Press.
23. Ecker, U. K. H. et al. (2014). 'The effects of subtle misinformation in news headlines', *Journal of Experimental Psychology: Applied*, 323–35, https://doi.org/10.1037/xap0000028
24. Stephens, G.J. et al. (2010). 'Speaker–listener neural coupling underlies successful communication', *Proceedings of the National Academy of Sciences*, August, 14425–30.
25. Zak, P. (2013). 'How stories change the brain', *Mind and Body*, December. greatergood.berkley.edu
26. Campbell, J. (2012). *The Hero with a Thousand Faces*. Novato, CA: New World Library.

'All things are subject to interpretation.'

FRIEDRICH NIETZSCHE
Philosopher, critic, poet and philologist (1844–1900)

chapter six

Our Brain and Visual Perception

Our eyes take in most of the information that comes into our brain. We cannot deal with every single visual input that we receive and so our visual perception is a continuous process of filtering, selecting and interpreting what we see.

In order to make sense of what we take in through our eyes, our brain uses its store of knowledge, beliefs, experiences and expectations as a reference guide. This means that we tend to screen in visual information that supports our view of the world, and screen out information that contradicts it. In effect, we see what we want and expect to see.

Visual processing is a key cognitive process in the brain. This chapter explains how our brain perceives visual information and constructs what we know as our reality.

Part 1: The science explained

How do we see?

Our vision accounts for two-thirds of the electrical activity of the brain, and half of our neural tissue is directly or indirectly related to vision.[1] Vision is so dominant in the brain that it can affect, distort or even overwhelm our other senses.

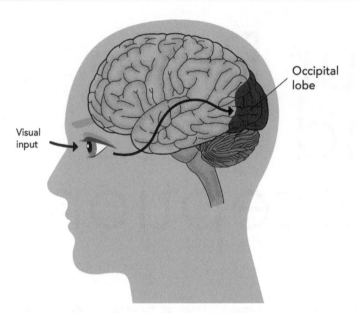

FIGURE 6.1: How our brain *sees*

Our ability to take in visual information depends on two of our organs: 1) our *eyes* to receive visual stimuli and 2) our *brain* to make sense of these stimuli. Our eyes generate a two-dimensional image, but our brain needs a three-dimensional understanding in order for us to interact with the world around us.

The area most involved in visual processing is the primary visual cortex, which is one of the most important parts of our occipital lobe (see Figure 6.1) situated at the back of the brain, as explained in Chapter 1, Our Brain.

The occipital lobe works with the other lobes to identify and place incoming visual information, as shown in Figure 6.2.

The **dorsal stream** (the 'where' pathway) visually guides our movement and locates *where* objects are.

The **ventral stream** (the 'what' pathway) helps us identify *what* we are looking at.

When we receive a visual image from our optic nerve, the brain then adds two extra elements to this image: our existing memory and our interpretation of the image that we are currently seeing.

We are constantly comparing what we see with what we already know, and we often see only what we expect to see. This can make us blind to other items or objects in our visual field, as Chapter 4, Our Brain and Attention, discusses in more detail.

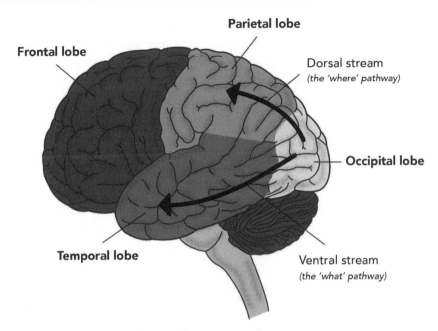

FIGURE 6.2: Two visual pathways that act together

Bottom-up or top-down?

Psychologists distinguish between two types of visual processing (see Figure 6.3). These are also referred to in Chapter 4, Our Brain and Attention.

Bottom-up processing	Perception is direct and data-driven: what we see is what we get. Proposed by James Gibson,[2] this view proposed the sensory information we receive from the environment is sufficient for us to act. It is therefore also known as the Ecological Theory.
Top-down processing	According to Richard Gregory,[3] our visual perception is indirect and is shaped both by our experiences and expectations, which enable us to make inferences about what is in front of us. Because most of the visual information that we receive is lost by the time our brain processes it, our memories enable us to create best guesses or hypotheses. This process is known as top-down processing and it makes our reality almost entirely subjective.

FIGURE 6.3: Bottom-up and top-down processing

Both theories have their strengths and weaknesses. The bottom-up theory acknowledges the richness of sensory information available to us and it also explains how animals and babies are able to make accurate judgements of perception; but it does not explain perception errors, such as in visual illusions. The top-down theory suggests that our sensory experience on its own is insufficient and that we need our prior knowledge to construct our perception.

Neither view explains perception all the time and both theories are dependent on the amount and clarity of the information available in the first place.

Visual perception: a complex process

Knowledge of our visual system was advanced in the late 1950s by the pioneering work of two neuroscientists, David Hubel and Torsten Wiesel, who won a Nobel Prize for their work in this field. They explained that when we view the world around us, specific neurons in the brain are dedicated to processing as well as recognising particular details about what we see.

Recent research into the mouse visual system has uncovered that our seeing brain is actually even more complex than previous studies would suggest.[4] It now seems that, of all the neurons in the visual cortex, only 10% of the neurons in this region actually activate to perceive objects in our outside world. What is not clear is the exact function of the remaining 90%. It seems that we have yet to complete the picture of how actually see.

We see the whole first and details second

When we see an object, our brain is able to process it in as little as 13 milliseconds.[5] The image is then stored for later recall.

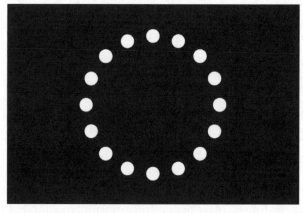

FIGURE 6.4 A circle or just a collection of dots?

For example, if we look at Figure 6.4, we see a circle rather than a collection of dots.

Much of our understanding of how and why we perceive objects comes from *Gestalt psychology* (*gestalt* is from the German word for 'form' or 'shape'). The principle of Gestalt psychology is that we form wholes from parts of objects that can be separated and analysed. So the whole is different from the sum of its parts.

FIGURE 6.5 Figure-ground perception

The *figure–ground* picture in Figure 6.5 can be perceived as two different images depending on how we see it: there are two faces looking at each other or a white vase. The figure is the object we perceive, while the ground is everything that is in the background. Our eyes separate the figure(s) from the background in order to understand what is being seen.

Many famous logos take advantage of the Gestalt psychology principle:

In the **FedEx** logo, look for the arrow between the 'E' and the 'X'.
In the **Formula 1** logo, look for the hidden number 1 between the letter 'F' and the speed lines.
In the **Carrefour** logo, look for the white 'C' in the middle.
In the **Hershey's Kisses** logo, look for the chocolate 'kiss' between the 'K' and the 'I'.
In the **Toblerone** logo, look in the picture of the Matterhorn for the image of the bear, the symbol of the Swiss city of Berne.
In the **Tour de France** logo, look for the cycling man; the yellow circle is a wheel.

When we look at an object, each of our eyes sees a slightly different picture. Our brain then brings together both versions. We use cues, such as shadows, textures and prior knowledge, to help us to judge depth and distance.

We see faces everywhere

One of the reasons that we have survived as a species is because we can perceive and recognise *faces*.

As Chapter 2, Our Brain and Emotion, explains, we have an area of the brain dedicated to seeing faces. This area is called the *fusiform face area* (FFA) and it means, among other things, that we can quickly recognise someone we know, even from different perspectives.

We see faces everywhere – in clouds, shapes of leaves, drinks and food.[6] This phenomenon, called *pareidolia,* is believed to be a result of the brain's top-down processing tendency to use what is known and familiar.

Faces are encountered in every aspect of our life.

We see faces in trees.

We see faces in buildings.

We see faces in food.

We see faces in cars.

Courtesy of Kent Area Midget & Sprite Club representative.

When we think we see a face in other objects, the activity in our brain – in both the *occipital lobe*, which processes visual information, and the *frontal lobe*, which is involved in planning and decision-making – is exactly the same as if we were in fact looking at a real person. This may explain why we really believe we have seen a face.

Our tendency to see faces everywhere may be a survival instinct: our existence has depended on our ability to interact and cooperate with other human beings (and avoid dangerous animals). We are therefore hardwired to seek out other people in our environment.

In fact, the wider our social network, the more the fusiform face area grows in the brain. So our brain continues to adapt to be able to recognise the people around us.

In 2004, Diane Duyser in Florida, USA, made a toasted cheese sandwich and said that, when she looked at it before eating it, she saw a lady looking back at her.

Ten years later, the cheese sandwich was sold on eBay for $28,000 to an online casino that claimed that it would take the sandwich on a world tour and donate the money to charity.

Blindness in our brain

People with damage to certain areas of the brain can develop a form of brain blindness, known as *agnosia* (from the Greek word meaning 'ignorance'). Those who suffer from agnosia will be able to describe the features of an object such as a table, but will not be able to recognise it as a table.

For example, someone with agnosia may describe a rose as 'about six inches in length, a convoluted red form with a linear green attachment', but they do not know it as a *rose*.

One form of agnosia is a failure to recognise faces. This face blindness is known as *prosopagnosia* (from the Greek *prosopon*, meaning 'face' and *agnosia*, meaning 'ignorance'). People with prosopagnosia need to rely on other features such as voice, hairstyle or clothes to recognise people.

Prosopagnosia was explained in depth by neurologist Oliver Sachs, who described a patient suffering from prosopagnosia; the patient confused his wife's head with a hat and tried to put it (his wife's head) on his own head.[7]

We take shortcuts to simplify what we see

In order to help us concentrate on what is important, our brain takes shortcuts and simplifies the information our eyes receive. These shortcuts compensate for the delay in our brain's visual processing time. The simpler the object, the easier and faster it is for the brain to interpret what it is.

Even when we observe something complex, we still reorganise it into something simpler.

Consider the diagram below:

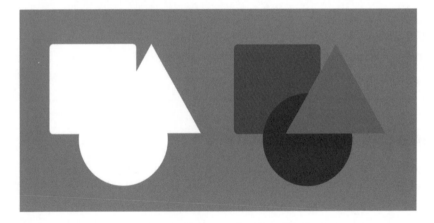

Compare the three separate objects (triangle, square, circle) on the right to the complex-looking white object on the left.

You may find that the three objects on the right are easier to distinguish than the object on the left, which appears to have no recognisable form.

How do we see colour?

The human brain can recognise over a million different colours.

Colour vision starts with the eye, which contains three types of specialised nerve cells called photoreceptors. These photoreceptors are on the retina, the layer of tissue at the back of the eye and are sensitive to different wavelengths of light. There are two types of photoreceptors: rods and cones. Rods distinguish between black and white and cones enables us to see colour.

When light hits these photoreceptors, electrical signals are sent to the brain. The photoreceptors have to work together to help us see a range of colour; when one or more photoreceptor is damaged or lacking, we may suffer from colour blindness.

The exact process of how the brain synthesises information from the photoreceptors has, up until very recently, not been entirely clear. However, scientists in Colombia have recently identified a special brain circuit in fruit flies that compares signals it receives from the eye, and it seems that this system is very similar in humans.[8] The hope is that future breakthroughs could help to address problems with vision or even enable computers to recognise colour.

Part 2: Impact on our daily life

We fill in the gaps

The brain likes to see a whole image first, before dealing with the composite details, as already discussed in this chapter.

Although we use our store of knowledge and memories to interpret new visual inputs, sometimes there is not an exact match between what we see and our stored information. In other words, there is a gap. To help us to bridge this gap and complete the picture, we find a near match and use our brain to make associations. The less information we are given, the more we provide our own material to address any disparities.

This is why we can construct a meaningful image from random shapes, as illustrated by our ability to form a panda's face from just some black shapes:

Our search for whole patterns is highlighted by the fact that we can make sense of the passage below:

> Aoccdrnig to rscheearch at Cmabrigde Uinervtisy, it deosn't mttaer in waht oredr the ltteers in a wrod are, the olny iprmoetnt tihng is taht the frist and lsat ltteer be at the rghit pclae. The rset can be a toatl mses and you can sitll raed it wouthit porbelm. Tihs is bcuseae the huamn mnid deos not raed ervey lteter by istlef, but the wrod as a wlohe.

Visual perception is therefore dependent on context. Whether we see random shapes or a collection of letters or words, our brain will jump to a conclusion about what comes next; it then fills in the gaps to help us make sense of it.

Why are we susceptible to visual illusions?

The word *illusion* comes from the Latin word *illudere*, which means 'to mock'. When we see a visual illusion we often feel that our eyes are playing tricks on us.

Because of the speed at which our brain works, as well as the shortcuts it has to take to interpret visual information quickly, our brains are susceptible to being deceived.

An example of this is the *Müller-Lyer illusion* (Figure 6.6), which distorts our perception of the lower line to make it look longer than the line above it.

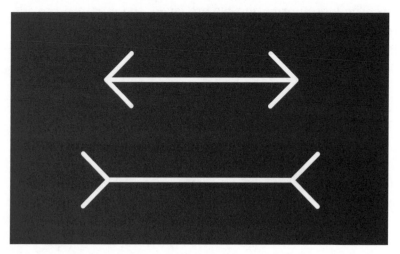

FIGURE 6.6: Müller-Lyer illusion

In the *Herring illusion* (Figure 6.7), the black left-to-right lines look warped, even though they are actually straight.

FIGURE 6.7: Herring illusion

Edward Adelson, Professor of Vision Science at the Massachusetts Institute of Technology (MIT), designed the chequerboard illusion (Figure 6.8) in 1995 to highlight how we determine colour with shadow.

Our brain knows that shadows make objects darker and then tries to compensate for this by interpreting shadowy objects as lighter than they actually are.

In the case of the chequerboard, we therefore assume that the square marked B is slightly darker than it should be because of the impact of the shadow. In fact A is the same colour as B.

If you still do not believe it, cut square B out of this book and put it on top of square A. You will see that they are in fact the same colour!

Our visual perception protects us . . .

We are very good at picking out similarities and differences in our world.

Our basic human instinct to protect ourselves from danger has stimulated our craving for similarity and sharpened our ability to detect anything different or unknown in our visual field.

Studies have even demonstrated that the more diverse our environment, the more we are drawn to and seek out people who are like us.[9] This may explain why many married couples look quite similar!

FIGURE 6.8: Chequerboard illusion

Credit: Professor Edward Adelson, MIT.

Being able to spot similarity across a range of people is known as the *similarity-attraction effect* (SAE). A recent study has shown that people are even likely to pick partners who share a similar DNA.[10]

Our experience of similarity also affects our assumptions about trustworthiness. Research shows that we are more likely to trust and treat favourably people who look like us, perhaps because we feel a greater genetic affiliation to them.

The reverse is also true: we are more likely to perceive facial similarity in those whom we consider trustworthy.[11]

. . . but can also prevent new thinking

The downside of our preference for similarity is that we may surround ourselves with a comfort zone of homogeneity and limit ourselves to interacting only with people who feel familiar to us.

The implications of this are significant, particularly in the light of research that reveals the strong relationship between diverse social networks and innovation – the more diverse the social network, the more innovation will occur.[12]

And so our natural inclination to feel safe and familiar may lead to constrained personal networks and reduced learning opportunities, compared to people from diverse backgrounds.

Our truth is subjective

Our lens of perception turns neutral information into events that are meaningful for us. This collectively constitutes our *truth*. This truth then becomes an internal guide of what we think is right, even though it may not be representative of what is actually there.

Our truth colours and distorts our perceptions to the extent that each of us might look at the same thing, but we will all see something different.

The truth that we constantly project on to the world around us helps direct our attention to what is important and relevant.

> A group of young boys, some from wealthy families and some from poor families, were all asked to look carefully at a coin.[13] The coin was then taken away and all the boys were asked to draw a picture of it.
>
> The boys from the wealthy families drew a smaller-sized coin than the boys from the poor families.
>
> The boys' perception of the coin was therefore affected to some extent by the degree of importance given to money within each family.

This is explained in more depth in Chapter 4, Our Brain and Attention.

We do not see ourselves accurately

Our view of ourselves develops over time and is influenced by our culture, our experiences and our interactions with others.

In Western societies, it is now a social norm for women and men to be dissatisfied with their body shape and believe that their bodies are never thin or fit enough.[14] In fact, this social norm has extended to other countries such as Fiji, where the ideal physical female shape has shifted dramatically from voluptuous to thin – resulting in an extraordinary increase in eating disorders.[15]

Across the world, the reported increase in eating disorders and psychological problems such as body dysmorphic disorder (where we become unable to see ourselves accurately) are often blamed on the widespread influence of traditional and social media. The tragedy is that, according to a report by the Professional Association for Childcare and Early Years (PACEY) in 2016, children as young as three years old now have body confidence issues.

Dr Jacqueline Harding, child development expert, comments:

'More research is needed in this area but contributing factors are likely to include: images on TV; images in storybooks and animations; the general chat by adults about their bodies, dieting, cosmetic surgery etc. There is little doubt that low levels of self-esteem appear to contribute significantly to negative perceptions of body image.'

Mirror, mirror on the wall

Our distorted view of our body also extends to our face. But it seems that here we are more likely to perceive ourselves in a more favourable light. When looking at pictures of our face, we identify ourselves more quickly with an image that has been airbrushed to look more attractive than an unaltered image.[16]

This distortion does not extend to our perception of others, whom we easily recognise from non-airbrushed images.

So it seems that we are inclined towards a more attractive version of ourselves.

But what happens when mirrors on the wall reflect our image back?

Research has shown that people taking a test in a room with a mirror are less likely to cheat compared with control groups performing the same exercises in rooms without mirrors.

Mirrored settings, it seems, increase our ethical behaviour and the effort we put into our work.

Part 3: Stories and top tips

Our reality is what we are used to

In the 1800s, Scottish missionary Robert Laws showed a picture to East Africans living in the country that is now Malawi.

While Westerners saw a family sitting in a cornered room with a window looking out on to a tree outside, East Africans saw a family sitting outside under a tree in the background and a woman carrying a box on her head.

Our perception of the world is shaped by our reality.

What should we believe?

Over the last 50 years, the world's media has had a pervasive influence over what we believe. The advent of the Internet has sparked an explosion of real-time information on a global level. More information means more control and so the media operates like a giant brain, shaping our perceptions and opinions, determining the flow and content of messages.

For example, on 1 September 2016, the *Wall Street Journal* published two opposing headlines, both with the same picture:

Trump Softens His Tone

Trump Talks Tough on Wall

Claims were then made on the Internet that the *Wall Street Journal* had deliberately attempted to sway Republican readers with the first headline, 'Trump Softens His Tone', in a pro-Trump area and to use the other headline, 'Trump Talks Tough on Wall', in a non-Trump area in order to bolster Democratic support.

In fact, the two editions of the *Wall Street Journal* were published at different times of the day. The first was published after Trump's meeting with Mexican president Enrique Peña Nieto. The second was published later in the day, after Trump had delivered a speech about immigration and the building of a wall along Mexico's border with the United States.

So not only is our frame of reference constructed by the media, but the Internet is now also contributing an additional dynamic to the way we interpret the news we are given. Newspaper headlines shape our views initially and then citizen journalism provides another dimension.

Whatever their guise and format, the various media channels effectively control our reality. Our view of the world is continually being influenced, directed, manipulated and distorted by what we read and hear.

For instance, our views of various recent events across the world, such as the 2016 presidential election in the United States, Brexit and the Syrian crisis, are fashioned by the techniques used by all forms of media and Internet communications. Our emotions are regularly aroused and manipulated and we create heroes and villains on the strength of selective reporting and public mass-messaging.

Because we are so easily swayed by the views of others, sometimes without even realising it, we find ourselves being swept along and adopting their opinions as our own.

Fact, fiction or just fake?

Fake news describes online articles and stories that look like authentic journalism but are completely fabricated to resemble journalism and attract as much attention as possible. The recent circulation of fake news typifies the danger of believing what we read.

One of the best-known examples of fake news is the story that aired in December 2016, about a man brandishing a gun in a Washington pizzeria that had been reported as being the headquarters of a child sex ring run by Hillary Clinton. The story was reported on online message boards and a poll reported that 14% of Trump supporters believed its validity.

A BuzzFeed analysis has claimed that fake election news stories generated more interest and engagement on Facebook, where there is an audience of around 1.8 billion, than stories from traditional major news outlets such as the *New York Times, Washington Post, Huffington Post* and NBC News. Facebook has now announced that it will be providing tips to help readers spot fake news stories.

The Lab of Misfits: enabling people to perceive differently

Founded by Dr Beau Lotto, a world-renowned neuroscientist specialising in perception, The Lab of Misfits is a creative studio of perceptual neuroscience, bringing together experts in the field of science, art and technology. Senses are stimulated and realities are challenged to effect a deeper understanding of how we perceive the world in order to see things differently.

Since our brain is constantly evolving and adapting to the world that is in constant flux, it is critical that we are continually able to reassess and redefine how we see what is around us.

The dangers of our digital age

Our digital age may have created significant efficiencies in commerce and communication, but it has also brought with it a new kind of interaction that is no longer based on physical human presence.

Although our brain is still designed to look for and interpret facial expression, body language and tonal variation, the preferred mode of interaction now through social media means that people see and are seen virtually, and not face to face.

Perceptions, particularly among the younger generations, are now being managed almost entirely though social media. Connections are made in order to expand networks but are then narrowed down to shared interests. Friends are categorised, images are carefully crafted and managed, and the need to belong, be accepted and be admired is addictive.

But the proliferation of social media sites showing off personal images is exacerbating a need to look perfect. Images are airbrushed before being posted, and we are now caught in a complex paradox of wanting to fit in and to stand out, to wear make-up but also look natural, to follow others and be followed ourselves. We are more connected, but also more disconnected, than ever.

It is therefore crucial that we regularly give ourselves a healthy dose of reality. There will always be people who seem richer, thinner, cleverer, fitter and more successful than we are.

Being happy starts with accepting this and appreciating what we do have.

In the words of Lao Tzu:

'Be content with what you have; rejoice in the way things are. When you realise there is nothing lacking, the whole world belongs to you.'

Top Tips
Remember: **IMAGE**

Imagine new possibilities and approaches by looking around you and keeping your mind open and receptive. Learn something new on a regular basis. Challenge your truth and escape from the confines of your comfort zone, which may be blinkering your view of life.

Manage the way you receive information. Have checks and balances in place when looking at information. Our brains are prone to errors in perception. Find people who do not necessarily agree with you. Their lens may prevent you from making a mistake.

Accept who you are, with all your imperfections. We are all a work in progress! Some degree of self-criticism and humility are fundamental to learning and personal growth. At the same time, recognise the pressure that social media puts us all under when it comes to comparison with others. Even *perfect* people are not perfect! But we can all strive for fulfilment and satisfaction in everything we do.

Gain different perspectives by challenging your own truth and the way you look at a situation. Be careful of justifying your position and beliefs even in the face of contradictory evidence. It is easier to form a new belief than change an existing one. Question the way you perceive difficult situations: another approach may help you address these better.

Exercise and stretch your cognitive abilities by challenging your view of the world. Visual illusions, as well as being entertaining and fun, are effective ways to stretch our thinking. They also remind us that our mind is easily tricked and that our perception is not always matched by reality.

References for Chapter 6

1. Bowan, M.D. (1999). 'Integrating vision with the other senses', monograph chapter in OEP Foundation post-graduate curriculum, December, 1–10.
2. Gibson, J.J. (1972). 'A theory of direct visual perception' in J. Royce, W. Rozenboom (Eds.). *The Psychology of Knowing*. New York: Gordon & Breach.
3. Gregory, R. (1970). *The Intelligent Eye*. London: Weidenfeld and Nicolson.
4. De Vries, S.E.J et al. (2019). 'A large-scale standardized physiological survey reveals functional organization of the mouse visual cortex', *Nature Neuroscience*, December. doi:10.1038/s41593-019-0550-9
5. Potter, M.C. et al. (2014). 'Detecting meaning in RSVP at 13 ms per picture', *Attention, Perception and Psychophysics*, February, 270–79.
6. Liu, J. (2014). 'Seeing Jesus in toast: Neural and behavioral correlates of face pareidolia', *Cortex*, April, 60–77.
7. Sachs, O. (2015). *The Man Who Mistook His Wife for a Hat*. London: Picador.
8. Heath, S.L. et al. (2020). 'Circuit mechanisms underlying chromatic encoding in drosophila photoreceptors', *Current Biology*, January. doi:10.1016/j.cub.2019.11.075
9. Bahns, A. et al. (2011). 'Social ecology of similarity. Big schools, small schools and social relationships', *Group Processes and Intergroup Relations,* July, 119–31.
10. Domingue, B.W. (2014). 'Genetic and educational assortative mating among US adults', *Proceedings of the National Academy of Sciences,* April, 7996–8000.
11. Farmer, H. (2013). 'Trust in me: Trustworthy others are seen as more physically similar to the self', *Psychological Science,* October, 290–92.
12. Philips, K. (2014). 'How diversity makes us smarter: Being around people who are different from us makes us more creative, more diligent and harder-working', *Scientific American,* October, 311.
13. Bruner, J.S., & Goodman, C.C. (1947). 'Value and need as organizing factors in perception', *Journal of Abnormal and Social Psychology,* January, 33–44.
14. Salk, R., & Engeln-Maddox, E.E. (2011). '"If you're fat, then I'm humongous!" Frequency, content, and impact of fat talk among college women', *Psychology of Women Quarterly,* April, 18–28.
15. Gerbasi, M.E. et al. (2014). 'Globalization and eating disorder risk: Peer influence, perceived social norms, and adolescent disordered eating in Fiji', *International Journal of Eating Disorders,* November, 727–37.
16. Epley, N., & Whitchurch, W. (2008). 'Mirror, mirror on the wall: Enhancement in self-recognition', *Personality and Social Psychology Bulletin,* November, 1159–70.

There is no neutrality. There is only greater or lesser awareness of one's bias.

PHYLLIS ROSE

Literary critic, essayist, biographer and educator (1942–)

chapter seven

Our Brain and Biases

Being biased is a human phenomenon. We are all biased and we use our biases every day, often unconsciously, to help us make decisions.

Biases are the beliefs, attitudes and preferences that we form about ourselves and other people. We pick up these biases through our culture, background and education and they are pervasive influences over how we see the world and make decisions.

Our brain has to predict rapidly what is safe or harmful in our environment. To help our brain do this, our biases quickly shortcut new information. The problem is that they intervene so quickly that we may make a bad choice or overlook a crucial detail.

This chapter explains how biases work in our brain and shows how our biases may distort our thinking or prevent us from forming an accurate view of the world.

Part 1: The science explained

A psychological immune system in the brain

Our biases are human adaptive responses to our environment and provide an immediate frame of reference for fast interpretation and action.

In a sense, our biases are our brain's psychological immune system and prevent us from decision paralysis.[1] If we were unable to respond quickly to our surroundings we would not have been able to survive as a species.

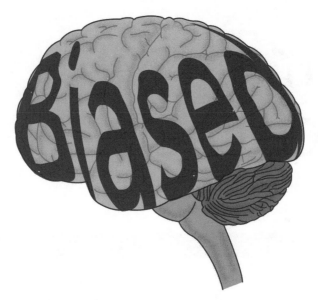

FIGURE 7.1: We are all biased

Why are our biases so powerful?

Our biases (Figure 7.1) play a more powerful role in our decision-making than many of us realise, particularly when we have limited information or when we are in a heightened emotional state. Our biases step in to fill any gaps or to make us feel more certain about a decision, often without our realising it.

Two psychological phenomena feed and strengthen our biases:

1. *Cognitive dissonance* occurs when, faced with evidence that may call certain existing beliefs into question, our brain suffers an uncomfortable tension between the new and stored information.

> The term **cognitive dissonance** was devised as a term in the 1950s by Leon Festinger who was studying a doomsday cult that believed that the earth was going to be destroyed by a flood.[2] When the flood did not materialise, members of the cult rationalised this by saying that there was another prophecy that the world would now be 'saved'.

2. *Motivated reasoning* helps us to reduce cognitive dissonance through finding evidence to support the original beliefs and any decision arising from these beliefs. Even if subsequent information completely contradicts

our first response, we generally find a way to make this new evidence fit with our original belief, however incongruent it is. And if we cannot make it fit, we will either ignore it or dismiss it altogether, even if it is staring us in the face.[3] This is explored later in the chapter in the section on *Confirmation bias*. The more polarised our views are, the less value we place on facts that threaten them. In politically motivated reasoning, we may even resort to conspiratorial thinking that helps us cement our views about the other side. It is easier for us to assume a cover-up of information than to change a deeply entrenched belief.

As humans, we have an excellent ability to make excuses and justify our actions. We don't exercise regularly ('I am too tired'; 'I have too much to do'), we eat food we know is unhealthy ('I don't have the time to cook'; 'I will do better next week') and we smoke ('More people die in road accidents than from smoking-related diseases'; 'My family all smoke and they have lived to old age').

Ironically, our own biases may prevent other people from challenging them because they are so deeply-rooted in who we are and the decisions we have made throughout life. But because we are often blind to our own biases, we do not know the extent to which they have taken hold.[4] This blindness is known as our *bias blind spot*.

Types of biases

Loss aversion

One of our strongest biases is called *loss aversion*. **Loss aversion** is based on the fact that our brain has to minimise uncertainty about the future and places more urgency on avoiding threats than realising gains.[5]

Whenever we can, we try to avoid losses, and we hate losing more than we like winning. Consequently, we do not weigh gains against losses equally. It is also mentally harder for people to convert from losses to gains: once people have developed a negative view of something it takes a long time for them to consider the same thing in a positive way.

As a result of loss aversion, we are persuaded to spend money on something if we know that we could lose out by not making the investment. Language of loss ('You are paying too much'; 'You are losing out on this deal') motivates us to act more effectively than language of gain ('Get our best product'; 'You will save money on this'). This is also covered in Chapter 5, Our Brain and Language.

Some studies suggest that psychological losses are generally twice as powerful as gains. When we buy something, we like to feel that our pain of loss (paying) must be offset by what we will gain.

Loss aversion is responsible for the *sunk-cost fallacy,* which means that the more we invest in something, the harder it becomes to abandon it. This is why we often convince ourselves that further investment is justified because the resources already invested will otherwise be lost. And that is not taking into consideration the overall losses involved in the further investment.

The sunk-cost fallacy explains why projects are kept going for longer than they should: we cannot face the thought of having to stop them after so much investment has already been made.

> The sunk-cost fallacy is sometimes called the *Concorde fallacy.* Concorde was the world's first commercial supersonic aeroplane and was a joint venture between Air France and British Airways. Despite early predictions that it would be a financial failure, the project was continued. People's psychological attachment to their initial investment meant that no one wanted to give up, even after huge losses of time, effort and money.

Confirmation bias

Confirmation bias is a form of selection bias, whereby we look for and choose information that confirms or reinforces our existing beliefs. We tend to assign more weight to supporting evidence and ignore or downplay any contradictory evidence we receive. **Confirmation bias** originates from the influence of our desire to prove our beliefs: when we want or expect something to be true, we often make it true.

With confirmation bias enabled, we see only what we expect or want to see. As a result, we respond more to the behaviour of those who confirm our own views. In this way, if we assume that people will behave negatively towards us, we will tend to interpret their behaviour, even if it is neutral, as hostile.

Confirmation bias can be dangerous since it can blind us to other avenues or possibilities. The past is not always the best predictor of the future and it may prevent us from seeking different information, or even lead us to the wrong conclusion.

Specialists and experts are particularly susceptible to confirmation bias. For example, a doctor may jump straight to a particular hypothesis about a certain illness and then ask the patient questions that help to confirm that hypothesis. The doctor may also ignore any evidence the patient might provide that may contradict the hypothesis. Similarly, lawyers taking on a new case may see shared traits with a previous case and look for details to support the assumption that both are the same – even when they are not.

> During Hurricane Katrina in 2005, thousands of residents of New Orleans ignored signs that the levee system was collapsing. They did not believe that this could happen and so were unable to interpret any information that contradicted their beliefs. Consequently, they stayed in their homes, which were directly in the line of the oncoming water. Katrina claimed nearly 2,000 lives.

Hindsight bias

Hindsight bias has been widely researched as one of our most common biases, particularly in the business world, although it is also frequently used in sports, politics and medicine.

It describes our 'I knew it all along' tendency, when we claim that we could have predicted what would happen, after we know the outcome. We fall prey to hindsight bias when there is an unclear relationship between decisions and outcomes. A successful outcome, for example, can lead us to believe that we really did know the answer all along, and we fail to remember exactly what we did think at the time we made the decision.

Hindsight bias can lead to overconfidence. So, because we think we have successfully predicted the past we then believe that we can foresee what is coming; our overconfidence in our predictive ability may then lead us to take unnecessary risks. In order to reduce this confidence, researchers Neal Roese and Kathleen Vohs suggest considering other outcomes that were not anticipated in order to weigh all possibilities together.[6]

Richard Thaler, who was awarded the Nobel Prize in 2017 for his work in psychology and economic behaviour, recommends writing down how decisions are made at the time that they are made.[7] A real-time record serves as a reminder of the assumptions underlying any decision made and will address any memory errors in the future.

Optimism bias

Optimism bias leads us to overestimating our likelihood of experiencing good events in our lives and underestimating our likelihood of experiencing bad events. **Optimism bias** also means that we are over-optimistic about ourselves in particular – and rarely about other people. And it's often the case that we are oblivious to this fact.

The benefit of optimism bias is that it can protect and inspire us – and it keeps us moving forward. For instance, when we are successful, we believe it is because of our ability and when we fail, we blame circumstances beyond our control – which prevents us from giving up.

When we are optimistic, we look into the future with hope. This is why many of us prefer a working day such as Friday, which brings with it the anticipation of the weekend, over a day of holiday such as Sunday, which heralds the beginning of the working week. In other words, optimism bias feeds our anticipation for what is coming rather than our pleasure in what is right in front of us. Being optimistic also helps us to reduce anxiety and stress.

However, unrealistic optimism can lead to risky behaviour such as smoking, despite scientific evidence and statistics that clearly point to its harmful effects. Unrealistic optimism can even underpin poor financial planning and inaccurate estimates about the cost and duration of projects.

A study asked a sample of smokers and non-smokers to estimate the likelihood that they would live to age 75 or longer.[8] Researchers compared the estimates with a representative sample of death certificates.

The estimates were accurate except for those submitted by heavy smokers: men reported a 50% likelihood of living to age 75 and women reported a 60% likelihood of living to age 75.

When compared with the death certificates, the results showed that only 26% of men and 30% of such women would actually survive to age 75.

Overconfidence bias

Closely linked to optimism bias is *overconfidence bias*. **Overconfidence bias** is observed when we make judgements about ourselves relative to other people.

When we are overconfident about our abilities to make good judgements, we often do a poor job of estimating probability and make bad decisions as a result. This bias is sometimes referred to as the *illusion of knowledge* bias because we are more confident in our knowledge and ability than we deserve to be.

Overconfidence bias may explain why only 10% of New Year's resolutions made in January will be maintained until the following December.

And if we think that we are not affected in any way by the overconfidence bias, it means we are overconfident!

In 2015, a leadership consultancy conducted a large research project involving 69,000 leaders and 750,000 employees.[9] Leaders were asked to rate their skills and abilities, then their ratings were compared to how their employees viewed them.

The results showed that there was little positive correlation between leaders' and employees' ratings. In fact, those leaders who believed that they were exceptional were judged by employees to be among the worst leadership performers.

Conversely, leaders who underestimated how good they were turned out to be best at their jobs in the eyes of their employees.

The more they underrated themselves, the higher other people rated them.

Self-awareness and emotional intelligence are frequently touted in boardrooms as essential leadership skills – but perhaps leaders also need a healthy dose of self-criticism too.

Present bias

We do not do a good job of planning for the future. This has been illustrated in studies that ask people their decisions about the future versus the present.

Present bias describes our tendency to place more emphasis on benefits that are lodged in the present time when considering a trade-off with a future point in time.

Present bias is related to a cognitive trap known as *hyperbolic discounting*, where we are less likely to consider the consequences of our choices the further in the future those choices are. This is why we often struggle to save money today, or why our food choices today may look significantly different to the savings and food choices that we plan for the future. For example, we are more likely to choose food that gives us pleasure today – such as chocolate – over food that offers less pleasure but is considered a healthier option.

Because we have such a strong present bias and often feel disconnected from the future, researchers have looked at what it would take to get us to save more money now.[10]

People were shown either images of their current self or aged images depicting how they may look in the future. They were then asked to allocate $1,000 among four options:
1. Buying something nice for someone special
2. Investing in a retirement fund
3. Planning a fun event
4. Putting money into a savings account

Those who saw an image of their aged self put twice as much money into the retirement fund as those who saw the image of their current self.

In-group and out-group bias

Our brain is designed to seek out similarities and differences in others, as Chapter 6, Our Brain and Visual Perception, explains. We naturally and subconsciously favour people in our own social group because similarity feels familiar and safe.

Our *in-groups* are people with whom we feel we share several traits or interests, such as our family and people from the same culture. *Out-groups* are people who are different from us. As Chapter 2, Our Brain and Emotion discusses, our empathy for others is selective and predicated on the connections we have forged with the people around us.

Social prejudice and racism are rooted in in-group bias. Some scientists believe that this bias is hardwired in our brains.

The neuroscientist Dr David Eagleman conducted a functional magnetic resonance imaging (fMRI) study where he asked 130 participants to look at six labelled hands that were then randomly stabbed by a syringe.[11] This stabbing activated a brain response. Researchers wanted to see whether people would care differently if they observed someone from their in-group being stabbed versus someone from their out-group.

There was a strong brain response when observing any in-group member being stabbed by the syringe, and no response when the out-group member was stabbed.

The study shows that we find it more difficult to empathise with those whom we believe are different to us.

Negativity bias

Our brain reacts more intensely to negative than positive stimuli. This feeds our natural *negativity bias*. We are more likely to reach for bad news than good news and we also attribute more weight and significance to negative rather than positive comments.

From an evolutionary point of view, our **negativity bias** is a protective measure that has ensured our survival. We have adapted to be able to spot threat and danger in our world so that we can stay alive. Despite this, we need to be vigilant as this bias can sometimes cloud our thinking by making us assume the worst.

When we apply our negativity bias to our own life, it can promote negative self-esteem that can even affect our physical health. This was shown in a study about normal-sized teenagers who believed themselves to be overweight – they were found to be more likely to become obese in later life.[12]

Our negativity bias is therefore far-reaching and can infiltrate all aspects of our life: our self-esteem, our relationships and the language we use.

> **Can a positive or negative attitude affect team performance?**
>
> This question was considered in a study that looked at the performance of 60 business teams.[13] The study examined the relationship among the number of positive/negative comments made among team members and the team performance overall.
>
> The findings showed a marked correlation between team performance and positive comments. In fact, the positive comments in the high-performing teams outweighed negative comments by nearly six to one. The medium-performing teams showed a ratio of nearly two positive comments to one negative comment. The low-performing teams showed that three negative comments were made for every positive one.

Authority bias

We have *authority bias* instilled in us from early childhood. A number of factors increase our susceptibility to authority bias:

The authority figure is viewed as legitimate (wearing a uniform influences this perception).
The environment is impressive (such as expensive offices or inspirational academic institutions).
We do not need to take responsibility for our actions; this responsibility is assumed by the authority figure.
We cannot directly see the impact of our action and are removed from touching or seeing them.
Other people are also obeying orders alongside us.
The authority figure is in close proximity.

Our compulsion to obey authority is a fundamental building block of society: we need a system around us to support, educate and guide us. The main problem with the authority bias is that it may lead us to follow orders, even when we believe them to be wrong. This is a theme that is also explored in Chapter 11, Our Brain and Leadership.

In the wake of the Second World War, a number of psychologists explored the basis for our treatment of each other. One of the most famous studies in this area was Stanley Milgram's on obedience, which began in the 1960s, soon after the Nuremberg Trials.[14] Stanley Milgram was a psychologist at Yale University and wanted to explore how far humans would go when following orders to harm each other.

Participants (all men aged between 20–50 years) were paired with each other and given specific roles: a *teacher* and a *learner* (who was really an actor) and placed in separate rooms. The 'learner' was strapped to a chair with electrodes and the 'teacher's' role was to ask the learner questions and administer shocks (in reality these were fake) increasing the voltage each time, whenever the learner gave the wrong answer. As the learners shouted out in pain from the other room, the teachers became more uncomfortable, but were prompted to continue by the researcher who was sitting behind them wearing a white lab coat. Two thirds of the participants continued to the highest level of 460 volts, which would have been fatal if they had been real.

Although Stanley Milgram's experiments cannot be replicated today on ethical grounds, due to the the emotional distress caused to the participants, several subsequent studies have attempted to test authority bias, whilst also protecting participants' well being. More recent studies have yielded similar results to the original experiments,[15] with one reporting even higher levels of obedience.[16]

Groupthink

As well as being biased towards authority, we also strive for consensus within a group. *Groupthink* is a bias that we adopt when we set aside our own personal beliefs in order to adopt the opinion of the rest of the group. This can lead to people being overly optimistic, engaging in risk-taking, and ignoring possible moral problems, warning signs or consequences.

Groupthink can lead to faulty decisions by the collective. A team or group will be particularly vulnerable to groupthink when that group is highly cohesive, isolated from external influences, lacking leadership and when its members are from similar backgrounds.

In the 1950s Dr Solomon Asch conducted a series of psychological experiments to examine the power of group opinion over an individual's opinion.[17] People were shown a line drawing (Exhibit 1) and asked to select a matching line from a group of lines of different lengths (Exhibit 2).

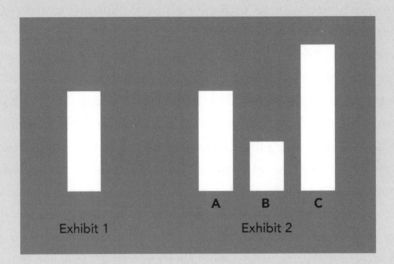

Exhibit 1   Exhibit 2

Participants were asked in a group to select the matching line. Actors were present within the group and were briefed to choose a different line at certain intervals – even though their choice was an obviously incorrect answer. On the occasions that the actors selected the wrong answer, the participants were unwilling to challenge the group and were more prepared to give an incorrect answer in order to fit in, even though they knew the answer was wrong.

When they were asked why they had conformed to the wishes of the group, some admitted knowing that the answer was wrong but said they did not want to be ridiculed; others said that they thought that the rest of the group must be correct.

Dr Asch's experiment shows the degree to which groupthink and a desire to conform is driven by both a need to fit in and a belief that other people collectively must be better informed.

Anticipation of regret

An *a priori* or *anticipation of possible regret* can influence our decision-making. This is often seen in buying decisions where we may later regret not choosing one of the options that was available. **Anticipation of regret** can therefore influence choices made at the time and can lead to faulty decision-making, even outweighing risk perception.

We can see this tendency in bidding behaviour at auctions. We behave differently when we cannot see the price that others are offering, compared to when we see what others are offering, particularly in incremental stages. When we can see what other people are bidding, we are more likely to offer a higher figure than we had previously intended, in order to avoid the feeling that we have just missed out on something. We are therefore trying to mitigate the regret we may otherwise have felt, had we lost the bidding war.

Anticipation of regret was observed in 1998 when Andrew Wakefield and colleagues published an article in *The Lancet*, highlighting a link between autism and bowel disorders with the measles, mumps and rubella (MMR) inoculation.[18]

Parents anticipated the regret that they felt they would have if they had their child inoculated. It was better, in their eyes, to do nothing (and risk measles, mumps and rubella for their child) than feel that they were the potential cause of autism or a bowel disorder by having the child vaccinated, even though there was scientific evidence proving that the triple vaccination was safe.

The Lancet article was later retracted.

Learned helplessness

Learned helplessness is a psychological trap and a form of conditioning whereby people feel that they have no control over their situation and so behave in a helpless manner. This inactive state can prevent them from seeing opportunities for relief or change.

The concept of **learned helplessness** was discovered by accident in dogs by two psychologists, Martin Seligman and Steven Maier.[19] The dogs had been conditioned to expect an electrical shock after hearing a certain tone.

After the conditioning, the dogs were placed in a box that contained two compartments separated by a low barrier. The floor in one of the compartments was electrified and the dogs only had to jump over the barrier to escape being given an electric shock. But the dogs did not jump. Further experiments showed that these dogs had developed a cognitive expectation that nothing they did would prevent or eliminate the shocks. They therefore made no attempt to escape the shocks.

Since this experiment, this phenomenon has been observed in various situations involving humans, where an earlier failure leads to feelings of powerlessness and impotence that affect future performance.

Learned helplessness can induce the *pessimism-attribution bias* that leads to distorted thinking and self-beliefs. For example, when we have failed at something we may then become convinced that nothing we do from then on will have any effect on future performance.

This is often the reason why people stay in the wrong job or the wrong relationship, or why they do nothing to improve their health. To an outsider, a solution may seem simple, but for people suffering from this bias it is often difficult to escape the bad situation because they feel that it is beyond their control.

Part 2: Impact on our daily life

We think other people are more biased than we are

Many of us would like to believe that our opinions and decisions have been carefully and rationally formed. But all of us are biased to some degree or other – and all of us will experience some or all of the biases explained above. Yet, ironically, many of us think other people are more biased than we are!

Much of the time we are unaware of our own biases. This is known as *unconscious* or *implicit bias*. Even if we do recognise that we may be biased, we rarely question or confront the biases we carry inside us. Nevertheless, our biases continue to influence how we live and interact with those around us.

Despite being aware of our biases, we can never fully overcome our biased thinking; but we can try to interrupt it, slow it down and minimise its effects on our decision-making. The key point to remember is that no amount of training will fully eradicate biased thinking. The best we can do is to become more self-aware and recognise that we have biases, so that we can challenge our own thinking and assumptions.

We hate being wrong

Although we like to think that we make good decisions and that if we were presented with contradictory facts we would change our views, in fact, the opposite is true.

As discussed earlier in this chapter, when we are provided with evidence to counter an original opinion or belief, we stick even more rigidly to our original belief, rather than believe the new contradictory (but correct) evidence.

We are so afraid of being wrong that we lose our ability to reason when someone or something contradicts our convictions. Not even the proof of Barack Obama's birth certificate has been sufficient to change some people's belief that he was not born in the United States. By the same token, many of the parents who were convinced by the link between the MMR vaccine and autism did not change their views even after this link was found to be false; in fact, many parents became even less likely to vaccinate their children.

Our brain avoids complexity

The more choices we have, the more we avoid complexity and the less likely we are to make a decision. Because most of us dislike uncertainty, and our brain is continually attempting to predict and protect, when there are too many unknowns we look for the simplest solution to help us make a fast decision.

When we have to choose between multiple outcomes, our brain cannot cope and becomes distracted. However, when we have just two outcomes, we are able to make a much faster choice.

More choice is not always better for our brain! In a study, shoppers in a food store saw a display stand with 24 varieties of jam being offered.[20] Later in the week, shoppers saw a similar stand but with only six varieties of jam.

Although the larger stand initially attracted more interest than the smaller stand, people were ten times more likely to purchase a jar of jam from the smaller rather than the larger display.

Having too many choices also makes us tired and can even lead to us avoiding having to make a decision altogether. This is called *choice overload* and can lead us to *choice paralysis,* where we avoid making important decisions.[21]

As the number of options increases, the more the degree of certainty is reduced concerning the choice we have. As a result, we are more likely to suffer from anticipation of regret about the choice we may then go on to make.

We are easily influenced

Our brain is often influenced in ways of which we are not aware. This has promoted interest in a topic known as *behavioural economics* or *decision science*. In fact, Harvard University now offers an executive programme in Behavioural Economics in recognition of its importance.

Anchoring

Numbers matter! Our brain *anchors* itself to the highest available number. The initial figure we set for anything tends to influence the final price that is agreed. Our brain uses the initial number as the reference point. This is why we are more likely to pay more for something if we see a higher figure first. This explains why car prices in garages are so high: when the salesman then reduces the price, we feel like we have a deal. We can see the same effect when negotiating our salary for a new job and why we, not our new employer, should open negotiations. The higher we set the initial anchor, the higher the final agreed salary will be.

Framing

We can use language to *frame* choices that highlight either the positive or negative aspects of the same concept, which can then lead to different decisions. For example, would we prefer to undergo surgery with a 10% failure rate, or surgery with a 90% success rate?

Frames make the buying decision easy for the brain. Negative framing is used a great deal in marketing (playing to our loss aversion) – we are often told what we stand to lose if we choose not to purchase something. This has been discussed in Chapter 5, Our Brain and Language.

If we are buying a bottle of shampoo, we may have the chance to buy one bottle at a 20% discount or another bottle at full price with free conditioner. Because of our loss aversion, we are more likely to choose the bottle with the free gift, even though the value of the conditioner may be less than that of the discount. This is because we do not want to lose out on the free gift.

Priming

Priming is a form of implicit or nondeclarative memory (explained in more detail in Chapter 3, Our Brain and Memory) and it describes certain associations that we make based on the information we have already stored in our brain. For example, a person who hears the word *red* and is then asked to name a fruit may be more inclined to say 'strawberry' or 'apple' than a fruit that is not red.

We are constantly being primed in various ways.

At the **cinema**, we are often primed to buy drinks, both as we walk into the cinema and during the commercials.
In **wine merchants**, the music being played may influence us to buy wine from the same country as the music.
In **supermarkets**, the smell of bread at the back of a store primes us to walk through the whole store.
Smells associated with **hygiene** (such as citrus) may induce more hygienic behaviour.
The colours **green** and **blue** can promote creative thinking. Offices that look out over green fields, rather than over concrete buildings, can have an impact on our ability to think up new ideas.
Even putting a **pen in our mouth** horizontally can create a smile expression, which will make us feel happier and help us find jokes funnier!

Nudge theory

Nudge theory is an aspect of behavioural economics where our behaviour can be *nudged* in a specific direction. The direction can be either good or bad.

In 2010, the government in the United Kingdom set up the Behavioural Insights Team, also known as the Nudge Unit, which has worked with Richard Thaler whose best-selling books, *Nudge* and *Misbehaving*, reinforce the same philosophy.[22, 23]

In 2012, after winning the Civil Service Award, the Behavioural Insights Team published its **EAST** framework:

Easy	Make it as straightforward as possible for people to pay tax, debts or take up a service. Provide default options or pre-populated forms. Simplify the language used.
Attractive	Draw people's attention to important information or actions required of them up front. Design compelling rewards. Personalise language and make the message relevant to them.
Social	Describe what other people are doing, such as '9 out of 10 people pay their tax on time'. Actively incentivise or reward behaviour that saves time or money.
Timely	Prompt people when they are most receptive and likely to be honest. Give people the costs and benefits of their action and help them plan.

Among the initiatives of the Behavioural Insights Team has been one nudging people into paying their car's road tax using a letter written in simple English. It states: 'Pay your tax or lose your car.' In some cases, a photograph of the recipient's own car has been attached. This letter alone has doubled the number of people paying the tax, with the number tripling with the addition of the photograph.

Similar outcomes have been seen elsewhere.

> Children may also be nudged. *The Economist* cites a study in French schools that found that if the subject was called 'geometry', boys excelled, but if it was called 'drawing', girls did just as well as the boys – or even better.[24]

Workplace studies have shown that managers who believe their company has a reputation for supporting women in more male-dominated fields of science and technology are more likely to hire, develop and promote women.[25]

The downside of nudge is that we can be manipulated in the same way by the nudging of others. By not paying attention to whether something is an *opt-in* or *opt-out*, we may find ourselves committing unknowingly to initiatives without even realising that we have done so.

For example, our tendency to accept default options means that we are more likely to enrol in schemes that have an opt-out rather than an opt-in clause. Taking organ donation as an example, a scheme that requires donors to state positively that they want their organs to be used (opt-in) has a lower sign-up rate than if donors are required to state if they do not want their organs to be used (opt-out).

Similarly, in order to increase retirement savings, British legislation now supports the default option for corporate pension plans, which automatically enrols employees unless they choose to opt out.

Part 3: Stories and top tips

Even children become biased quickly

In the United States in 1968, the day after the assassination of Martin Luther King, one of the most significant social studies on in-group/out-group bias was carried out in an Iowa classroom.[26]

The teacher, Jane Elliot, decided to demonstrate racial prejudice by dividing her third-grade class into groups on the basis of eye colour. Elliot told the blue-eyed children that they were 'better' than the brown-eyed children and within minutes the blue-eyed children started calling their brown-eyed classmates 'stupid' and refused to play with them. The next day she reversed the situation and observed the brown-eyed children doing exactly the same to their blue-eyed classmates.

The impact of her classroom study had lasting effects: her pupils later showed significantly less racism than other children their own age, and this effect lasted as they grew to adulthood.

Jane Elliot has since run similar experiments on adults and has found that adults demonstrate even greater racist tendencies than children.

Who are our friends?

Many of us are living examples of in-group/out-group bias. We only have to look at the people we socialise with to observe this. Even when we think we have expanded horizons and have a heterogeneous social circle, we will nevertheless generally revert to what feels familiar and similar whenever our comfort zone is threatened.

In other words, we will naturally and automatically seek out people with whom we can identify and share some commonality, even in diverse surroundings.

Our friends therefore often reflect the type of people that we are ourselves.

Do we ever learn from our mistakes?

In 1672, a group of young girls in Salem Village in colonial Massachusetts started to blame their own bad behaviour on other people, whom they accused of being witches.

The Puritan community to which these girls belonged had formed a cohesive group, united by harsh winters, recent conflict, strong religious convictions and their belief in the occult.

Most of those accused were women who did not conform with the rest of the group and who were viewed as a threat to the community because they wore different clothes, challenged their husbands or, as widows, owned property. As a result of the legal trials in Salem, some 20 people and one dog were executed, with a further 200 people imprisoned.

None of these trials were based on any scientific evidence but rather were the result of widespread scapegoating and group polarisation by a community that was swept along on a wave of mass hysteria and accusation.

Centuries later, during the 1950s, Senator John McCarthy conducted a series of witch-hunts in search of communist sympathisers. Those who were accused were told to testify or risk losing their jobs and social standing. They were also offered the chance to cooperate and accuse some of their own friends and colleagues of being communists. Few people dared to challenge McCarthy's accusations.

During this time, people were suspicious and paranoid. The Cold War was the perfect breeding ground for groupthink and mass hysteria. Few people dared to speak out against McCarthy or his supporters, and no one at the time challenged the inaccurate reporting of the media or the death sentences, even though they were based on spurious evidence.

The McCarthy era, as it become known, prompted Arthur Miller to write *The Crucible* to highlight the parallels between McCarthyism and the events in Salem so many years earlier. Although we like to think we learn from the past, we rarely do.

Nudges or dark patterns?

It is not uncommon these days to be in the middle of booking something on the internet when a message tells us how many people are looking at the same thing or that it is the last one left. However, a recent investigation by a cyber-security researcher who decided to look more closely at one such figure unveiled that the figure had in fact been randomly generated.

This technique of using verbal nudges to push customers towards making certain buying decisions is known as *dark patterns*, a term coined by Harry Brignall, a design consultant in 2010.[27]

A study at Princeton in 2019 looked at 11,000 shopping websites and discovered 1,818 dark patterns and 15 different types currently in use.[28]

To address growing concerns, the Norwegian Consumer Council published a report in 2018 advocating greater transparency and honesty for firms promoting to customers online.[29] There are websites that publish accurate data about viewing numbers, but there are still many that employ dark patterns to increase sales, eroding public trust and retailers' reputations.

Nudges are now commonly used to drive consumer marketing behaviour, but the problem comes when information is manipulated or misleading to the public. Calls for increased regulation will become more frequent as we learn more about the techniques being used to influence the choices we make every day.

Being human makes us biased

During the 2016 US presidential election, Donald Trump's running mate Governor Mike Pence criticised Hillary Clinton for accusing police officers of having implicit biases, saying that it was demeaning and racist.

However, according to researchers such as Alexis McGill Johnson of the Perception Institute, Pence has confused implicit or unconscious bias with explicit or overt racism: having implicit bias is very much part of being human.

Although initiatives in recent years have focused on providing education in social institutions such as schools and businesses on implicit or unconscious bias, it is a concept that nevertheless remains misunderstood in certain circles.

But accepting that we are all biased does not give us carte blanche to behave in a racist or bigoted manner, or relieve us of social responsibility. Even the best intentioned among us hold implicit biases. This does not mean that we are racist and are going to violate the rights of others; we all simply need to recognise that we naturally absorb these biases from the people and culture around us, and we often do so without questioning the biases' validity or morality.

We see outcomes and not probabilities

Our brains are wired to downgrade familiar risks. Every day many of us travel in a car without worrying about the potential threat to our life. When it comes to risk assessment, our brain resorts to instinct rather than logic. Although it is difficult to assess danger, our brain does it anyway, translating fear into action.

When we encounter a potential risk, we evaluate it rapidly by comparing it to our store of memories (as discussed in more detail in Chapter 3, Our Brain and Memory). But our memories may either not be appropriate to the situation or they can lead us to draw the wrong conclusions. For example, if there are two aeroplane crashes in quick succession, we conclude that flying is dangerous, even though statistics tell us it is safer than driving.

We are especially bad at judging low-probability, high-risk threats such as terrorism, or we perceive that vaccination's greater risks of possible side effects outweigh the benefits of protection. And so we either over-react or under-react. With the recent pandemic of the COVID-19 coronavirus, there is understandable fear across the world. But we barely register the survivor numbers and instead we focus on the fatalities as a primary outcome. Media headlines (as explained in Chapter 5, Our Brain and Language) fuel our fears further with language that grips us emotionally and distorts our thinking. And the greater the pain or pleasure associated with the risk, the greater our expectation that it will happen to us.

In addition, our strong *novelty bias* means that we pay attention to anything new or unusual (remember the word 'new' in Chapter 5, Our Brain and Language) and so broadcasts of a new threat sensitises us all the more to any information related to that threat.

In an experiment, people were asked how much they would pay to: a) avoid a 1% chance of a 'short, painful, but not dangerous electric shock' or b) avoid a 99% chance of getting such a shock.[30]

To avoid a 1% chance of an electric shock, people were willing to pay on average $7, but to avoid a 99% chance, the number was not much higher at $10.

The experiment showed that we are more concerned with outcomes than probability, especially when the outcome carries a strong emotional element. This is also why people play the lottery; although the probability of winning is low, the potential outcome is powerful.

Can we beat our biases?

We will never be without our biases completely, but we can certainly become more aware of them.

Because biases can lead us into decision traps, they tend to be viewed in a negative light. But they can also sometimes help us make accurate judgements.

Since they activate quickly, we are not always aware of when they may be driving us towards a right or wrong decision. Knowing where we may be biased is a first step. The Harvard Implicit Association Test (IAT) is a popular tool that measures subconscious associations among different groups of people and moral evaluations. Although the IAT has been criticised for not being an accurate predictor of biases on an individual level,[31] it can provide an aggregate score of implicit intolerances if the tool is taken multiple times.

Training in diversity and implicit or unconscious bias has had mixed reviews,[32] with some programmes even reported to worsen existing biases.[33] Recent research advises against one-off initiatives and advocates a review of practices that include recruitment and performance reviews, as well as tracking data on attitude and behaviours in additional to the usual organisational metrics.[34]

Whatever our biases, slowing down our responses sufficiently to evaluate and question *why* will move us closer to making more intentional decisions.

Top Tips
Remember: **ANGLE**

Accept that biases exist in all of us – they make us human. You will then be more open to challenging your own biases. Question your judgements about others by flipping your stereotypes. Imagine alternative outcomes, including possible failures, to broaden your view. Record decisions at the time they are made, together with their underpinning assumptions. This will protect you from memory errors and overconfidence in the future.

Nurture diversity in your world and travel as much as possible to learn about different cultures and customs. Our brain will adapt to different influences, such as diverse environments and multicultural perspectives.

Give your brain fewer options. This will help your decision-making. Think about how you are being nudged or influenced. Prime yourself with positive emotions, words and images.

Listen to the way you communicate with other people and pay constant attention to your own natural negativity bias. Behaviour influences thoughts, and thoughts influence behaviour. Be warm and positive in the way you act towards people and you will foster positive relationships, even with those you may previously have disregarded or written off.

Encourage healthy debate and disagreement. This will help defend against groupthink. Challenge your own expectations and beliefs about people. Beware of labelling individuals and of contributing towards stereotypical thinking. People normally behave in the way we expect them to behave.

References for Chapter 7

1. Gilbert, D. et al. (1998). 'Immune neglect: A source of durability bias in affective forecasting', *Journal of Personality and Social Psychology*, September, 617–38.
2. Festinger, L. et al. (1956). *When Prophecy Fails: A Social and Psychological Study of a Modern Group That Predicted the Destruction of the World*. London: Harper Torchbooks.
3. Palminteri, S. et al. (2017). 'Confirmation bias in human reinforcement learning: Evidence from counterfactual feedback processing', *PLoS*, August. https://doi.org/10.1371/journal.pcbi.1005684
4. Scopelliti, I. et al. (2015). 'Bias blind spot: Structure, measurement and consequences', *Management Science*, April. https://doi.org/10.1287/mnsc.2014.2096
5. Kahneman, D. (2012). *Thinking Fast and Slow*. London: Penguin Books.
6. Roese, N.J., & Vohs, K.D. (2012). 'Hindsight bias', *Perspectives on Psychological Science*, September, 411–26. https://doi.org/10.1177/1745691612454303
7. Javetski, B., & Koller, T. (2018). 'Debiasing the corporation: An interview with Nobel laureate Richard Thaler', *McKinsey Quarterly*, May.
8. Schoenbaum, M. (1997). 'Do smokers understand the mortality effects of smoking? Evidence from the Health and Retirement Survey', *American Journal of Public Health*, May, 755–59.
9. Zenger, J., & Folkman, J. (2015). 'We like leaders who underrate themselves', *Harvard Business Review*, November, 2–6.
10. Ersner-Hershfield, H. (2013). 'You make better decisions if you "see" your senior self', *Harvard Business Review*, June, 3–4.
11. Eagleman, D. (2016). 'Why do I need you?', Episode 5 of *The Brain*, aired February, BBC Four.
12. Sutin, A., & Terracciano, A. (2013). '"Weightism" increases risk for becoming, staying obese', *PLOS ONE*, 24 July. doi.org/10.1371/journal.pone.0070048
13. Fredrickson, B.L., & Losada, M.F. (2011). 'Positive affect and the complex dynamics of human flourishing', *American Psychologist*, October, 678–86.
14. Milgram, S. (1963). 'Behavioural study of obedience', *Journal of Abnormal and Social Psychology*, 371–78
15. Burger, J. (2009). 'Replicating Milgram: Would people still obey today?' *The American Psychologist*, 1–11. https://doi.org/10.1037/a0010932
16. Doliński, D. et al. (2017). 'Would you deliver an electric shock in 2015? Obedience in the experimental paradigm developed by Stanley Milgram in the 50 years following the original studies', *Social Psychological and Personality Science*. https://doi.org/10.1177/1948550617693060
17. Asch, S. (1955). 'Opinions and social pressure', *Scientific American*, November, 31–35.
18. Wakefield, A.J. (1998). 'RETRACTED: Ileal-lymphoid-nodular hyperplasia, non-specific colitis, and pervasive developmental disorder in children', *Lancet*, February, 637–41.
19. Seligman, M., & Maier, S. (1967). 'Failure to escape traumatic shock', *Journal of Experimental Psychology*, May, 1–9.
20. Lyengar, S., & Lepper, M. (2000). 'When choice is demotivating: Can one desire too much of a good thing?' *Personality Processes and Individual Differences*, December, 995–1006.
21. Chernev, A. et al. (2015). 'Choice overload: A conceptual review and meta-analysis', *Journal of Consumer Psychology*, August, 333–58.

22. Thaler, R. (2009). *Nudge: Improving Decisions about Health, Wealth and Happiness*. London: Penguin Books.

23. Thaler, R. (2016). *Misbehaving: The Making of Behavioral Economics*. New York: W.W. Norton.

24. The Economist. (2012). 'Nudge, nudge, think, think', May. economist.com

25. Braun, S., & Turner, R.A. (2014). 'Attitudes and company practices as predictors of managers' intentions to hire, develop, and promote women in science, engineering, and technology professions', *Consulting Psychology Journal: Practice and Research*, June, 93–117.

26. Peters, E.S. (1987). *A Class Divided: Then and Now*. London: Yale University Press.

27. Brignall, H. (2019). https://www.darkpatterns.org

28. Mathur, A. et al. (2019). Dark Patterns at Scale: Findings from a Crawl of 11K Shopping Websites. *Proceedings of the ACM on Human Computer Interaction archive*. https://doi.org/10.1145/3359183

29. DECEIVED BY DESIGN How tech companies use dark patterns to discourage us from exercising our rights to privacy, 27 June 2018.

30. Rottenstreich, Y., & Hsee, C.K. (2001). 'Money, kisses, and electric shocks: On the affective psychology of risk', *Psychological Science*, May, 185–90.

31. Blanton, H. et al. (2009). 'Strong Claims and Weak Evidence: Reassessing the Predictive Validity of the IAT' Faculty Scholarship Paper 1532. http://scholarship.law.upenn.edu/faculty_scholarship/1532

32. Dobbin, F., & Kalev, A. (2016). 'Why diversity programs fail' *Harvard Business Review*, July–August.

33. Kulik, C. et al. (2007). 'The rich get richer: Predicting participation in voluntary diversity training' *Journal of Organizational Behavior* August, 753–69. doi: 10.1002/job.44433.

34. Chang, E. (2019). The mixed effects of online diversity training PNAS, April, 7778–83, https://doi.org/10.1073/pnas.1816076116

"Every child is an artist. The problem is staying an artist when you grow up."

PABLO PICASSO
Painter, sculptor, poet and playwright (1881–1973)

Our Brain and Creativity

Our ability to think creatively has ensured our survival as a species. We have a natural curiosity that has led to new discoveries, and we have continued to forge new ways of living, communicating, eating, travelling and learning.

In recent years, as certain organisations have failed to keep up with or ahead of competitors, *creativity* and *innovation* have become popular concepts that are now generally viewed as the panacea for business success. The World Economic Forum has even listed creativity as one of the top three skills that professionals will need for the future.

This emphasis on instilling or accessing a creative mind-set has prompted researchers, educators and business leaders to look more deeply at what *creativity* actually means and whether, in fact, everyone is capable of being creative.

This chapter discusses what creativity is and how it works in our brain. The underpinning premise is that we all have a creative spark, which, in many of us, just needs to be reignited.

Part 1: The science explained

How does creativity work in our brain?

Creativity comprises the conception, testing and verifying of an idea. Creativity often happens when we are daydreaming, allowing our mind to wander or even

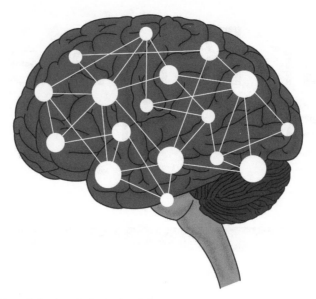

FIGURE 8.1: Creativity is a 'whole-brain' process

trying to imagine what other people are thinking. And an idea can come to us when we least expect it.

There are many mistaken beliefs about creativity. We convince ourselves that creativity is something other *creative* people are born with, that we have to be right-brained or left-handed or that it is all about intellect. However, a commonly held view among researchers, innovators and artists is that, whoever we are and whatever our skill, we can all be creative; we just need courage, perseverance and the willingness to fail.

Chapter 1, Our Brain, describes our brain as bilaterally organised to process different types of information, with creativity featured on the right side. Although the right side of our brain is heavily involved in generating new insights, the full creative process is actually a whole-brain skill (see Figure 8.1). In other words, our creative ability depends on dynamic interactions across a number of different brain regions.[1]

The areas of our brain responsible for creativity have been collectively described as our *imagination network,* a term that was first proposed in 2001. This network largely involves the *frontal, parietal* and *temporal* lobes of our brain.[2]

Creativity relies on in the way that all of these lobes interact with each other:

The **temporal and parietal lobes** store specialised knowledge.

The **frontal lobe** is involved in the development of alternative solutions or perspectives.

A recent study using the brain scans of 500 volunteers has also shown that there is a link between our brain structure and creativity.[3]

The findings highlight that those who were more open, creative and receptive to new ideas had a thinner, larger and more wrinkled cortex (outer layer of the brain) compared to the other participants.

The thinner cortex may point to a high level of synaptic pruning, which is a neurological process linked to improved connectivity and cognitive efficiency, as discussed in Chapter 1, Our Brain.

Creativity is messy and contradictory

Most psychologists today agree that creativity is multifaceted in nature. On a neurological level, creativity is even deemed to be messy. This is because our imagination network is essentially full of contradiction.

On one hand, our imagination network helps us entertain abstract thoughts and allows our mind to wander in time or space. On the other hand, it allows us to focus sharply and deal with the here and now.

In short, the imagination network moves between the rational and the emotional sides of the brain, turning networks on and off.

How are new ideas formed?

When our brain creates anything that is different from what we already know, certain brain regions are activated and work together.

In 2015, a study was carried out at the University of Haifa to examine the creative process in the brain.[4]

Participants were given half a minute to devise a new and original use for different objects. A functional magnetic resonance imaging (fMRI) scanner examined their brain activity while they formulated their idea. The ideas that cropped up less frequently were scored high on originality, while more commonly occurring ideas were given a lower score.

It was found that in the participants who generated the highest degree of originality, brain activity was strong in an area that we use to daydream. In addition to this, another region towards the front of the brain was active – the part that we use for rules and social norms.

The stronger the collaboration between these two brain regions, the higher the level of original thinking.

But this collaboration in the brain needs to be carefully managed: when we judge too much or too early, it may hinder or dampen the creative process. When our brain needs to run totally free and randomly, it cannot be stifled by rules or evaluation. And so it has to switch off the frontal lobe that we use for critical analysis.

Later on, we may consciously activate these frontal lobe regions in order to assess the viability of the ideas that have been generated.

Researchers in California have measured the brain activity of rappers and other musicians whose work involves creative improvisation.[5]

The musicians played a small keyboard while inside a fMRI scanner to monitor their brain activity. Through their music, they were asked to convey positive emotions and then negative emotions, and at the same time were shown happy and sad images.

The researchers observed deactivation of the brain's *dorsolateral prefrontal cortex* (DLPFC), which helps to plan and monitor behaviour, when conveying positive emotions, suggesting that the musicians were allowing their minds to be unconstrained. When conveying sad emotions, the part of the brain that is linked to reward was activated.

This study highlighted the relationship between creativity and emotion, again proving the involvement of different regions of the brain in the creative process.

Why is a eureka moment not 'out of the blue'?

When we experience a sudden insight or moment of inspiration that seems to come to us from nowhere, it is actually the result of different brain regions working together, connecting pieces of information over a period of time.

Although we take information into both our left and right hemispheres, the neurons on our right are wider reaching and can pull in ideas that are further away and unrelated in our brain. Brain studies using electroencephalography (EEG) and fMRI show that our brain experiences bursts of high frequency just prior to one of these eureka moments.[6]

In particular, the activation of an area of the brain located in the right hemisphere known as the *right anterior superior temporal gyrus*, which is involved in musical processing and spatial perception, enables us to connect unrelated objects or concepts.

Examples of eureka moments	
Microwave	In 1945, Percy Spencer was experimenting with a new vacuum tube when he noticed that the chocolate bar in his pocket was melting. He realised that microwaves being emitted by the vacuum tube could penetrate the exterior of a food and cook it *from the inside out* instead of *from the outside in*. Two years later, the first microwave oven was manufactured, although it was not until 1967 that it was made smaller and more affordable.
Velcro	In 1948, Swiss engineer George de Mestral went hiking in the woods and noticed that burrs from plants he had walked into had stuck to his clothing. After examining a burr under a microscope and discovering that they were covered in tiny hooks that allowed them to attach to clothes and fur, he created what is now known as Velcro.
Post-its	In 1968, Spencer Silver at 3M discovered a glue that would not stick. But the company did not pursue the idea until 1974, when another 3M employee, Arthur Fry, used the low-tack glue for bookmarks in his hymn book. Now Post-its are sold all over the world.
Hypodermic needle	In 2011, scientists in Japan developed a hypodermic needle that is based on a mosquito's proboscis.[7] Instead of being a smooth needle that comes into contact with a considerable amount of skin, causing pain, this new model is serrated and barely touches the skin. The needle mimics the mosquito's mouthparts and breaks the skin in such a way as to reduce the pain normally caused by a syringe – in much the same way as we rarely feel a mosquito bite!

So if we constantly feed our brain with new information and then allow it to make links and associations, an idea may suddenly come to us when we are least expecting it, or while we are doing something completely unrelated.

Are creative people different from everyone else?

The question above has been baffling scientists for decades. Just as our creative brain is contradictory and multidirectional, so too it seems that people in creative professions can exhibit a range of complex behaviours.

During the 1960s, a series of experiments was conducted on some well-known thinkers of the time to investigate their creativity.[8] Among these thinkers were writers, architects, scientists, entrepreneurs and mathematicians. They were invited to spend time meeting each other and being tested, interviewed and observed. The researchers wanted to assess their personality, mental stability and creativity.

The study found that creativity comprised a range of intellectual, emotional, motivational and moral factors.

What everyone had in common was a willingness to share personal detail, a preference for ambiguity, an unusually high tolerance for disorder, independence and unconventionality, and a willingness to take risks.

To some extent, it seems that people who spend their time engaged in creative pursuits do stand out from others in a number of aspects: they combine introspection with emotional expression, they are rational and emotional, deliberate and spontaneous, disorderly and organised. These inner conflicts may lead them to create.[9]

In essence, people who are deemed to be creative have allowed themselves to engage in a range of experiences, many of which are reflected in their work. Their heightened sense of self seems to sensitise them to life's ups and downs, and some – such as creative writers – even score high in terms of symptoms of mental illness.

A recent study has considered the creative process by looking at Fields Medallists, Pulitzer Prize winners and six Nobel laureates, examining their personal histories and conducting neuroimaging on their brains.[10]

The study concluded that creative people:

- Prefer to teach themselves rather than be taught, and they find standard ways of teaching unhelpful.

- Love both the arts and the sciences, while traditional education often encourages a divide between the two.

- Are resilient in the face of scepticism and rejection – although they may suffer anxiety if these factors persist. This persistence might breed psychological pain, which can manifest as depression or anxiety.

- Have bad ideas as well as good ideas. But they may also see connections and possibilities that no one else can see and have the tenacity to try them out.

Nancy Andreasen, who conducted the study, states:

'You cannot force creativity to happen – every creative person can attest to that. But the essence of creativity is making connections and solving puzzles.'

But creativity is also in the small stuff

Being creative does not always have to be linked with great works of art or achievement. We can also be creative with everyday issues, such as how to decorate a table, how to keep children entertained at the weekend, how to present data and how to communicate with our boss.

While many of us have not followed a career path that we would typically associate with creativity, we can nevertheless find a multitude of opportunities to think differently, remove obstacles, see novelty and find possibility in what we do every day.

'Discovery is seeing what everybody else has seen, and thinking what nobody else has thought.'

Albert Szent-Györgyi
Nobel prize-winning biochemist known for isolating vitamin C

A number of the greatest inventions have arisen from the ability to imagine another possibility:

Thomas Edison invented the first multiplex telegraph by observing a water pump.
Willis Carrier invented air conditioners after he saw water condensing on the side of a window.
The physician René Laënnec invented the stethoscope after observing two children sending signals to each other by tapping on a piece of wood with a pin.

Our senses affect our creativity

Because creativity depends on our ability to make new connections and associations, the more input we receive through our senses, the more material there is for our brain to work with.

People who experience heightened sensory input and an intermingling of the senses may have hyperconnectivity of certain brain regions. This is a condition called *synaesthesia,* which affects one in 2,000 people. Synaesthetes may experience conjoined sensory input, such as seeing numbers in different colours, or tasting strawberries when they hear the word 'book'.

The symptoms of synaesthesia are considered to be genetic, although other researchers have suggested that the condition is a result of earlier pruning issues in the brain. It has been found to be more common in artists, poets and writers, leading researchers to make the association between synaesthesia with high brain interconnectivity and creativity.[11]

Sight:	Daylight has a better impact on our cognitive performance than artificial light,[12] but dim lighting can enhance our creative performance.[13]
Smell:	Smell is a powerful enhancer of emotion and brain agility:[14] – Lemon and jasmine can improve cognitive functioning. – Vanilla and cinnamon can help enhance creativity. – Rosemary and grapefruit are energising and stimulating.
Sound:	Focus sometimes does require silence and freedom from any distraction, but a moderate level of ambient noise (such as background conversation) can also sometimes boost our creative powers.[15]
Taste:	Fresh fruit and vegetables can stimulate positive changes in mood and are effective fuel for creative thinking.[16]
Touch:	Temperature impacts cognitive performance. A warmer workspace is more conducive to cognitive efficiency than a cold one. When our workspace is too cold, we are using our energy and resources in trying to stay warm, and we make more errors.[17] This is explained further in Chapter 11, Our Brain and Leadership.

Is intelligence linked to creativity?

Intelligence can be summarised as our capacity for learning, reasoning and understanding.

Some researchers believe that there is a positive relationship between intelligence and creativity. It makes sense that intelligence and the ability to store more information may then provide more for the brain to work with and connect – thereby becoming more creative.

The *Threshold Theory* suggests that highly creative people have an intelligence quotient (IQ) of about 120 (see Figure 8.2 for ranges).[18]

IQ Range	Classification
Above 145	Genius or near genius
130–144	Very superior
115–129	Superior
85–114	Normal

FIGURE 8.2: IQ ranges

With anything that is above that, the relationship between IQ and creativity is not as evident. This may suggest that a very high IQ may not necessarily mean high creativity.[19]

Part 2: Impact on our daily life

Can we learn to be creative?

The short answer is yes! Creativity is not a fixed ability that we are born with. It emerges through a number of processes that lead to new ways of thinking.

But many of us need to train our minds to produce new ideas. In order to do this, we have to rethink our view of creativity as being due purely to genius and instead see it as a thinking skill that we can all learn.

And so creativity is less about *who people are* and more about *what people do*. When we accept this we are able to allow our brains to enjoy the creative process as much as those whom we consider to be truly creative.

We can all boost our creativity by consciously deciding to engage in cognitive techniques that stretch our thinking (see Figure 8.3).[20]

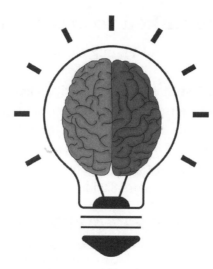

The actor and comedian John Cleese describes our brain as being like a tortoise: a tortoise pokes its head out to check that the environment is safe before it fully emerges. For creativity to take hold, we therefore need to create a safe place like a tortoise's shell.

Creativity will emerge only when it feels that the time is right and that it will not be threatened by other thoughts.

Creative skill	Creative action
Connection	Allow random thoughts and ideas to enter your mind and your brain will start to piece them together. We need to see connections and relationships between different facts, ideas or existing components.
Daydreaming	Give your brain time and space to think, reflect and entertain abstact thought. Find creative space. When we daydream and relax, our alpha brainwaves are prominent and sensory input is minimised. This state is called *optimal inattention* and is also achieved during meditation and mindfulness.
Shifting	Break away from your work for five minutes and generate as many ideas as possible on your own (for example, find different words to rename something). This is a more effective way of producing different ideas than brainstorming, which has limited value because of the power of *groupthink* or collective judgement. Groups are better at idea selection than idea creation.
Thinking like a child	We need to combine work and play. Experiment – without judgement or criticism. Our brain works best when it is relaxed, happy and free to explore possibilities.
Persistence	We need to motivate ourselves to try, endure failure and try again. As Tom Peters said, we need to 'Fail Fast – Learn Fast – Fix Fast'.
Using our nose	Of all of our senses, our sense of smell provides the most powerful link to memory. This phenomenon, known as the Proust effect, can often trigger lost memories and emotions from the past to inspire and create new ideas.

FIGURE 8.3: Cognitive techniques that boost creativity

Creativity is not fragile: we need to challenge it!

We need to work on our ideas, test them and even criticise them. Our ideas can handle it! Ideas need work, scrutiny, judgement and expansion. In allowing ourselves to work on an idea, we may find ourselves discovering different dimensions and possibilities. We should not treat ideas as if they were fragile.

Overcoming challenges can create the right conditions for creativity to flourish. Failure can ignite the creative regions of the brain, and we will then try even harder to compensate for not succeeding the first time. According to Shane Snow the teams that solve problems most successfully are not necessarily the most talented, but they are the teams whose members use their diverse experiences, skills, knowledge to debate and stretch each other's thinking.[21]

Convergent versus divergent thinking

Creativity needs us to think *divergently* rather than *convergently*. However, as humans, we are more convergent than divergent thinkers.

Convergent thinking (see Figure 8.4) is mainly focused on providing the right answer or solution, rather than on how to solve a problem. We effectively *converge* on the best approach and address any deviation from the correct path. Convergent thinking relies on plans and logic. Most corporate strategies are developed from convergent thinking.

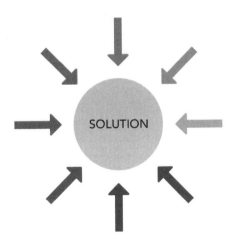

FIGURE 8.4: Convergent thinking

449 Failures!

In the 1960s, Unilever – a company known for manufacturing laundry detergent – had a major problem. The nozzle that they used to turn chemicals into a powder kept blocking.

Unilever's mathematicians could not fix the problem.

Finally, Unilever asked their biologists, who, using a different, evolutionary-based approach, made a series of smaller incremental adjustments. After 45 different models and 449 failures they created a nozzle that worked.[22]

And Dyson failed over 5,000 times!

Thirty years ago, James Dyson imagined redesigning the vacuum cleaner. Frustrated with how the vacuum bag clogged with dust, he decided to replace it with a fastspinning motor that created a cyclone of air that, in turn, created suction.

Some 5,127 designs later, Dyson's first vacuum cleaner was rejected by British retailers. The first models were sold only in Japan, where they were very successful. By the mid-90s, Dyson's vacuum cleaner had become a bestseller in the United Kingdom.

As James Dyson says:

'We fail every day. Failure is the best medicine – as long as you learn something.'

Divergent thinking (see Figure 8.5) looks for alternatives and widens our spectrum of available ideas. Divergent thinking opens up our thinking to consider arbitrary concepts. It feels more chaotic and disorganised, but it is often the source of additional ideas. Divergent thinking enables us to consider unusual combinations and multiple possibilities. It tests notions and sees where they take us.

We cannot use both convergent and divergent thinking at the same time. Each process requires us to use our brain differently. We need to devote time to one, and then the other. Our brain needs space to create and come up with ideas freely, and only when divergent thinking has exhausted all random possibilities should we apply convergent thinking to evaluate and select the best ideas.

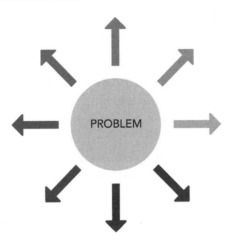

FIGURE 8.5: Divergent thinking

We should guard against moving too quickly into convergent thinking simply because we need quick answers now. Ideas need to be generated and then connected, challenged and tested. This can take time.

Twitter is a result of divergent thinking. When Twitter was developed, it did not have an obvious practical application. There was no clear underpinning strategy or formula for success.

Twitter was launched to see what the take-up would be. The aim was to refine the application only after determining how many people used it.

After testing the market and seeing where the idea could go, Twitter has gone on to become one of the world's most popular and widely used social networking services.

Creativity helps us to imagine the future

As Chapter 7, Our Brains and Biases, discusses, we have a strong *present bias* and, the further away the future seems, the more difficult it is for us to imagine it. *Distal imagination* is the term given to conceiving ideas or experiences beyond our current situation. Although most people find this difficult, recent research has shown that those who are involved in creative pursuits are better able to do this compared with less creatively driven individuals.[23] And when envisioning the future, only creative people automatically activate a particular neural system in the brain. This system is known as the *default mode network* that is made up of different brain regions (the *medial prefrontal cortex, the posterior cingulate cortex, the angular gyrus* and *the hippocampus*) that all work together when we daydream, access our memories and consider other people's feelings and intentions.

Creativity therefore helps us to transcend our own current reality to conjure up new possibilities and alternative perspectives.

Why do many of us stop being creative?

As will be discussed in Chapter 12, Our Brain and Lifestyle, our brain is a muscle, and the more we use it, the fitter and stronger it becomes. Creativity is a brain skill that many of us have stopped using; consequently, our ability to be creative weakens and we believe that we are not creative.

The difference between people who are creative and those who think they are not creative is that creative people have not given up and stopped using their imagination.

We can all generate original ideas, but often we do not allow these ideas to take hold. We convince ourselves either that we are too busy or that our idea is worthless. And when the ideas we put forward are rejected or overlooked, we revert to behaviour that is more successful, which often means quick answers that have obvious benefits. This weakens our creative connections over time.

Having to be practical can also be an obstruction to the creative process. We spend so much of our time focusing on relevance and application that we do not value the more abstract exercise of simply letting our minds wander.

We first need to let our mind explore what is possible before determining the pragmatic benefit of this. Creativity needs to be able to flow naturally without the boundaries of time and the pressures of problem-solving.

Why does brainstorming not always work?

Concepts such as brainstorming are designed to facilitate a broader way of thinking, but the very process is often constricted by the necessity to think about a specific solution.

When we are under pressure to brainstorm ideas for a solution, we are not relaxed. Our brain does not respond creatively to this forced method of idea generation. If we want to get the best out of the creative process, we need to minimise anxiety and relax our brain.

We also need to be away from the judgement of others. Group brainstorming can sometimes turn into an ideas-critiquing session, which defeats its purpose. We have much better ideas when we are free to explore any possibility, however crazy it may seem. It may just lead us to the right solution.

How we crush creativity early on

One of the most-watched TED talks of all time is by Sir Ken Robinson, an author, speaker and international advisor on education. Sir Ken decries the lack of creative opportunities for children in education and describes research highlighting how divergent thinking falls away as we get older. He claims that:

If we look at young children, we can see that they are naturally creative. They explore, experiment, laugh and have fun while they are coming up with new ideas. But, by the time children are ready to move to secondary school, this creative spark has all too often been extinguished.

'We are educating people out of their creative capacities.'

Sir Ken describes creativity as the *genetic code of education,* citing it as a critical tool in modern life.

Creativity needs freedom: freedom to play, freedom to think, freedom to draw, freedom to imagine. This is equally true of the adult world, but the creative freedom that is present in the young child is all too often crushed by an environment of over-control, over-measurement and over-reward.

Our early years of divergent thinking are instructed out of us as education systems give us fewer options, reduce our horizons and teach us to converge on one correct answer.

The other issue is that children today have never been busier: their after-school schedules are crammed with activities and they have no room in their lives to create on their own.

Feeling bored is good for children because they explore ways to reduce their boredom. They also learn to be intrinsically motivated and driven less by external rewards and more by the joy they find in doing something for themselves.

In 1968, the author and general systems scientist, Dr George Land, tested the creativity of 1,600 children aged around five years old using the same test he devised for NASA to help select engineers and scientists.[24] He retested the same children at 10 years of age, and again at 15 years of age. The results are illustrated in the bar chart below.

98% of the younger children could think imaginatively, with the percentage declining sharply five and ten years later. When the same test was then used with 200,000 25 year-olds, only 2% could apply divergent thinking.

As Dr Land stated:

'Non-creative behavior is learned.'

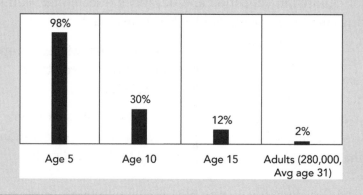

The biggest problems we all have are our over-reliance on technology and the sedentary lifestyles many of us now lead. Our addiction to our electronic devices means that we are not physically mobile, and when our body is still, then our brain activity drops.

Children will regain their natural creativity and curiosity by being encouraged to run around and play. Not only will their brains will love it; their bodies will too!

Reigniting and harnessing the creative spark

If our creative spark is to be reignited and harnessed by educators, leaders, policy-makers and parents, some attention needs to be paid to the conditions under which we expect people to thrive.

But while many enterprises expound the need for creativity in their people, they find themselves caught up in the dilemma of whether to increase efficiency and raise productivity or encourage the complex, unpredictable and messy exploration of ideas. The question is: are both of these activities possible at the same time? When times are tough, is room created for the free flow of ideas, or is emphasis placed instead on cost-cutting and the removal of anything that is non-essential to the bottom line?

A great deal of research has been carried out over the years to assess the relationship between creativity or *innovation* (which is a creative idea that has been turned into a replicable product or service that satisfies a specific need) with managing for profitable growth. Few organisations, it seems, have been able to master the two disciplines concurrently.

One notable exception is the software company SAS Institute, which regularly features in *Fortune*'s 100 Best Companies to Work For list.[25] In the 2017 list, *Fortune* cites one SAS employee as saying:

'They simply want to make life easy and carefree for us because that's the key to innovation.'

SAS believes that employees do their best when they are intellectually engaged and free from distractions like day care, healthcare and dry-cleaning, which are all provided on site. There is no distinction between the *creative* people and *non-creative* people: *everyone is creative*. Even the CEO still writes code. Managers are responsible for promoting and fostering the right environment for creative thinking and for ensuring that people take regular breaks. Long hours are frowned upon. People are trusted to manage their own workload and experiment in a spirit of collaboration. Moreover, the organisation has consistently enjoyed revenue growth.

Creativity is inconvenient and often disruptive. It gets in the way of our day-to-day work and interrupts our established methods and processes. To harness creativity means to let go of old ideas, systems and methods – a concept that is hard to practise in most organisations. And the fact that organisations like SAS are outside the norm means that the majority of us do not benefit from environments that encourage freedom of expression, tolerance of failure and enthusiasm for learning.

We still have a long way to go before organisations universally embrace a creative paradigm and allow for the genesis and nourishment of ideas on a continual and often chaotic basis.

Why are bad ideas still good ideas?

Having many bad ideas also means we will have a lot of good ideas! The trick is to keep having ideas – and enjoy the process while it is happening. Creativity thrives in a fun atmosphere where we turn normal thinking on its head.

When we feel that we are allowed to have only good ideas, we often block our creative flow and deny ourselves any ideas that we think may not be considered good.

Creativity needs space, practice and exercise. We need to exercise our creative muscle. The more ideas we have, the better they will become. Sometimes bad ideas turn into good ideas – or at least a bad idea may sow the seeds for a good idea to grow.

Deliberately generating bad ideas allows people to engage in an unfettered form of reverse brainstorming. Bad ideas can then be reversed, in order to see whether the opposite idea may lead somewhere.

Divergent thinking can be practised regularly and easily. One exercise that stimulates divergent thinking is to list as many different uses as possible for a common object, like a fork or a paper clip, in a few minutes. New research into group co-creativity, such as engaging in improvisation and spontaneous tasks like random storytelling or imagining a shared experience together, has been shown to boost divergent thinking and even improve psychological health.[27]

> '**Every day I write down ideas.**
>
> **I write down so many ideas that it hurts my head to come up with one more. Then I try to write down five more.**
>
> **The other day I tried to write 100 alternatives kids can do other than go to college. I wrote down eight, which I wrote about here. I couldn't come up with any more.**
>
> **Then the next day I came up with another 40. It definitely stretched my head.'**
>
> James Altucher[26]
> (investor, writer and entrepreneur)

Green is good for creativity

A number of recent studies have explored how exposure to green space can boost creativity and cognitive skills. In Spain, an association has been established between green surroundings and measures of cognitive development in 2,593 primary schoolchildren aged between seven and ten years.[28]

Green scenes can also have a restorative effect on our brain and boost our concentration. A study involving 150 students has shown how the brain is stimulated and enhanced by a short view of a flowering green meadow compared to a bare concrete roof.[29]

The same study also emphasised the importance of short mental breaks for our ability to focus and reactivate our brain. Just a 40-second intermission, to reset our thinking about the task in hand, can make a considerable difference to our cognitive performance.

> **'Alice laughed: "There's no use trying," she said; "one can't believe impossible things."**

Thinking creatively together

Edward de Bono's *Six Thinking Hats* is a simple and efficient thinking tool,[30] designed to consider issues or problems from different angles and to prevent convergent or critical thinking from taking hold too early.

First published in 1985, the book features six hats, each representing a separate category of thinking style (see Figure 8.6), and everyone mentally wears the same hat at the same time before moving onto the next hat. This technique is known as *parallel thinking*.

> **"I daresay you haven't had much practice," said the Queen. "When I was younger, I always did it for half an hour a day. Why, sometimes I've believed as many as six impossible things before breakfast." '**
>
> Lewis Carroll

Hat	Purpose	Details
White hat	Facts	Focus on the available data, historic trends and any missing knowledge or information
Red hat	Feelings	Explore feelings and intuition, gut reaction, subjective opinion and emotional responses to others
Black hat	Judgement	Consider the difficulties, errors, risks or pitfalls of an approach in order to make the plan more robust
Yellow hat	Optimism	See the positive aspects and benefits of an idea and provide the reasons why an idea is valuable and might work
Green hat	Creativity	Develop alternatives, possibilities and solutions by removing obstacles and encouraging a free flow of ideas
Blue hat	Process	Control the facilitation of thinking skills, the sequence, timing and use of hats

FIGURE 8.6: Edward de Bono's six thinking hats

Part 3: Stories and top tips

Sleepiness removes constraints . . .

To create his surreal paintings, Salvador Dalí experimented with the time period between sleep and wakefulness. This period is when different sensations and perceptions from the day appear to us as *hypnagogic* images (the word *hypnagogic* comes from the Greek for 'leading to sleep') or light dreams and abstract thoughts.

Dalí wanted to capture these for his paintings.

One of the techniques he used was to sit beside a tin plate on the floor while he held a spoon in his hand over the plate. As he relaxed or fell asleep, the spoon would fall from his fingers and on to the plate and wake him up. During the ensuing hypnagogic period, images would connect with other completely unrelated images in Dalí's brain – and these are what he painted.

When we are awake, we rely on known connections, but as we enter sleep, our brain is able to be freer and make new and different associations.

. . . but sometimes constraint is good

In 1960, the publishing company Random House bet an author $50 that he would not be able to write a children's book in fewer than 50 words. The author accepted the bet and won it. The book was *Green Eggs and Ham* and the author was Dr Seuss.

Green Eggs and Ham is one of the best-selling children's books in history and has sold over 200 million copies.

Dr Seuss's creativity was ignited because of the 50-word limit. It was so successful that he applied the same strategy to *The Cat in the Hat,* using a vocabulary list of only 236 very simple words.

Limits and boundaries can help the creative process by forcing us to find solutions that may otherwise not have occurred to us; we seek ways of making something work within given restrictions. Our brain loves a challenge!

Do the opposite to what people expect

Apple's first Macintosh commercial, directed by Ridley Scott (who had already directed *Blade Runner* and *Alien* and went on to direct *Thelma and Louise, Gladiator* and a number of other high-profile films), is a powerful example of how to challenge accepted and expected norms. Designed to be disruptive and to jolt people out of what they were used to, the commercial contrasted the newcomer Apple with the existing world of computing, dominated at that time by IBM. The result was ground-breaking.

Both Apple's commercial and computer represented something completely different. The Macintosh computer was the first personal computer to include a graphical-user interface and its ease of use appealed to the less technologically savvy, as well as those who wanted to be at the edge of innovation.

Innovator or fast follower?

Recent research suggests that those we often label pioneers have, in reality, been fast followers. It is very difficult to enter a brand-new market or present a brand-new product. The failure rate is high. A more strategically sound approach may be to exploit what is already out there and then adjust it for greater success.

For example, many of Apple's remarkable achievements lie not in an ability to innovate in the pure sense of the word, but in the skill of improving products already on the market. The iPod was not the first MP3 player, but it was viewed as being better than existing devices because it was priced and sized differently, with the added benefit of the iTunes service. And every year, iPads and iPhones slim down or shape up, offering better screens and faster systems. The key, it seems, is to follow the competition, faster and better than before.

In the words of the Scottish–American industrialist Andrew Carnegie:

'It is better to be a follower than a pioneer. The pioneers get scalped.'

Top Tips
Remember: **IDEAS**

Inspire yourself by looking at the world around you. Make connections and think of possibilities using random objects and ideas. Go for a walk in natural surroundings and take in the sights, sounds and smells of your environment. The next good idea is often found in the unlikeliest place. Let your mind run free.

Disrupt your habitual thought patterns. Get out of your comfort zone and do the opposite of what you would normally do. Give your brain a jolt! Criticise your own ideas and give them a workout. Think of bad ideas as well as good ideas. Sometimes a bad idea reversed can become a very good idea!

Enjoy abstract thoughts, especially when you feel tired. Sometimes creative ideas come when your brain is not trying to compete with other pressures and thoughts. When our brain is relaxed, ideas will often come to us.

Allow your mind to wander and daydream. Imagine 'What if?' or 'Why not?' This will activate your imagination network. Build on other people's ideas and let the process develop organically. Support and build on other people's creative suggestions. Sometimes it is the second person to speak that determines the fate of any idea.

Sleep on a problem. If you cannot find a solution, relax and let sleep go to work on it for you. You may find that you have the answer in the morning. Your brain will be more creative when it is relaxed. Our dreams will work on ideas while we are asleep.

References for Chapter 8

1. Gregoire, C., & Kaufman, S.B. (2016). *Wired to Create: Unraveling the Mysteries of the Creative Mind*. New York: TarcherPerigee.
2. Raichle, M. et al. (2001). 'A default mode of brain function', *PNAS,* January, 676–82.
3. Riccelli, R. et al. (2017). 'Surface-based morphometry reveals the neuroanatomical basis of the five-factor model of personality', *Social Cognitive and Affective Neuroscience,* April, 671–84.
4. Mayseless, N. et al. (2015). 'How does our brain form creative and original ideas?' *Science Daily*, 19 November. www.sciencedaily.com/releases/2015/11/151119104105.htm
5. Limb, C. et al. (2016). 'Emotional intent modulates the neural substrates of creativity: An fMRI study of emotionally targeted improvisation in jazz musicians', *Scientific Reports,* January. doi. org/10.1038/srep18460
6. Kounios, J., & Beeman, M. (2014). 'The cognitive neuroscience of insight', *Annual Review of Psychology*, 65 and 71–93.
7. Izumi H. et al. (2011). 'Realistic imitation of mosquito's proboscis: Electrochemically etched sharp and jagged needles and the cooperative inserting motion', *Sensor and Actuators: A Physical Journal*, January, 115–23.
8. Barron, F. (1963). *Creativity and Psychological Health: Origins of Personality and Creative Freedom*. Princeton, NJ: Van Nostrand.
9. Csikszentmihalyi, M. (1996). *Creativity: Flow and the Psychology of Discovery and Invention*. New York: HarperCollins.
10. Andreasen, N. (2014). 'Secrets of the creative brain', *The Atlantic,* July–August, 15–20.
11. Ramachandran, V.S., & Brang, D. (2011). 'Survival of the synesthesia gene: Why do people hear colors and taste words', *PLOS Biology,* 22 November. doi.org/10.1371/journal.pbio.1001205
12. Münch, M. et al. (2012). 'Effects of prior light exposure on early evening performance, subjective sleepiness, and hormonal secretion', *Behavioral Neuroscience,* February, 196–203.
13. Steidle, A., & Werth, L. (2013). 'Freedom from constraints: Darkness and dim illumination promote creativity', *Journal of Environmental Psychology*, September, 67–80.
14. Augustin, S. (2009). 'The smell is right – using scents to enhance life', *Psychology Today,* 23 December. psychologytoday.com
15. Mehta, R. et al. (2012). 'Is noise always bad? Exploring the effects of ambient noise on creative cognition', *Journal of Consumer Research*, December, 784–99.
16. Conner, T.S. et al. (2017). 'Let them eat fruit! The effect of fruit and vegetable consumption on psychological well-being in young adults: a randomized controlled trial', *PLOS ONE,* 3 February. doi/org/10.1371/journal.pone.0171206
17. Hedge, A. (2005). 'Thermal effects on office productivity' in *Proceedings of the Human Factors and Ergonomics Society Annual Meeting,* September, 823–27.
18. Torrance E.P. (1966). *Torrance Tests of Creative Thinking: Norms and Technical Manual-Research Edition*. Princeton, NJ: Personnel Press.
19. Jauk, E. et al. (2013). 'The relationship between intelligence and creativity', *Intelligence,* July, 212–21.
20. Epstein, R. (2016). 'How to enhance the creativity of a person and figuring out the mysteries of the creative process', *Psychology Today,* 9 June. psychologytoday.com
21. Snow, S. (2018). *Dream Teams. Working Together without Falling Apart*. London: Piatkus.

22. Syed, M. (2015). *Black Box Thinking: Marginal Gains and the Secrets of High Performance.* London: John Murray.
23. Meyer, M.L. et al (2019). 'Creative expertise is associated with transcending the here and now', *Journal of Personality and Social Psychology*. doi: 10.1037/pspa0000148
24. Land, G., & Jarman, B. (1992). *Breakpoint and Beyond: Mastering the Future Today.* New York: Harpercollins Publishers.
25. Florida, R., & Goodnight, J. (2005). 'Managing for creativity', *Harvard Business Review*, July–August, 124–31.
26. Altucher, J. (2011). 'How to be THE LUCKIEST GUY ON THE PLANET in 4 easy steps', *Business Insider*, 25 February. businessinsider.com
27. Felsman, P. et al. (2020). 'Improv experience promotes divergent thinking, uncertainty tolerance, and affective well-being', *Thinking Skills and Creativity*, March. https://doi.org/10.1016/j.tsc.2020.100632.
28. Dadvand, P. et al. (2015). 'Green spaces and cognitive development in primary schoolchildren', *PNAS*, June, 7937–42.
29. Lee, K.E. et al. (2015). '40-second green roof views sustain attention: The role of micro-breaks in attention restoration', *Journal of Environmental Psychology*, June, 182–89.
30. De Bono, E. (2016). *Six Thinking Hats.* London: Penguin Books Ltd.

"Progress is impossible without change and those who cannot change their minds cannot change anything."

GEORGE BERNARD SHAW
Playwright and socialist (1856–1950)

chapter nine

Our Brain and Change

The world is changing faster than ever. New is everywhere: new technologies, new devices, new possibilities, new demands – effectively new ways of living, learning and working.

But most of us do not like change. We find comfort in routines, habits and what feels familiar. Even the changes that we choose for ourselves pose some difficulty and need readjustment. Although most of us accept that competitive advantage depends on our ability to adapt quickly, change is not a phenomenon that we readily embrace.

This chapter considers what change means both for individuals and for organisations. It offers insights into how habits are formed and changed, what is needed to help people manage change in themselves and others, and why resilience is a vital ingredient in our increasingly turbulent world.

A better understanding of how our brain handles change will help us to handle the unexpected and unpredictable around us.

Part 1: The science explained

Change is painful for the brain

We naturally resist change because change represents uncertainty – and uncertainty is threatening and painful for a brain that wants to keep us safe and alive. Although many of today's threats are no longer life-or-death situations, our brain still protects us as if they were just that.

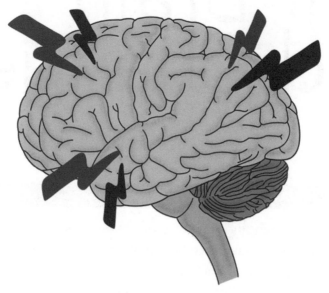

FIGURE 9.1: Change means pain for the brain

A threat does not even need to be a real one; it is how we view the threat that affects the way our brain responds to it. Psychological pain and physical pain are registered in our brain in exactly the same way (see Figure 9.1).[1] Research has even shown that *acetaminophen* (the active ingredient in Paracetamol and Tylenol) dampens feelings of social rejection.[2] This is further highlighted in Chapter 11, Our Brain and Leadership.

When we feel uncertain or anxious, our fight or flight mechanisms are mobilised. Resources are diverted from our *frontal lobe* and we focus instead on survival. When this happens, there is increased activity in 1) the *anterior cingulate cortex* (worry), 2) the *orbital frontal cortex* (error prediction), 3) the *insula* (pain and disgust) and 4) the *amygdala* (anxiety).

As soon as these four regions of the brain are engaged, resources are diverted from the frontal lobe area, which we use for higher-level intellectual functioning, and become focused instead on survival.

Our capacity for rational thought is thus diminished, and even when the change is a good idea, we still resist it.

Our response to change may be summarised as follows:

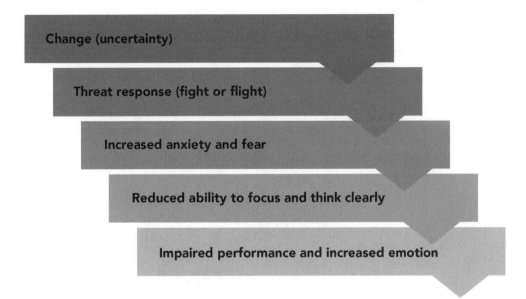

Change (uncertainty)

Threat response (fight or flight)

Increased anxiety and fear

Reduced ability to focus and think clearly

Impaired performance and increased emotion

Anxiety is contagious

As explained in Chapter 7, Our Brain and Biases, we do a great deal to avoid loss. When we think we are at risk of loss – loss of our job, loss of the skill we have spent years mastering, loss of our reputation – we become anxious. And when we are anxious, it spreads like a contagion across our social groups.

Recent Gallup analysis highlights the finding that the wellbeing of leaders and the wellbeing of their teams are interdependent.[3] The emotional state of each affects the emotional state of the other.

In times of change, therefore, our anxious state can influence and exacerbate the states of those around us. This can even lead to a heightened pattern of thought, known as *cognitive vulnerability,* which is also contagious.

College students were randomly assigned to a roommate. The higher the level of cognitive vulnerability in one of the students, the more likely the other was to develop higher levels of cognitive vulnerability. The students whose cognitive vulnerability increased also later showed higher levels of depressive symptoms.[4]

Why do our brains love routine and habits?

Our routine activities use an area of the brain with a group of neurons in the temporal lobe called the *basal ganglia* (see Figure 9.2), which plays a significant role in the formation of long-standing habits. The basal ganglia are activated by familiar and repetitive activity to which we no longer have to pay attention.

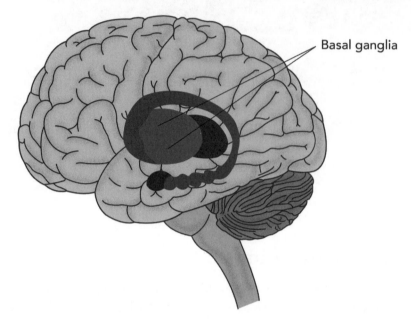

Basal ganglia

FIGURE 9.2: The basal ganglia

This area of the brain requires much less energy than our working memory (which is what we use to pay attention to new information) because it uses brain circuits that have already been shaped and defined by experience.

All activities that are repeated eventually become orchestrated by the basal ganglia, thereby freeing up the prefrontal cortex to focus on fresh inputs.

Practice and routine therefore become hardwired into our brain and any habit, good or bad, is hard for our brain to override. Although bad habits often linger in the brain, it is possible to replace them over time with good habits that are more powerful.

We are all lazy

Sir Isaac Newton's First Law of Motion is *the law of inertia*: a body at rest tends to remain at rest; a body in motion tends to stay in motion. The term *inertia* (from the Latin for 'lack of skill' or 'inactive') was devised by the German astronomer Johannes Kepler in the 16th century.

In studies of patients who have undergone heart bypass surgery, only 10%, on average, adopt healthier habits to prevent a relapse.[5]

As humans, we suffer from natural inertia: we are inherently lazy. Studies prove that when we physically move, we find the most energy efficient way to do it and burn as few calories as possible.[6] Our autonomic nervous system continually monitors how much energy we use and ensures that our muscles work in an optimal way, even when we decide to go for a run.

In the past, this may have served as an important energy-conserving purpose, especially when food was not readily on hand. But today, when such inactivity is no longer beneficial to our survival, it seems that our brain is predisposed to being sedentary and even undermines our best intentions to be more active.

In a recent study, scientists in Switzerland looked at 29 people who wanted to engage in more activity but were struggling to do so.[7] Participants were asked to choose between images of physical activity or inactivity while their brains were observed by the researchers using electroencephalography (EEG).

The results showed that participants were faster choosing the active images, but the EEG readings also showed that the brain had to work harder to avoid the inactive images. It therefore takes more effort for the brain to override its inclination to expend less effort.

On a psychological level, this laziness underlies why we find it difficult to change and this is known as *cognitive inertia*. **Cognitive inertia** is the reason we are susceptible to *confirmation bias* (which is explained in more detail in Chapter 7, Our Brain and Biases) and it is also the cause of businesses failing to change their corporate routines and practices.

Cognitive inertia is the reason we find it easier to stick with the status quo. We stick to what we know: we eat the same food, we wear the same clothes and we have the same friends. On a positive level, cognitive inertia prevents us from suffering from decision fatigue and it frees up our brain to take on other matters. But there are times when we need to break this inertia, when what we are doing no longer has any use or relevance. This requires applying a force to jolt us into a new direction. Sometimes a small push can generate its own momentum.

And, as Newton's Law also states, once something is in motion, it can take a great effort to halt it.

Ernest Hemingway explains that his technique was to write:

'one true sentence and go on from there.'[8]

How do we combat inertia?

Change is difficult to achieve when it comes to both starting or stopping anything.

Combatting inertia in ourselves and others is not always easy, but it is possible. We can all override our brain's natural inclinations: we simply need a good reason to make the change.

As the Harvard Business School Professor Rosabeth Moss Kanter says:

'Doing something, almost anything, is energizing.'[9]

Experience and expectation are interlinked

Because we are constantly using previously stored knowledge to help us deal with new information, as has been explained in other chapters, our expectations will therefore generally drive our experiences.

This is particularly true of pain and pain relief, which is why the *placebo effect* is so powerful. This effect, whereby an inactive substance like sugar or distilled water can sometimes improve a patient's condition simply because the patient expects to benefit, has been shown to have the ability to improve our breathing (our lungs dilate), heal ulcers and reduce blood pressure.

However, the reverse of this is more negative. When it comes to pain itself, we often experience more pain when we expect in advance that something will be painful. This is called the *nocebo effect*. The suggestion of pain is enough to stimulate the experience of pain, which is why doctors and dentists need to be cognisant of the language they use with patients, as discussed in Chapter 5, Our Brain and Language.

Our expectation of a new change initiative is often coloured by a bad or difficult experience of previous change. Our sensitivity to the pain of the change is intensified accordingly. Similarly, if we expect a change programme to be positive, we will actually increase its likelihood of success.

So when we repeatedly focus on something being either painful or pain-free, our neural circuits will strengthen in either direction. We can increase or decrease our own discomfort, depending on where we choose to direct our thoughts.

A study found that people's expectations of less pain brought about a reduction of 28.4% in perceived pain.[10] This result was comparable to the effects of an actual drug, morphine.

When we expect pain to be lower, we will therefore perceive it as lower, but the experience of what is painful seems to be slightly different for men and women.[11] Studies have found that male participants are able to endure pain for longer than female participants, and that women are more willing to report pain than men are.

This has significant implications in a changing environment where leaders need to stay abreast of any issues among the individuals involved. If the environment is male-dominated, for example, there may be a higher degree of silent acceptance and stoicism, which may not be helpful in the long term.

How does the brain make and change decisions?

Decision-making can happen rapidly in the brain. When we make a decision and are faced with different choices our brain considers the difference in value between them.[12] The larger the difference in value, the faster we make the decision. But when the options are similar in value, it can take much longer. Current research is now focusing on how our brain uses memories to make a decision and what happens when there are no memories available.

But what happens when we want to reverse a decision?

It is difficult for the brain to change its plans. Even if we change our mind, it does not necessarily mean that we can change our behaviour.

Changing a behaviour involves complex neural coordination among multiple brain areas, but if we do not do it quickly it is often too late.[13] The longer a decision stays in the brain, the harder it is to change it.

Using functional magnetic resonance imaging (fMRI) researchers have found that reversing a decision involves rapid coordination between two specific zones, the *prefrontal cortex* and the *frontal eye field* (FEF). The FEF is a region situated just behind the prefrontal cortex that is involved in controlling eye movements and visual awareness. We can only successfully reverse our decision when we change our mind within 100 milliseconds of making it. If we wait any longer, it is less likely that we will be able to change.

As we get older, the communication between the prefrontal cortex and the frontal eye field slows down and it becomes even more difficult to change our mind at the last minute. Scientists are now exploring ways of improving our ability to change a decision quickly, so that we can exert more control over our choices.

Part 2: Impact on our daily life

Why does most change fail in organisations?

Most leaders do not fully understand the impact of change on their people. Many change efforts fail because people's need for certainty is not properly addressed by the provision of adequate information for the duration of a change initiative. Communication can be spurious or concerned solely with hard facts and logic, while the emotional aspects of the change are often dismissed or completely overlooked. All too frequently, any change-related messages are posted on an intranet portal with the expectation that everyone will automatically read and understand them.

Change is difficult because it effectively means a rewiring of our brain, and this cannot happen overnight. To effect real change, leaders need to be supportive and, above all, to exercise patience and understanding. Change therefore takes time.

Leaders regularly underestimate the pain that is being experienced throughout an organisation because their vantage point is different. Not surprisingly, the implementation and assimilation of new practices and routines are not at all straightforward.

Successful change needs the right leadership

The success of any change initiative largely depends on how much energy and enthusiasm is demonstrated by leaders. So much has already been published about the leader's role during change, yet still this continues to be a real issue.

Leaders often miss emotional signs of resistance or distress because they are so focused on polished presentations and correct messaging. And they do not have the time to devote to dealing with personal concerns and individual issues.

But our natural negativity bias ensures that negative emotions spread far more quickly than positive emotions, which means that leadership effort must be dedicated to dealing with this fallout. And so the best gift leaders can give to their people is their time. Listening is crucial – and when people feel that they are being heard, then they are more likely to listen in return.

As well as engaging in listening, leaders also need to put thought into the language they use with the people around them. The more positive and encouraging the language, and the greater the focus on team effort and collaboration, the more our reward network is activated, spurring us on to greater endeavour. There are certain words to which our brain responds positively or negatively – a topic that was explored in more depth in Chapter 5, Our Brain and Language.

Leading change: dealing with the push-back first

When we tell our brain what to do, it automatically resists and behaves just like a naughty child.

Leaders need to recognise the power of the *push-back* from employees when any change initiative is first announced, as well as later, during the various forms and methods of communication that occur.

As Newton's third law of motion states:

'For every action, there is an equal and opposite reaction.'

This push-back is highlighted in a useful model called *Force Field Analysis* (see Figure 9.3), which illustrates how resisting forces (people's worries, anxieties and emotions) will arise for every driving force (reasons for the change, such as improved efficiency, reduced headcount, automation of certain processes):

FIGURE 9.3: Force Field Analysis

Unless the resisting forces are first defused, before time and resources are spent pushing the driving forces on to people, the planned change will never fully achieve its desired outcome.

Resisting forces are also weakened when there is better communication, consultation and listening. Chapter 11, Our Brain and Leadership, considers the role of leadership in keeping people motivated and focused. During times of change, this leadership role is even more critical.

We like the challenge of change – if we are given enough freedom

William Glasser states that we are genetically driven to satisfy our basic needs of survival, love and belonging, power, freedom and fun.[14]

Having the freedom to think, develop our own insights and make our own choices will activate our reward network and enhance our personal satisfaction. We are then motivated to repeat this experience, so change can therefore become a series of sequential, energising activities.

Feelings of achievement will then prevent the brain from resisting change and nullify the effect of the amygdala's threat response. We accept and support something much more if we have chosen it ourselves.

When we make our own choices, we are motivated intrinsically and find pleasure in what we do. *Intrinsic motivation* relies on autonomy, but granting this autonomy is often a challenge for leaders, whose job it is to set the direction and distribute the work.

The good news is that we only need to *feel* that we have a choice in order to ignite our intrinsic motivation. And in any case, leaders can do a great deal to provide their people with opportunities to make choices within the parameters of the business goals.

Explain the *why*
Leaders do not need to focus on the *what*. The *why* is enough to give us a sense of purpose and direction. We can then work out the *how* for ourselves.

Test ideas and solutions
Leaders can involve their teams in generating ideas and solutions, and then in the testing of these. When we feel part of any solution, we are more likely to contribute towards its implementation.

We need other people around us

We are social beings. In our modern world, which has been dehumanised to a large extent by technology, our fundamental need for closeness to and acceptance by others is stronger than ever.

During times of change and uncertainty, our social networks are an important source of reassurance and comfort, but becoming attuned to the mental and emotional state of others relies on personal rather than virtual contact. It is only when we spend time with people that we can pick up emotional cues that may otherwise have gone undetected. This is true of all age groups.

A study has shown that even the younger generation that has grown up in the digital age needs real people.[15]

Eleven-year-olds were divided into two groups:

Group 1 experienced a normal week with access to computers.

Group 2 went to a nature/science camp with no access to computers for a week. The children had to spend their time interacting with each other and with the adults at the camp.

At the end of the week, the children at the camp (Group 2) were able to detect emotions more accurately and read people more accurately than Group 1 could.

And so even in a world where the new normal is constant access to technology, we cannot deny our instinctive need to bond with others on an emotional level.

Information is essential during change

Although this book has made positive reference to Apple in the context of creativity, there is nevertheless a dark aspect to the way the majority of Apple employees work: secrecy.

Much has been made of Steve Jobs' method of guarding the detail of a new product until the moment of its unveiling. An article on 22 June 2009 in the *New York Times* describes how Apple's secrecy even extended to Jobs' own health problems.

But while Apple's clandestine culture has become an effective marketing ploy that thrills customers and delights investors, it is not a strategy that works well for most of us. Our brain responds well to transparency and has a strong need to feel informed, involved and included.

We crave certainty and, as soon as we get it, we activate our brain's reward centre, releasing the neurotransmitter *dopamine*. As Chapter 1, Our Brain, explains, dopamine is associated with a number of brain functions such as learning, working memory and voluntary movement. Dopamine is also our *motivation molecule* and is fired in anticipation of reward. In other words, dopamine mobilises us to act – and it makes us feel good.

Information gives us certainty – and any information is better than no information. When our brain receives information, especially after a period of uncertainty, we stop worrying and instead find that we have more energy and drive.

We also like to see the whole picture – the context. When we cannot see the whole picture, we start to feel uncertain and anxious and we do whatever we can to fill in the missing parts. This is why there is so much misinformation when a situation is ambiguous. If we do not receive sufficient amounts of the right information, we supplement what we do get with our own assumptions, opinions and interpretations.

> The way anxiety can be manipulated has been researched for decades.
> A study has shown that, when we anticipate an event that is unpredictable and therefore threatening, our experience of pain is enhanced.[16]

Information is therefore critical during periods of change. The more people are consulted and informed, the greater the reduction in their anxiety levels – and the more accurately messages are circulated.

Change rewires our brain

Our brain's plasticity means that it will adapt to new activities or routines over time and it will reshape and reorganise itself accordingly.

Change can therefore stimulate our brain in the right way. When we decide to change and make an effort to learn something new and then stick at it, our brain starts to change. It literally rewires itself.

Habits mean that our brain has made certain cognitive processes automatic. We are creatures of routine: we stick to what we know because it feels comfortable and safe. Chapters 3 and 4, on memory and attention, have discussed what happens when our behaviour becomes hardwired into the neural structure of our brain.

When we practise new behaviours and activities, our brain adapts by creating new neural pathways over time. This is how our brain hardwires a new habit.

New behaviours also need to become rooted in the norms and values of an organisation, whereupon they become an embedded part of the new culture. When leaders try to lead change, they often overlook the hardwiring of existing habits and the fact that it will take time and sustained repetition for people to learn how to rewire new habits into their brain.

We need to stay fit and healthy

Change depletes our resources and can be exhausting. It is even more important during these periods of change that we focus on our physical health and maintain an upbeat mood when times feel challenging.

Sleep and exercise are particularly important for our brain, since they help to maintain healthy cognitive function and also keep the body in balance. This is covered in Chapter 12, Our Brain and Lifestyle.

The importance of resilience

Resilience is our ability to recover or bounce back from a difficulty or challenge. Resilience has been a topic of research since the 1960s and it continues to be an area of interest in a number of different contexts.

We love stories of resilience – such as J.K. Rowling's remarkable ability to write her first Harry Potter book while struggling financially and then to cope with multiple rejections before her eventual publication and worldwide success.

Resilience is very personal and can vary from situation to situation. It is a significant aspect of how an individual will deal with change, and for this reason it is becoming an increasingly important ingredient in organisational success.

Psychologists believe that, while it seems that some people are naturally more resilient than others, we can nevertheless learn to develop resilience over our lifetime.

In the 1970s, Carol Dweck, now Professor of Psychology at Stanford, studied how children deal with failure. She observed that, from an early age, most people manifest either a *fixed mindset or a growth mindset.*[17]

- A **fixed mindset** describes the belief that we cannot change, that our character and abilities are inherent and that success or failure is dependent on innate intelligence.
- A **growth mindset** refers to the view that effort and perseverance are linked to achievement and that failure is a means of growth and discovery. Most successful people have a growth mindset and an appetite for lifelong learning.

In reality, we are all a mixture of both fixed and growth mindsets. Even those who feel that they are predominately of a growth mindset may, at times, fall into a fixed mindset and become stubborn, defensive or self-justifying.

Our environment, at home and at work, may trigger fixed mindset tendencies. It is important that we recognise early warning signs, stay open to new experiences and pursue opportunities that stretch and challenge our brain.

A resilient outlook stems from being able to view the world through a positive lens and cope with setbacks and adversity. Resilience is also bolstered by an ability to find solutions as problems arise, and to view even the most difficult situations as opportunities to learn and grow.

Endorphins are critical to a resilient system and these are released when we exercise and laugh. Endorphins diminish the perception of pain and reduce anxiety. They are discussed in more detail in Chapter 2, Our Brain and Emotion.

Create the right conditions for change

The power of the *push-back*, or resisting forces, during times of change means that we are not good at being told what to do. A more effective technique is to encourage people to make changes for themselves by fostering the right conditions for these changes to take place.

Robert Cialdini's work on persuasion and influence highlights six principles that drive any new behaviour (see Figure 9.4):[18]

Reciprocity	We will respond to people who do us a favour. When this favour is unexpected, it is even more powerful. John McFarlane, former CEO of ANZ Bank, sent a bottle of champagne to all employees at Christmas with a card thanking them for their work on the company's *Perform, Grow and Break-out* change programme. Rewards have a disproportionately positive impact on change motivation and often the effect will last for months, if not years.
Social Proof	Sometimes we just need to see what other people have done first. Amazon, for example, does this effectively by showing us what choices other people have made. We look to others, especially when we feel uncertain ourselves. This is why all change initiatives need *early adopters* and small successes at the beginning – to help to convince others.
Consistency	If we commit publicly to doing something, we are more likely to follow through and do it. When we say 'yes' to something in front of other people, for example, in a team meeting, we are less likely to back out from that committment.
Liking	We like people who are like us (we are drawn to similarity because it feels nonthreatening). We will be motivated to do something new if someone we like asks us to do it.
Authority	We respect authority and often do not question it. Uncertainty drives a strong need to look for expert advice and guidance. When respected figures endorse a change, it tends to be accepted more readily.
Scarcity	We often want what we cannot have. This is linked to our *loss aversion bias* (explained in more detail in Chapter 7, Our Brain and Biases). Statements phrased in terms of loss are: 'You will lose out if you don't do this.' 'We will miss this opportunity if we don't act now.' These statements may drive us to change, in order to avoid a perceived loss.

FIGURE 9.4: Robert Cialdini's six principles of persuasion

Part 3: Stories and top tips

We need to change, even when life is good!

Change does not occur solely in response to a crisis. Those organisations that enable both continuous reflection and improvement, even when business is good, and take frequent adaptive measures to help meet shifting challenges, are often the most successful.

One of the worst phrases we can use is 'Why fix it if it ain't broke?', which implies that we need to wait for something to break before we address it.

The key to managing ongoing regular changes – both big and small – is a dynamic and agile culture whereby business models and strategies are revisited, reviewed and revised as circumstances change.

All this requires an ability to read early warning signals and respond rapidly. New ideas are the currency of the future. But in order to generate new ideas, many organisations will need to rethink their ways of working, and may even need to give up their attachment to what made them successful in the first place. There will inevitably come a point when previous success is no longer a guarantee of future success.

Madonna is a good example of relentless reinvention and innovation. She is now over 60 years old and her career has been a series of reincarnations, each one more provocative than the last. Madonna has continued to court controversy and flout tradition, attracting both positive attention and condemnation – but always staying one step ahead.

We need to change our thinking in order to change

We will often not change unless we feel the need to change. But we all have *cognitive hurdles* to overcome. These are thoughts and phrases that we resort to in order to entrench a belief or a point of view. Overcoming these cognitive hurdles requires that we look at the world around us through a different lens.

In the 1980s, the New York subway was considered one of the most dangerous places in the city. Murders on the subway were considered an inevitable aspect of urban life. The New York police force, most of whom did not regularly use the subway, tried to downplay people's anxieties and fears.

However, this all changed in 1990 when Bill Bratton became head of the Transit Police in New York. Bratton was a supporter of the *broken window theory*, posited by criminologists George Kelling and James Wilson, which says that even minor acts of vandalism will lead to more serious crime. Kelling and Wilson believed that by addressing minor offences, rates of more violent crime would be lowered.

Bratton insisted that all New York police officers, including himself, use the subway in order to experience the problems for themselves. Having observed the conditions that were creating the crimes, the police officers felt more inclined to change what was happening.

Make change easy for people

One example of making change easy for people is the encouragement by some businesses of the concept of *bring your own device* (BYOD) to engage their employees on a deeper level.

If, for example, we are accustomed to using a Mac, the BYOD initiative means that we do not spend time and effort adjusting to a PC. Using devices that are available and familiar means that time can instead be focused on the application of the technology to enhance the customer experience and business productivity.

Of course, there are serious concerns around security of data, loss of devices, risk of cyber attacks and greater exposure to viruses. And even though a BYOD approach may reduce hardware costs, there may be additional investment needed to support a range of different devices.

However, with technology continuing to dominate the way we work, organisations need to think more flexibly about how they keep their people engaged and productive while the technology and working landscape shifts beneath them. When people feel self-sufficient and able to work well, they are more likely to do a good job.

Employee mobility can be a good thing

Low employee turnover is not necessarily a good thing, especially for the individuals concerned. Traditionally, we have believed that moving jobs on a regular basis signified lack of commitment. Nowadays, it is becoming a more acceptable part of working life.

The longer we stay in any organisation, the more out of touch with the external world we become. Our vision narrows and we become victims of our organisation's orthodoxies or deeply ingrained beliefs. We start to believe our own propaganda and do not see any need to change.

Our brain needs new challenges and experiences to keep it active and agile. If we surround ourselves constantly with the familiar, we become stale and stagnant. Old habits dominate and suppress our desire to enquire and to learn.

Changing jobs or even career means feeling incompetent and uncomfortable again. Most of us do not enjoy this stage in learning, but it is actually very good for us. When we feel incompetent, we strive to acquire new knowledge and skills, and the new neural connections we make keep our brain healthy and resilient. The more used we get to personal change, the better we are at dealing with organisational change.

Successful change goes beyond facts

Our brain cannot be changed simply because we are given facts. Only when change messages resonate on an emotional level do we feel motivated to move away from old practices and routines.

Dr Dean Ornish is a professor of medicine at the University of California at San Francisco and founder of the Preventative Medicine Research Institute. In 1993, he conducted a year-long trial with patients who were suffering from clogged arteries and were due to have surgery.[19] Dr Ornish's trial treated the patients with a variety of methods, including psychological sessions, meditation, yoga, exercise and relaxation. After three years, 77% of the patients had changed their lifestyle and no longer needed surgery.

Dr Ornish explains that when we tell people that they will die if they do not change their lifestyle, they become more short-term focused, living day-to-day with the same safer and easier patterns of behaviour. But by helping people focus on the 'joy of living' and giving them a range of support structures to help them achieve this, they feel better about themselves and feel inspired to drive change personally.

When we can see and feel the benefits of doing something different, we are even more driven to make it work. The same is true in the business world. Change initiatives need to build connections and confidence.

Dr John Kotter, Professor Emeritus of Leadership at Harvard Business School, advocates:

'victories that nourish faith in the change effort, emotionally reward the hard workers, keep the critics at bay and build momentum.'[20]

Culture is key

Organisations may have the best strategy in the world, but culture is what really counts. If a strong and positive organisational culture is not in place, strategic plans become worthless.

Successful change depends on a supportive and collaborative culture. As organisations grow, it is critical that good cultures are preserved.

The shoe company Zappos spends time carefully evaluating candidates at interview for cultural fit. New employees are offered $2,000 to leave after the first week of training if they decide that they are not in the right job. Zappos is prepared to invest in the wrong people leaving as well as in the right people staying.

The values of the company represent a fundamental part of employees' training, and a substantial portion of leaders' budgets is dedicated to team development activities. As a result, Zappos' employees feel valued, motivated and productive. And Zappos' customers are happy, too.

Southwest Airlines is another organisation that spends time on ensuring good cultural fit. For 43 years, it has enjoyed enormous success because of the culture it has created.

Southwest Airlines has been the subject of two PhD theses, which gave rise to the book *NUTS*. The book details the uniquely positive elements of the airline's culture.[21] An example is how the now-retired founder, chairman and CEO Herb Kelleher famously used to ask pilots to drop their trousers during job interviews to see if they had a sense of humour.

The organisation's underpinning philosophy is that great employees offer great service to customers.

Southwest Airlines empowers its employees to keep customers happy and it has a number of recognition awards and programmes that reinforce positive behaviour. For example, the airline's magazine *Southwest Spirit* features a story every month of an employee who has delivered exceptional customer service.

Over the years, Southwest Airlines has managed to weather increasing competition and rising fuel prices by adapting to a changing environment with a constant focus on customers and employees.

Instead of resorting to cost-cutting, the airline has looked for ways to boost revenues. For example, when other airlines imposed a baggage charge, Southwest Airlines introduced a 'Bags Fly Free' policy, which attracted new customers.

Throughout its growth, Southwest Airlines has kept a close eye on its culture and has been very selective about who is brought into the fold. The airline has consistently been ranked as one of the best places to work by *Forbes, Fortune* and others.

Change is essential for a healthy brain

As mentioned throughout this book, our brain is constantly changing and adapting. Our habits and routines are reflected in the brain's size and shape.

Dr Michael Merzenich, Professor Emeritus in neuroscience at the University of California, describes how flute players have enlarged regions in the brain that control their fingers, tongue and lips.[22]

In business, we carve our expertise into the structure of our brain, and overriding this expertise can feel arduous. But a healthy brain requires the new neural connections that change brings. Learning continually is critical to keeping our brain adaptable to the world around us.

As a final point, we should beware of using labels and putting people in boxes in the belief that this will help us predict behaviour. We have the potential to be so much more than the constraints we impose, however well intentioned they may be.

Curiosity and courage to challenge ourselves and others are important allies as we change and grow throughout life. Change is not just a business imperative; it is critical for the long-term health of our brain.

Top Tips
Remember: ADAPT

Accept that expectations often drive results. Listen to the language that you use with others; this will often reveal your expectations of how the change will be. Become more aware of your own feelings, thoughts and responses to any change that you are experiencing. Remember that if you expect something to be good it is more likely to turn out that way.

Decide to change something in your life. It does not have to be a big change: any change is good. Try eating something different, take a new route to work, talk to someone you do not know very well. Above all, break simple routines on a regular basis. If we make regular changes in our life, we stay agile, flexible, open-minded and robust.

Acquire good habits that keep you healthy and strong. These include sleep and exercise. Personal resilience is essential when life becomes more unpredictable and uncertain. Make sure that the people in your life support decisions that you make involving change. A caring and encouraging social network is essential to your happiness and wellbeing.

Picture a future state that takes you away from your present comfort zone. Find something about the future that could be rewarding in order to motivate you to keep moving forward, even when you feel tempted to revert to what you already know. Lasting change depends on persistence and tenacity.

Transform your negative thoughts and words. Use the language of hope and aspiration when you talk about your own plans and ambitions. Challenge your own cognitive hurdles and try to see the world through a different lens.

References for Chapter 9

1. Eisenberger, N. (2012). 'The neural bases of social pain: Evidence for shared representations with physical pain', *Psychosomatic Medicine*, February, 126–35.
2. Dewall, C. N. (2010). 'Acetaminophen reduces social pain: Behavioral and neural experience', *Psychological Sciences*, July, 931–37. doi: 10.1177/0956797610374741
3. Robison, J. (2012). 'Wellbeing is contagious (for better or worse): How one employee's wellbeing affects that of the entire team', *Gallup Business Journal*, 27 November. gallup.com
4. Haeffel, G.J., & Hames, J.L. (2013). 'Cognitive vulnerability to depression can be contagious', *Clinical Psychological Science*, April, 75–85.
5. Deutschman, A. (2005). 'Change or Die'. *Fast Company*.
6. Selinger, J.C. et al. (2015). 'Humans can continuously optimize energetic cost during walking', *Current Biology*, September, 2452–56. https://doi.org/10.1016/j.cub.2015.08.016
7. Cheval, B. et al. (2018). 'Avoiding sedentary behaviors requires more cortical resources than avoiding physical activity: An EEG study', *Neuropsychologia*, October, 68–80. https://doi.org/10.1016/j.neuropsychologia.2018.07.029
8. Hemingway, E. (2010). *A Moveable Feast: The Restored Edition*. New York: Scribner.
9. Moss Kanter, R. (2020). *Think Outside the Building: How Advanced Leaders Can Change the World One Smart Innovation at a Time*. New York: PublicAffairs.
10. Coghill, R.C. et al. (2003). 'Neural correlates of interindividual differences in the subjective experience of pain', *Proceedings of the National Academy of Sciences*, July, 8538–42.
11. Wise, E. et al. (2002). 'Gender role expectations of pain: Relationship to experimental pain perception', *Pain*, April 335–42.
12. Tajima, S. et al. (2019). 'Optimal policy for multi-alternative decisions', *Nature Neuroscience*, September. doi: 10.1038/s41593-019-0453-9.
13. Xu, K.Z. et al. (2017). 'Neural basis of cognitive control over movement inhibition: Human fMRI and primate electrophysiology evidence', *Neuron*. doi: 10.1016/j.neuron.2017.11.010
14. Glasser, W. (1998). *Choice Theory: A New Psychology of Personal Freedom*. New York: HarperCollins.
15. Uhls, Y.T. et al. (2014). 'Five days at outdoor education camp without screens improves preteen skills with nonverbal emotion cues', *Computers in Human Behaviour*, October, 387–92.
16. Rhudy, J.L., & Meaghe, M.W. (2000). 'Fear and anxiety: Divergent effects on human pain thresholds', *Pain*, January, 65–75.
17. Dweck, C. S. (2007). *Mindset. The New Psychology of Success*. New York: Ballantine Books.
18. Cialdini, R. (2007). *Influence: The Psychology of Persuasion*. New York: Collins.
19. Ornish, D. et al. (1998). 'Intensive lifestyle changes for reversal of coronary heart disease', *JAMA*, December, 2001–2007.
20. Kotter, J.P. (2012). *The Heart of Change: Real-Life Stories of How People Change Their Organizations*. Boston: Harvard Business Review Press.
21. Frieberg, K., & Frieberg, J. (1998). *NUTS! Southwest Airlines' Crazy Recipe for Business and Personal Success*. New York: Broadway Books.
22. Merzenich, M. (2013). *Soft-Wired: How the New Science of Brain Plasticity Can Change Your Life*. San Francisco: Parnassus Publishing.

When stress is the basic state of mind, even good things stress us out. We have to learn to let go.

SAKYONG MIPHAM
Head of the Shambhala Buddhist lineage and Shambhala
International (1962–)

chapter ten

Our Brain and Stress

ABOUT THIS CHAPTER

Stress is a highly subjective phenomenon and is different for everyone. We do not all find the same things stressful, and there is considerable variation in the way we each respond to stress.

With the pressures of today's world, stress is pervasive and the term *stress* is frequently used to describe numerous conditions. Most of us are so used to feeling stressed that it has become a norm that we no longer question. But, sadly, despite growing awareness in this field, many people still feel unable to discuss feeling stressed and feel ill-equipped to deal with symptoms they are experiencing.

There are different symptoms of stress, including cognitive, behavioural, physiological and physical indicators.

This chapter discusses the signs and impact of stress on our brain and body, and offers tips to enable us to deal with stressors in our world.

Part 1: The science explained

What is stress?

Stress is a biological and psychological response that we experience when we encounter a threat that we feel we do not have the resources to deal with.

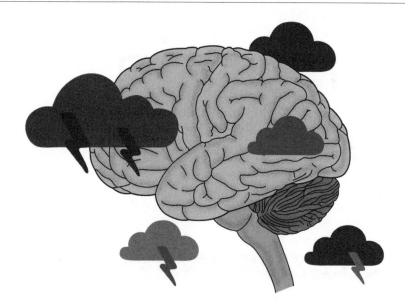

Stress was first referred to in 1936 by Dr Hans Selye,[1] a Hungarian endocrinologist.

He explained that any threat or *stressor* which is challenging, threatening or demanding (for example, public presentation, examination, divorce, death, moving, job loss) can result in a three-stage response:

Dr Hans Selye defines stress as:

'the non-specific response of the body to any demand for change.'

1 Alarm	When we encounter a stressor, our body reacts with the *fight or flight* response and our *sympathetic nervous system* is activated. Hormones such as *cortisol* and *adrenaline* are released into the bloodstream to give our body additional strength and energy to meet the stressor.
2 Resistance	Our body focuses resources against the stressor. Our blood glucose levels remain high, and cortisol and adrenaline continue to circulate at elevated levels. Our body remains in a state of high alertness, with heart rate and breathing accelerated.
3 Exhaustion	If the stressor continues beyond our body's capacity to respond or cope, we exhaust our resources and run out of defences, becoming susceptible to disease and death.

How do we get stressed?

Our brain and body assess whether or not a situation is stressful. This decision is made based on how we receive and process new sensory inputs and how our stored memories inform us about the last time we were in a similar situation.

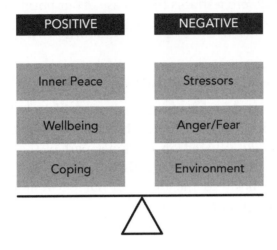

Overall, we need to maintain a regular balance, or *homeostasis*.

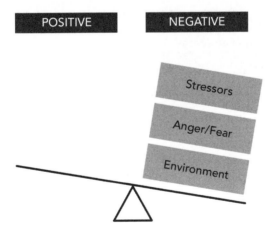

When we do not have homeostasis, such as when we are out of balance, we feel the effects of stress.

Where does stress start in the brain?

The *hypothalamus* is in charge of our stress response. Located at the base of the brain, the hypothalamus connects with several other regions of the brain to regulate homeostasis, as mentioned earlier. The hypothalamus also controls the pituitary gland, which orchestrates the release of our hormones from our body's endocrine glands. There are two components of our stress response (see Figure 10.1):

1) Sympathetic-adrenal-medullary (SAM) system

When we encounter a stressful situation, the amygdala sends an alarm to the hypothalamus, which activates the sympathetic nervous system. Signals are sent to the *adrenal medulla*, situated on the inner part of the *adrenal gland*. This produces hormones such as *adrenaline* (also known as *epinephrine*), which helps our body respond quickly to the threat in our environment. The body then undergoes the following changes:

Increase in heart rate
Increase of blood to the muscles
Increase in breathing
Increase of oxygen to the brain
Greater alertness and sharpened senses
Decrease in digestive activity
Release of glucose and fats for energy

As soon as adrenaline has been released, the hypothalamus activates the second part of the stress response.

2) Hypothalamic-pituitary-adrenal (HPA) axis

The *HPA axis* involves a network of glands: the hypothalamus, the pituitary gland and the adrenal glands. The hypothalamus stimulates the pituitary gland to activate the adrenal cortex, situated on the outer part of the adrenal gland, which produces hormones such as *cortisol*, which helps regulate our metabolism, and *aldosterone*, which helps to control blood pressure.

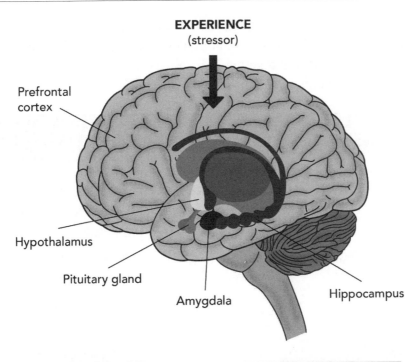

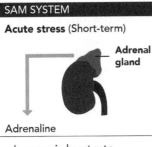

FIGURE 10.1: Our two stress pathways

Cortisol enables the body to maintain steady supplies of blood sugar so we can cope with the stressor on a prolonged basis. Cortisol also releases stored glucose from the liver (for energy) and helps control swelling after injury. The immune system is suppressed while this happens.

As soon as the perceived threat has passed, the *parasympathetic nervous system* takes control and restores balance in the body. The sympathetic and parasympathetic systems are designed to work together in balance (see Figure 10.2): when one part is working, the other stops as discussed in more detail in Chapter 1, Our Brain.

Parasympathetic 'Rest and Digest'	Body	Sympathetic 'Fight or Flight'
Pupils constrict	Eyes	Pupils dilate
Saliva production increases	Salivary glands	Saliva production reduces
Mucus production increases	Nose	Mucus production reduces
Heart rate slows	Heart	Heart rate increases
Bronchial muscles contract	Lung	Bronchial muscles relax
Gastric juices and digestion increase	Stomach	Digestion reduces
Normal function	Liver	Glucose increases
Urine increases	Kidneys	Urine decreases
Normal function	Adrenal glands	Adrenaline is released

FIGURE 10.2: The parasympathetic and sympathetic nervous systems

In relatively small amounts, stress can sharpen our concentration and help us to stay focused, energetic and alert. Stress can even give us extra strength to defend ourselves and overcome challenges.

However, a build-up of stress can cause major damage to our brain and body.

Over time, stress can directly and indirectly contribute to general or specific physiological and psychological disorders. Long-term stress raises adrenaline and cortisol levels in our body, which, in turn, increases heart rate, respiration and blood pressure, and places more physical stress on bodily organs (see Figure 10.3).

Elevated cortisol levels are especially harmful since cortisol suppresses the immune system by metabolising white blood cells. As the number of white blood cells lowers, the efficiency of the immune system decreases, leaving the body open to infection and disease. Blood pressure is also raised, resulting in hypertension and atherosclerosis, both precursors to cardiovascular disease.

And so, if our stress hormones are not metabolised, their cumulative build-up can be a contributing factor in heart disease, high blood pressure, stroke and other illnesses.

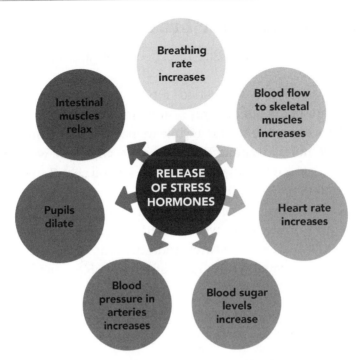

FIGURE 10.3: The effects of stress hormones on our body

Causes of stress

There are a number of factors that cause stress:

External	Internal
Biological and ecological factors (diet, pollution, working conditions)	Chronic worry
Major life changes	Pessimism
Work or school	Rigid thinking, lack of flexibility
Relationship difficulties	Negative self-talk
Financial problems	Unrealistic expectations/perfectionism
Being too busy	All-or-nothing attitude
Technostress (information overload, loss of privacy, reduced boundaries, digital divide)	
Children and family	
Occupational stress (uncertainty, demands, travel)	
Other (health, academic)	

Stress can shrink our brain

Research is increasingly highlighting the effect that stress has on the physical structure of our brain.

When we are stressed over a period of time, our brain adapts to the higher levels of cortisol present in our body and our hippocampus starts to shrink. This is why when we have been stressed for a while we become more forgetful.

Because we do not all respond to stress in the same way, we may experience different symptoms of stress. However, there are several common warning signs of stress, as highlighted in Figure 10.4.

The hippocampus is also one of the first areas of the brain to be affected by dementia. The fact that stressors over our lifetime could trigger the development of dementia is a key area of research today. A study has even revealed that people who have experienced significant stress are 65% more likely to develop dementia.[2]

Cognitive	• Memory problems • Inability to concentrate • Poor judgement • Seeing only the negative • Anxious or racing thoughts • Constant worrying
Emotional	• Moodiness • Irritability or short temper • Agitation, inability to relax • Feeling overwhelmed • Sense of loneliness and isolation • Depression or general unhappiness
Physical	• Aches and pains • Diarrhoea or constipation • Nausea, dizziness • Chest pain, rapid heartbeat • Loss of sex drive • Frequent colds
Behavioural	• Eating more or less • Sleeping too much or too little • Isolating yourself from others • Procrastinating or neglecting responsibilities • Using alcohol, cigarettes or drugs to relax • Nervous habits (for example, nail biting, pacing)

FIGURE 10.4: Warning signs of stress

Yale researchers looked at healthy participants who had experienced a stressful event such as the death of a loved one, loss of a home, loss of a job or divorce.[3]

Even those participants who had only recently experienced a stressful event showed reduced volume in the prefrontal cortex, the region of the brain that regulates emotions and self-control.

How do we measure stress?

There are many different ways of measuring stress. A variety of questionnaires assess the psychological and physiological factors associated with stress:

The **psychological factors** include feelings of wellbeing, self-efficacy (belief in our ability to exert control over our life) and cognitive ability.

The **physiological factors** include activation of the sympathetic nervous system, and sleep, gastrointestinal, upper-respiratory and cardio-pulmonary symptoms.

An objective measure of stress is to measure the stress hormones (cortisol and adrenaline) in blood, saliva, urine or hair. Cortisol is often used as a biological measure of chronic stress and is easily measured in saliva and, more recently, hair samples. Cortisol tends to fluctuate during the day and is higher in the morning, which is why hair samples tend to offer a more stable reading than urine or saliva.

Stress, inflammation and disease

Activation of our stress response is linked to 90% of all human diseases, of which inflammation is also a central component.

Recent research has looked more deeply at the nature of the relationship between stress, inflammation and disease.[4]

As mentioned earlier in the chapter, our stress response results in physiological changes such as an increased heart and respiratory rate, and higher levels of glucose, blood sugar and adrenaline. Cortisol is also produced, which suppresses the immune system and digestion. So our body is placed on high alert and normal functioning is placed on temporary shutdown.

But what happens if we are in this state on a chronic or long-term basis?

A state of chronic stress, as explained earlier in the chapter, may prolong cortisol secretion in our body. Over time, the body adapts to these repeated cortisol surges and eventually reduces the amount of cortisol released, leading to a dysfunctional or down-regulated system that becomes cortisol-resistant.[5]

And so excessive levels of cortisol compromise our entire stress response, the knock-on effect of which is widespread inflammation: pro-inflammatory neurotransmitters are released instead, and cortisol fails to function properly as an anti-inflammatory. Moreover, we are no longer able to turn off the amygdala and so our stressful experience is intensified.

The continuing cycle of stress and inflammation is exacerbated by the presence of pro-inflammatory *cytokines*, a group of proteins secreted by the cells in our immune system, which become acclimatised in the body where they can also spread. This disturbance of the immune system has been linked to stress-related diseases, all of which have inflammation in common: rheumatoid arthritis,[6] cardiovascular disease,[7] inflammatory bowel disease,[8] cancer[9] and depression.[10]

Although the exact causes of many diseases are still not fully clear – and, of course, we should also consider genetics, age and lifestyle – there is evidence that stress and inflammation may induce or worsen the symptoms.

Studies continue to publish findings linking stress-reducing strategies, such as aerobic exercise, yoga, meditation, walking in natural surroundings and social interaction with friends, with decreased inflammation.

Part 2: Impact on our daily life

What we think is stressful will be stressful

Our brain cannot always differentiate between the imagined and the real. It is enough for us to think that something is stressful for it to become stressful. Stress is therefore a subjective phenomenon. Whether the threat is real or not is irrelevant; the brain will respond in the same way to a difficult meeting with the boss as it would to a meeting with a wild animal!

We prepare ourselves for physical survival on a regular basis, even though our life is not actually under threat. We cannot eliminate the threat and fight (punch the boss) or flee (run out of a meeting room), and so we become more aggressive, impatient, anxious and hyper-reactive. And because we cannot actually do what we are primed to do (fight or flight) we use the excess blood in our hands and feet to point or fidget.

Can stress be good for us?

The *Yerkes–Dodson law* was developed in 1908 by the psychologists Robert Yerkes and John Dillingham Dodson.[11]

> Yerkes and Dodson used mild electrical shocks to motivate rats to run around a maze in the correct order. However, as the shocks intensified, the rats tried to escape by running in random directions.
>
> While the mild shocks were motivational, the intense shocks had the opposite effect.

The Yerkes–Dodson law suggests that there is a relationship between performance and stress. It states that a certain level of stress can help improve performance, but beyond a specific point, performance becomes impaired (shown in Figure 10.5).

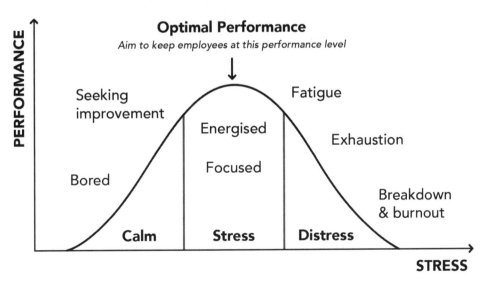

FIGURE 10.5: The Yerkes–Dodson Human Performance and Stress Curve

So stress enables most of us to sharpen our focus in the short term: we can study for exams, compete in a sporting event or deliver a presentation. But too much stress can overwhelm us and lead to breakdown or burnout.

The dividing line between enough and too much stress is different for each of us and will also depend on the complexity of the task. For simpler tasks, we may be able to cope with more pressure, while for more complex tasks that require more of our cognitive resources, we may find that our threshold is lower.

Our braking system

When we feel stressed and emotional, we lose our ability to think rationally: resources are diverted away from our frontal lobe, and we focus instead on defensive coping strategies.

But our brain has a *braking system,* which is situated in the right prefrontal cortex (see Figure 10.6).[12] The significance of this brain region is also discussed in Chapter 11, Our Brain and Leadership, as it is where we regulate our emotions.

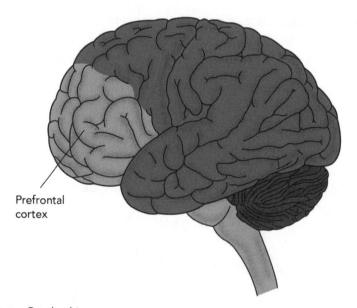

Prefrontal
cortex

FIGURE 10.6: Our braking system

Although this braking system has a limited capacity, it can be strengthened over time as we become more accustomed to dealing with emotional events. When we switch on our braking system, our emotional responses lose their intensity.

How can we apply the brakes?	
Label	The first step is to label the emotion. When we articulate and try to understand our emotions, we are applying rational thought and this activates our prefrontal cortex. When we suppress emotions, they tend to build up in our brain, taking on greater significance and often affecting later judgement and decision-making.
Reframe	The second step is to reframe what the stressful event means to us.

An experiment was conducted in which participants were shown a picture of people crying outside a church and were told that it was a picture of a funeral.

The participants were then asked to look at the same picture as a wedding ceremony.

When the participants reframed the scene as a wedding (this is called *cognitive reappraisal*), their brain activity changed. Their brains' emotional responses involving the amygdala reduced and their prefrontal lobe function became more active.[13]

The power of meditation and mindfulness

In recent years, *meditation* and *mindfulness* have been discussed and debated as interlinked and overlapping concepts. So what are the main differences between them and what do they do?

Both **meditation** and **mindfulness** are ancient practices originating in religion. Meditation encompasses a number of techniques aimed at regulating consciousness and concentration in order to transcend and manage emotions. Mindfulness is one of the techniques used in meditation and involves focusing completely on the present in order to reduce the intrusion of various emotions.

The underpinning philosophy of mindfulness is that a better awareness of the present leads to greater appreciation of our surroundings. We are also more equipped to notice signs of stress or anxiety earlier and therefore deal with them more quickly.

Various studies have highlighted the health benefits of meditation and mindfulness and, in particular, their usefulness in reducing stress-related conditions such as depression, anxiety, chronic pain, diabetes and high blood pressure.

A recent study investigated the impact of mindfulness on patients who were suffering from *generalised anxiety disorder* (GAD).[14]

After eight weeks of practising mindfulness, there was a significant reduction in patients' anxiety levels.

During mindfulness, our brainwaves slow down and move from a beta to an alpha rhythm. We move into alpha rhythms before sleep, as explained in Chapter 12, Our Brain and Lifestyle. Alpha rhythms have also been linked with creativity, as mentioned in Chapter 8, Our Brain and Creativity.

Alpha waves reduce the impact of distracting sensory information and help the brain to focus.[15] Brain-imaging studies even show that regular mindfulness meditation results in structural changes to the brain and increases the connections and blood flow between brain cells, leading to reduced depression and insomnia and increased compassion.[16]

A recent meta-analysis of 20 studies has highlighted how mindfulness meditation results in changes in two brain areas.[17] The first area, the *anterior cingulate cortex* (ACC), which is associated with emotional regulation, problem-solving and decision-making, and which is particularly important to us during periods of fast change, shows more activity after mindfulness meditation. The second area, the *hippocampus*, which is associated with memory and emotion and is susceptible to damage by chronic stress, shows greater volume of grey matter.

Mindfulness meditation is therefore instrumental in increasing our brain's overall performance and size.

However, it is also important to point out that mindfulness should not be viewed as a tool to help employers increase the productivity of their workforce, or an excuse to abdicate responsibility for fostering a healthy working environment. To do that would defeat its purpose as a means of disconnecting momentarily from the world in order to reflect and slow down.

Moreover, mindfulness is not a cure-all for stress and health issues. It has even been criticised for triggering traumatic memories, particularly among the hypersensitive or those suffering from post-traumatic stress disorder, where painful memories may resurface. Understanding that mindfulness is a therapeutic intervention that needs initial research is therefore an important first step towards engaging in any relevant techniques.

It is also useful to balance any stress management practice with other methods of relaxation, such as reading, spending time with friends and simply taking a break. While this may seem like common sense, it is often the last thing we feel like doing when we are feeling overwhelmed or at a low ebb.

> Magnetic resonance imaging (MRI) studies show how mindfulness causes the amygdala, the region of the brain involved in the body's stress response, to shrink.[18]
>
> The connections between the amygdala and other brain regions weaken, while the prefrontal cortex, which enables us to focus and pay attention, grows thicker.
>
> And so, as we practise exercising our thoughts and rotating our attention to the present, our primal responses become less relevant and influential.

Part 3: Stories and top tips

Are our jobs killing us?

In 1983, *Time* magazine's June cover story referred to stress as 'The Epidemic of the Eighties'.

Since then stress has become an ever-more pervasive term, with job stress being the number one source of stress for adults. The Japanese trend of *karoshi*, meaning 'death from overwork', is believed to be due to heart attack and stroke caused by high levels of stress. It is now estimated that the majority of visits to doctors are for stress-related problems.

Experts state that it is not easy to predict who will suffer from stress as a result of work-related pressures. Other factors should also be taken into consideration, such as social network, family life and genetic predisposition. However, there has recently been an increase in reports on stress and its impact on psychological and physical health.

The Health and Safety Executive (HSE) 2019 report estimates the costs of work-related stress to Great Britain to be over £5 billion a year, with stress,[19] depression or anxiety accounting for nearly 50% of all work-related ill health, with the causes attributed to workload, lack of managerial support and organisational change.

A study by Deloitte, published in January 2020,[20] finds that the costs of poor mental health to UK employers have increased by 16% since 2017, now costing up to £45 billion.

The 2019 report from the American Institute of Stress states that 83% of US workers suffer from work-related stress, with the US losing up to $300 billion a year to workplace stress.[21]

The 2019 Mental Health Information sheet by the World Health Organisation (WHO) lists the estimated cost of depression and anxiety to the global economy to be US$1 trillion per year in lost productivity.[22]

The 2019 European Survey of Enterprises on New and Emerging Risks (ESENER) has also found that there is a reluctance to talk openly about psychosocial issues such as stress.[23]

It is clear that the impact of stress is far-reaching, and has often been exacerbated by the recent economic difficulties.

After the financial crisis of 2008, reported incidents of mental illness and stress increased in line with people's worries about money and job insecurity. Executives still report feeling unable to cope or make simple decisions. Perhaps more worryingly, studies have shown that over time chronic long-term stress destroys brain cells and damages the hippocampus, the region of the brain involved in the formation and retrieval of memories. This may explain why the more pressure people feel they are under, the more forgetful they become.

Stress can affect anyone

Today's working environment is punishing for many executives. But admitting to being stressed has always carried a stigma, particularly in male-dominated, competitive environments where stress is sometimes associated with weakness or incompetence.

However, recent reports of senior executives having to take time off work to recover from stress-related illness have made the business world sit up and take note. Stress is no longer an affliction that hits the lower levels of the hierarchy involved in repetitive and routine tasks; even those at the top are not immune from suffering exhaustion and burnout.

Over the last few years, a number of organisations have focused on providing greater support to employees. However, technology now fuels the need to be available on a constant basis and employees, especially among the younger generations, are finding it difficult to switch off.

In 2011, when banks were still suffering from the effects of the banking crisis, Antonio Horta-Osorio, the group chief executive of Lloyds Banking Group, took eight weeks off work with exhaustion and work-related stress. After returning to work, he and his 65,000 employees participated in a full mental health awareness programme that was also supported by an online portal. Insurance coverage for mental health at the bank was then raised to the same level as that of physical health.

The cost of commitment

In the sporting world, it seems that managers and fans get so involved in watching games that it places stress on their hearts.

A Canadian study showed that just viewing a live hockey game was enough to increase spectators' heart rates to a level equalling vigorous physical stress.[24]

But, according to Dr Dorian Dugmore, chief executive of Wellness International in the UK, Football League managers are among the highest risk group of people for stress-related cardiovascular problems.[25]

Following the death of Jock Stein from a heart attack at a Wales-Scotland game in 1985, Dr Dugmore's research on Football League managers has uncovered a number of serious heart conditions, high blood pressure and dangerous levels of cholesterol. Several Premier League managers have even suffered heart attacks or other serious health problems. His first high-profile study was conducted in 2001 when two well-known managers, Sam Allardyce and Dave Bassett, were wired up to heart monitors during a match. Both managers showed dangerously high blood pressure responses and cardiac irregularities.

Today, with the support of the League Managers' Association and the Professional Footballers' Association, football managers are now enrolled in Dr Dugmore's 'Fit to Manage' programme, which monitors blood pressure and cholesterol levels and provides advice on nutrition and lifestyle.

It is not just the managers who are suffering the stress of watching the game; football fans too may be putting themselves at risk of a heart attack.

A study carried out by Oxford University researchers measured cortisol levels of 40 Brazilian fans before, during and after three matches during the 2014 World Cup.[26] The results showed that cortisol was particularly high during the semi-final when Brazil lost to Germany 7–1. But by the end of the game, the fans had reduced their cortisol levels by laughing together and hugging each other.

Dr Martha Newson, who led the study, recommends that clubs consider the extent to which fans identify with the players they are supporting, as well as the impact this has on their physiological and psychological wellbeing. Dr Newson also advocates creating a calming environment in the stadium after matches and suggests that stewards are trained to detect those fans most at risk of heart attacks.

We can all do something to help others

Yukio Shige is a 70-year-old retired police officer who patrols the Tojinbo cliffs in Fukui Prefecture, Japan, a popular tourist destination and a well-known spot for people to commit suicide. Over the last decade Mr Shige has prevented an estimated 500 suicides. After a friend tragically committed suicide, Mr Shige decided that he wanted to help others. Now known as the *Chotto matte* ('Hold on, wait') man, he goes to the cliffs every day, carrying binoculars and accompanied by his three volunteers.

Japan has one of the highest suicide rates in the world, with an estimated 30,000 people killing themselves every year. During the 1998 financial crisis, the number went up by a third. The numbers rose again after the 2008 worldwide financial crisis. Around 40% of young people in Japan are unable to find stable jobs and the fastest-growing suicide demographic is young men. In 2018 suicide was the top cause of death in Japan for those aged between 15 and 39.

Japanese culture discourages complaining or the expression of strong emotions from an early age. In particular, feelings that may be associated with weakness, such as anxiety or stress, are often suppressed. Different methods of stress relief have emerged over the years to enable people to release and share their emotions at work, such as the recent practice of hiring *ikemesos,* men who come into offices and show women emotive videos and pictures to encourage them to cry.[27]

For men it is more difficult. Cultural pressures, combined with high youth unemployment and technology-based communication, have led to the social phenomenon of *hikikomori* ('confined' or 'pulled inward') – young, mainly male, Japanese who withdraw from society. Similar cases have recently been reported in Western countries too.[28]

Mr Shige and his team do not just bring people back from the cliff edge; they also help people get their lives back. He has been reported as saying:

> **'If they're in debt, I take them to legal aid people; if they're out of work, I take them to the Hello Work employment agency; if they're homeless, I take them home with me.'**

Exercise reduces stress

Exercise reduces the effects of stress by lowering levels of the body's stress hormones, such as adrenaline and cortisol. Exercise also stimulates the production of endorphins, our natural painkillers.

Raising our heart rate can actually reverse damage to the brain caused by stressful events and can stimulate growth in the hippocampal region, which shrinks when we are stressed.

When we exercise, we also produce noradrenaline/norepinephrine, which is associated with improved cognitive function and learning.

The effects of exercise are immediate. Just after exercise our mood is better and our energy is higher. And even though exercise also produces cortisol, our level returns to normal very quickly afterwards.

According to Dr Robert Leahy, Director of the American Institute for Cognitive Therapy and author of *Beat the Blues Before They Beat You*:[29]

> **'Exercise is like free medicine. Medication may work more rapidly to lessen the symptoms of depression or stressed feelings, but the effects of regular exercise are longer lasting.'**

Top Tips →
Remember: **SMILE**

Set realistic goals and be patient with yourself. Pause regularly throughout the day: take a break from sitting at a desk every 20 to 30 minutes. Learn to prioritise what is really important. When we try to take on too much, we cause problems for ourselves and add to our stress levels.

Master your emotions and learn how to express and articulate how you feel. This will enable you to deal with your emotions more effectively. Know your own personal stress triggers and tolerance to stress, particularly when dealing with personal adversity. Seek to address these before they turn into bigger problems.

Introduce moments of calm and serenity into your day. Let your mind rest. Disconnect mentally from all the noise around you and especially from your technological devices. We should not be 'on' all the time. Use mindfulness techniques to focus on the present and reduce the impact of anxious thoughts. Breathe slowly – this will help you think more calmly and clearly.

Laugh with your social network of friends and family; share happy experiences and build positive memories together. Loneliness makes us more vulnerable to stress. An environment where we feel supported, nurtured and loved is essential to our mental wellbeing and ability to cope with life's pressures.

Elevate your mood with exercise. Carve out some personal time to focus on your health and wellbeing. Devote time and effort to building a strong, capable and resilient system that will enable you to manage life's challenges.

References for Chapter 10

1. Selye, H. (1978). *The Stress of Life*. New York: McGraw-Hill.
2. Johansson, L. et al. (2010). 'Midlife psychological stress and risk of dementia: A 35-year longitudinal population study', *Brain*, August, 2217–24.
3. Ansell, E.B. et al. (2012). 'Cumulative adversity and smaller gray matter volume in medial prefrontal, anterior cingulate, and insula regions', *Biological Psychiatry*, July, 57–64.
4. Liu, Y.Z. et al. (2017). 'Inflammation: The common pathway of stress-related diseases', *Frontiers in Human Neuroscience*, June. https://doi.org/10.3389/fnhum.2017.00316.
5. Hannibal K.E., & Bishop, M.D. (2014). 'Chronic stress, cortisol dysfunction, and pain: A psychoneuroendocrine rationale for stress management in pain rehabilitation', *Physical Therapies*, July, 1816–25. https://doi: 10.2522/ptj.20130597
6. Innala, L. et al. (2016). 'Co-morbidity in patients with early rheumatoidarthritis-inflammation matters', *Arthritis Research & Therapy*. https://doi.org/10.1186/s13075-016-0928-y
7. Tawakol, A.T. (2017). 'Relation between resting amygdala activity and cardiovascular events: A longitudinal and cohort study', *The Lancet*, February–March, 834–45. https:// www.sciencedirect .com/science/article/pii/S0140673616317147
8. Vannucchi, M. G. et al. (2018). 'Experimental models of irritable bowel syndrome and the role of the enteric neurotransmission', *Journal of Clinical Medicine*. https://doi.org/10.3390/jcm7010004
9. Yang, T. et al. (2019). 'Work stress and the risk of cancer: A meta-analysis of observational studies', *International Journal of Cancer*, May 2390–2400. doi: 10.1002/ijc.31955
10. Yang, L. et al. (2015). 'The effects of psychological stress on depression', *Current Neuropharmacology*, July 494–504. https://doi.org/10.2174/1570159x1304150831150507
11. Yerkes, R.M., & Dodson, J.D. (1908). 'The relation of strength of stimulus to rapidity of habit-formation', *Journal of Comparative Neurology and Psychology*, November. https://doi.org/ 10.1002/cne.920180503
12. Lieberman, M.D. (2009). 'The brain's braking system (and how to "use your words" to tap into it)', *NeuroLeadership*, September, 9–14.
13. Restak, R. (2006). *The Naked Brain*. New York: Three Rivers Press.
14. Majid, S.A. (2012). 'Effect of mindfulness-based stress management on reduction of generalized anxiety disorder', *Iranian Journal of Public Health*, October, 24–28.
15. Sacchet, M.D. et al. (2015). 'Attention drives synchronization of alpha and beta rhythms between right inferior frontal and primary sensory neocortex', *Journal of Neuroscience*, February, 2074–82.
16. Hölzel B. et al. (2011). 'Mindfulness practice leads to increases in regional brain gray matter density', *Psychiatry Research*, January, 36–43.
17. Congelton, C. et al. (2015). 'Mindfulness can literally change your brain', *Harvard Business Review*, January, 309–18.
18. Taren, A.A. et al. (2013). 'Dispositional mindfulness co-varies with smaller amygdala and caudate volumes in community adults', *PLOS ONE*, May. doi.org/10.1371/journal.pone.0064574
19. Health and Safety Executive Annual Statistics (October 2019).
20. Deloitte. (2020). 'Mental health and employers. Refreshing the case for investment', January.
21. Milenkovic, M. (2019). '42 Worrying Workplace Stress Statistics', *The American Institute of Stress*, September. https://www.stress.org/42-worrying-workplace-stress-statistics

22. WHO 'Mental health in the workplace', Information sheet, May 2019.

23. Third European Survey of Enterprises on New and Emerging Risks (ESENER 3), 2019.

24. Khairy L.T. et al. (2017). 'Heart rate response in spectators of the Montreal Canadiens hockey team', *Canadian Journal of Cardiology*, October, 1633–38. doi: https://doi.org/10.1016/j.cjca.2017.08.002.

25. Green, C. (2002). *The Sack Race. The Story of Football's Gaffers*. Edinburgh: Mainstream Publishing Company.

26. Newson, M. et al. (2020). 'Devoted fans release more cortisol when watching live soccer matches', *Stress and Health*, January. https://doi.org/10.1002/smi.2924

27. Paul, C. (2016). 'Behind the strange Japanese trend to cope with stress', *Time*, 10 August. time.com

28. Kato, T.A. et al. (2012). 'Does the "hikikomori" syndrome of social withdrawal exist outside Japan? A preliminary international investigation', *Social Psychiatry and Psychiatric Epidemiology*, July, 1061–75L.

29. Leahy, R. (2011). *Beat the Blues Before They Beat You: How to Overcome Depression*. London: Hay House.

'**The future depends on what we do in the present**'.

MAHATMA GANDHI
Lawyer, politician, social activist and writer (1869–1948)

chapter eleven

Our Brain and Leadership

ABOUT THIS CHAPTER

Our appetite for learning about leadership shows no sign of abating. From the latest theories presented by business schools, to the biographies of high achievers and self-help guides with easy-to-follow steps, we continue to reach for new tools and practical solutions based on others' tried and tested successes.

But can we really distil leadership into several key nuggets that can be replicated across a wider population? Consistent and effective leadership still seems to be an elusive concept that is hard to define and pin down.

This chapter discusses how our brain works within the context of the leadership role and why leaders could benefit from an understanding of the workings of the human brain.

Part 1: The science explained

Neuroscience and leadership

All leaders affect the brainpower of the people they lead (see Figure 11.1). It is therefore essential that leaders understand how the human brain works.

But finding good leaders appears to be a worldwide problem. A recent Global Workforce Leadership Survey found that as Baby Boomers (born between 1946 and 1964) retire, leadership will be the hardest skill to find in the

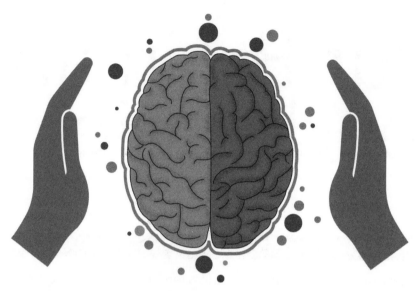

FIGURE 11.1: Leaders affect the brains of those they lead

remaining workforce.[1] A report entitled *Business Human Capital Challenges Today and in the Future,* from the Society of Human Resource Management (SHRM), also found that the availability of the next generation of leaders is a pressing concern for businesses today.[2]

Neuroscientists are now affording us a glimpse into how particular brain-coordinated activity, or *coherence,* may manifest itself in good leadership practices.[3] The higher the coherence, the better the brain is at executing complex tasks that require a high level of communication between its regions.

In one study, the brain activity of leaders was monitored using electrodes while they were asked a few questions about their goals for their companies.

Those leaders who were deemed by their employees to be inspirational were found to generate higher levels of activity in the *right frontal lobe*, an area responsible for interpersonal communication and social relationships.[4]

Right frontal lobe activity is now considered to be essential for inspirational leadership.

It is important to add that antisocial behaviours and poor social skills often arise from damage to the right frontal lobe.[5]

If we look at the leadership role as comprising several key activities, such as decision-making, communication and emotional self-regulation, these activities all require the multiple skills that constitute our executive functioning. And the seat of our executive functioning is the **frontal lobe**.

The frontal lobe helps us not only to make decisions, but also to make the correct decisions. In the wake of recent corporate scandals, ethical decision-making has received a great deal of attention. Some organisations have made a point of communicating their own moral compass to the world – consider Google's catchphrase 'Don't be evil'.

The way the frontal and temporal lobes communicate with each other is particularly significant to leadership as this communication involves the interpretation and management of emotional signals (see Figure 11.2). Our brain's ability to assess and use emotions appropriately is what is now referred to as *emotional intelligence*, a term that has been popularised by Daniel Goleman.[6]

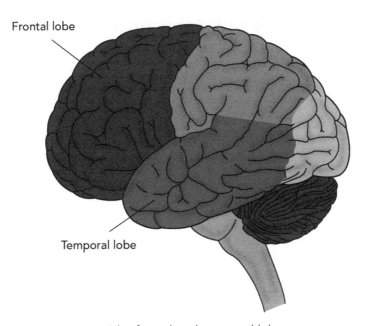

FIGURE 11.2: The frontal and temporal lobes

Are there chemicals of leadership?

Leaders need to manage the balance of chemicals that drive their behaviour and emotion.

Individuals high in *testosterone,* for example, are more likely to be seen as dominant and confident, and issues arise when leaders are overly competitive. High levels of testosterone and *dopamine* in overly competitive leaders reduce *oxytocin* levels, and, hence, the ability to be empathetic with others. This finding applies just as much to women as to men.

Equal balance needs to be found between *serotonin* (maintaining an upbeat mood), *oxytocin* (building trust), *dopamine* (motivation) and *noradrenaline* (alertness and focus).

Leaders can also promote chemical release in the people working around them, by reinforcing and rewarding certain behaviours.

When we are given the freedom to find solutions for ourselves, our brain rewards itself with neurotransmitters such as dopamine and noradrenaline. When we build positive relationships and forge bonds of trust, we release serotonin and oxytocin.

The cognitive cost of decisions

Why did Albert Einstein always wear different versions of the same grey suit?

Why did Steve Jobs always wear the same outfit?

Why does Mark Zuckerberg wear identical grey tee-shirts?

Any decision-making comes at a cognitive cost. Our brain's decision-making capability is finite, and when we make a decision, our ability to make further decisions is depleted.[7] The pre-frontal cortex, which we need to switch on to pay attention, expends a huge amount of energy but is easily exhausted. And so we pay the price if we allow this resource to become consumed by non-essential decisions, such as clothing choices.

Choosing between options, or switching between even simple tasks, can place even more strain on our brain's resources. So deciding whether or not to eat something in the morning can affect our ability to make an important decision later in the day.

As Barack Obama said, when he was US President:

'You also need to remove from your life the day-to-day problems that absorb most people for meaningful parts of their day. You'll see I wear only gray or blue suits. I'm trying to pare down decisions. I don't want to make decisions about what I'm eating or wearing, because I have too many other decisions to make.'

When we have to control our attention and activate our prefrontal lobe's executive functioning, we may later become more susceptible to cognitive traps and biased decision-making (as explained in Chapter 7, Our Brain and Biases). The influencing power of visual cues, such as decoy options, increases and we default to comparisons with inferior information or options, rather than devoting cognitive energy to proper choice evaluation.

This has important ramifications for leaders' decision-making. A tired brain cannot make good decisions, and so leaders must consider and prioritise the choices they make every day so as to get the best out of their own brainpower at the right time.

Researchers have found that participants who made more choices in a shopping mall were subsequently less likely to spend time trying to solve simple algebra problems.[8] The study also found that students suffering from decision fatigue caused by selecting degree courses made them more easily distracted and less inclined to study later.

Leaders can help us reshape our brain

When we focus our attention on anything over time, we create changes in the brain's structure, as explained in Chapter 4, Our Brain and Attention. Attention needs to be directed, and purposeful focus will prevent people from dwelling on what is unhelpful.

Environment is critical. If we are given the space to concentrate and pay attention, then our brain will create the right internal conditions to think, develop insights and make improvements. Our neural networks adapt to the work we do and the way we do it – and over time, we physically change our brain. This is known as *self-directed neuroplasticity*.

Leaders therefore have a significant role to play in the brain development of their people. The right or the wrong environment can have a neurological impact that should not be underestimated.

Expectations drive results

Leaders' expectations of their people are often the catalyst that can bring about good or bad performance in those same people. Leaders can either choose to see the spark in someone or they can choose not to. The same person who has been a failure under one leader can shine under another. It is often the expectation of the leader that drives results.

This is what we call the *Pygmalion* or *Expectation effect*. In Greek mythology, Pygmalion was a sculptor who fell in love with his own carving of a statue. Leaders' beliefs about their people quickly become reality.

In 1963, two researchers, Rosenthal and Jacobson, tested children at an elementary (primary) school in California with an IQ test called the Test of General Ability at the beginning of the school year.[9] The teachers were told that the test was a measure of academic 'blooming'.

In reality, the test had no such predictive validity. At the school, 18 teachers were informed of the students in their classes who had obtained scores in the top percentile. However, these students had actually been chosen by the researchers at random.

The teachers were told that at the end of the school year the same test would be used again to determine any differences in IQ.

The results were astounding. There was a marked difference in IQ test scores between the students labelled as 'blooming' and those who had not been labelled in this way. These results were strongest in the youngest children (aged between five and seven years old).

Rosenthal and Jacobson's results clearly demonstrate the power of expectation over results. This is what we call a *self-fulfilling prophecy*.

It was the expectations of the teachers that led to the pupils' increased (or decreased) performance, with the younger children being more susceptible to teaching influences than older children.

We become our labels

Chapter 8, Our Brain and Creativity, makes the point that we are far more than the labels we attribute to ourselves and others.

So why do we continue to use labels in the work place?

In almost every organisation today, labels are used to describe how people speak, think, behave and work: 'He is good with people'; 'She is analytical'; 'He is blue'; 'She is red'; 'I'm an introvert'; 'You're an extrovert'.

Many employers believe that this type of labelling enables better understanding of different communication styles and targeted development for employees. But labels can also be self-limiting and self-fulfilling.

In the wrong leaders' hands, labels can also be used as a means of assuming power over the individual and sanctioning treatment that fits the description.

Clinical psychologist, Dr Susan Heitler, warns:[10]

'Words have the power to define what we see, potentially blocking us from seeing aspects that differ from the label.'

When we believe that personality is fixed (*entity theory of personality*), we may create a negative environment that is more stressful and less productive than when we view personality as malleable and capable of change (*incremental theory of personality*).[11] Linked to this, Carol Dweck's work on fixed and growth mindsets are mentioned in Chapter 9, Our Brain and Change.

When leaders focus on a specific behaviour, rather than a general label, they are better placed to provide the right intervention to suit the individual and any desired change. Any label can be viewed in a positive and negative light and a strength can also be regarded as a weakness: 'perfectionism' to one person could be seen as 'pedantry' to another. And sometimes it is a new leader who is able to release a spark in an individual that a previous leader has failed to do.

If we believe that we can change, we are more likely to invest more effort into our personal growth; if our leaders believe that we can change, they will be more inclined to work with us towards a new future, rather than use labelling to apportion blame about the past.

We are defined not by labels, but by our behaviour.

Self-awareness is the hallmark of effective leadership

Much has been made about the importance of self-awareness in leadership. Self-awareness demands an ability to be open to feedback from others and sometimes to hear messages that are unexpected or even unwelcome. We do not always see ourselves the way other people see us.

As the Scottish poet Robert Burns said:

'O wad some Pow'r the giftie gie us To see oursels as ithers see us! It wad frae mony a blunder free us.'

How do we develop greater self-awareness?

Tools such as the *JoHari Window* are designed to encourage disclosure that people feel comfortable with.

Created by Joseph Luft and Harry Ingham in 1955, the **JoHari Window** is a tool that enables us to learn about aspects of ourselves that we may otherwise not have been aware of.[12]

The English translation is:

'And would some Power give us the gift To see ourselves as others see us! It would from many a blunder free us.'

The JoHari Window is based on a four-quadrant model (see Figure 11.3):

Open area	This represents information we know about ourselves and are willing to share. The more we feel able to disclose information about ourselves and can learn from others, the higher the level of trust we can build with them. We tend to be at our most effective and productive when we enlarge this open area.
Blind area	This represents information we do not know about ourselves but others can see. If we are able to accept feedback from others, we become more self-aware and open to advice.
Hidden area	This represents information that we are aware of but may not want others to know. There will always be some aspects of ourselves that we choose to keep private, but shared information is more likely to lead to increased communication and cooperation with others.
Unknown area	This represents information about ourselves that is currently unknown either to us or anyone else, such as untried abilities or skills. Collective or self-discovery through new opportunities enable this area to be reduced over time.

With different people, we choose different degrees of disclosure. The more we learn from other people about our own behaviour and impact, the more we increase our open area and reduce the blind area. And through self-discovery and

In 1997, a study of managers found that a training programme alone increased productivity by 28%.

When coaching was provided to support the training, productivity increased by 88%.[13]

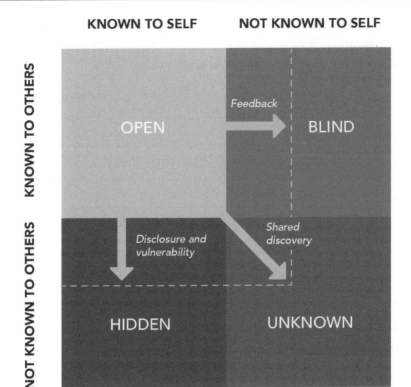

KNOWN TO SELF   **NOT KNOWN TO SELF**

KNOWN TO OTHERS

NOT KNOWN TO OTHERS

OPEN

Feedback

BLIND

Disclosure and vulnerability

Shared discovery

HIDDEN

UNKNOWN

FIGURE 11.3: The JoHari Window

collaboration with others, we are better able to build constructive networks that contribute to our continuing growth and development.

Coaching is an effective way of maintaining self-awareness and enhancing personal insight. If coaching is linked to and supports a development programme, it increases the chances of the new learning becoming embedded in new habits and skills.

The importance of trust and vulnerability

Trust oils the engines of communication: without trust, we cannot build and invest in meaningful relationships. But trust as a concept is difficult to pin down. We know it when we have it – and we are definitely aware of when it has been broken.

Dr Brené Brown, research professor at the University of Houston, has spent years researching into trust. She maintains that a healthy workplace is 'rumbling with vulnerability', and also that this vulnerability is necessary for trust.[14]

Dr Brown says:

'We need to trust to be vulnerable and we need to be vulnerable to build trust.'

But she is also keen to state that, while vulnerability involves emotional disclosure, it should not viewed as a reason for oversharing personal information.

Dr Brown's seven elements of trust are reflected in Figure 11.4: she believes that trust is about BRAVING connection.

Boundaries	We trust others if there is mutual respect about our boundaries.
Reliability	We trust people who honour their commitments and do what they say they will do.
Accountability	We trust those who own up to their mistakes, say sorry and then fix them.
Vault	We need to be certain that personal information is kept safe and treated confidentially.
Integrity	We trust those who embody the values they espouse and have the courage to do what is right.
Non-judgement	We need to feel that we can ask for help without being criticised or judged.
Generosity	We should look for and assume the positive in others' words and actions.

FIGURE 11.4: Brené Brown's Seven Elements of Trust

The face of leadership

Our brains are equipped with social antennae for determining how trustworthy others are. We rapidly determine whether someone is or is not trustworthy through the activation of our *mirror neurons* as discussed in Chapter 2, Our Brain and Emotion.

Our **mirror** neurons reflect the behaviour that someone else is exhibiting and then prompt a response in return. Anger, negativity or nervousness, for example, are recognised by others very quickly.

Our brain is designed to build trust gradually, and when we start building a bond with someone, we release oxytocin, which makes us trust that person even more.

We make a judgement within seconds whether we trust other people and we are heavily influenced by facial expression and face shape. Recent research has demonstrated that a face that looks happy, with upturned eyebrows and an upward curve to the mouth, is likely to be seen as trustworthy (see Figure 11.5). A face that looks angry, with downturned eyebrows, is viewed as untrustworthy.[15]

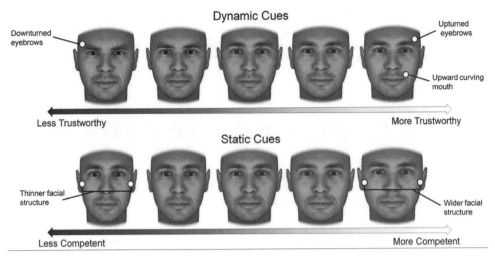

FIGURE 11.5: The face, trust and competence

Credit: Professor John Freeman, New York University.

Because trustworthiness can be inferred from facial expressions, it can sometimes be faked, which is why we may occasionally find ourselves trusting the wrong person.

We assess competence slightly differently – on the basis of facial width (also shown in Figure 11.5). The wider the face, the more competence is perceived. A wider face has been linked to higher levels of testosterone, and, hence, greater strength and aggression, which may have an evolutionary foundation: strength means a greater chance of survival.

The smile

Research into the smile has an interesting history. For four decades researchers have been associating the human smile with the chimpanzee *fear smile*, which is a submissive gesture used to defuse any potential aggression. When a chimp uses this fear smile, they are indicating that they are safe and do not pose a threat. Our human smile also has a submissive element because we often use it to defuse any potential hostility or when we are feeling nervous.

However, new evidence also suggests that our smile may also be linked to a joyful state of mind.[16] When comparing the chimpanzee smile used in play to the human smile, a number of similarities have been observed. While chimpanzees continue to use this smile in play conditions, the human smile has evolved into a more sophisticated communication tool.

The importance of the smile in business contexts must not be underestimated. The affirmative connotations of the smile mean that if leaders smile more, they are more likely to stimulate positive facial expressions, and, hence, positive feelings and trust in the people around them.

Part 2: Impact on our daily life

Environment is critical

Leaders are responsible for the environments they create around them and the communities that they encourage people to join. We all work best when we are part of a caring and inclusive network.

Our ability to interact with others has given us an evolutionary advantage over other animals, with the result that our brains have grown larger as we have developed social networks and learned to cooperate more with each other.[17]

But tough and competitive working environments, where there is a high risk of rejection, can be painful for us on a neurological as well as an emotional level. Our brain's pain receptors fire equally when stimulated by either social pain or physical pain (see Figure 11.6).[18]

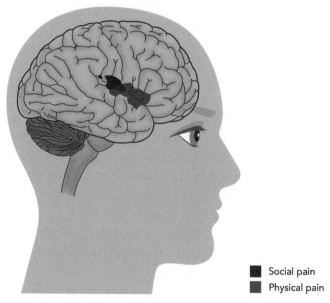

■ Social pain
■ Physical pain

FIGURE 11.6: Social and physical pain in the brain

Because we share the same neural pathways for physical and social pain, painkillers such as acetaminophen (Paracetemol/Tylenol) work on them similarly. As mentioned in Chapter 2, Our Brain and Emotion, painkillers may even dampen our ability to empathise with other people's pain.[19] And the effects of social pain often remain for much longer than the effects of purely physical pain.

According to the neuroscientist Dr David Rock, there are five key considerations that leaders should understand since they affect how we operate at work and with other people (see Figure 11.7).[20]

Status	Our sense of status is one of the most significant predictors of long-term health. Research has shown that, in monkeys, status is equal to survival.[21] When we perceive a threat to our status, we will respond defensively, as if we are facing a real threat.
	When we feel that we are learning, and when we are given positive feedback, our status goes up.
Certainty	Because our brain is a prediction machine, it craves certainty. Even a small amount of uncertainty can create the sensation in the *orbital frontal cortex* and the *anterior cingulate cortex* that 'something is wrong'. Certainty feels good because it is predictable.
	Being kept continually involved and informed with clear messages, particularly during times of change, increases our feelings of certainty.
Autonomy	When we feel that we have control over our work, we reduce our stress levels. Micromanagement, which reduces our feelings of control, can be threatening to us and may provoke a stress response in us.
	Feeling able to control our own workflow, manage our time at work and make decisions all contribute to a greater sense of autonomy.
Relatedness	We need to feel that we belong to a social group. We feel comfortable with people who are like us. Our brain searches for similarities because similarities make us feel safe. When we trust people, we collaborate with them. When we collaborate with other people, we share information.
	Small groups feel less intimidating than big groups because a small group offers more opportunities to connect with others.
Fairness	When we experience feelings of unfairness or injustice our *insula* activates. This is the region of the brain that is triggered when we experience disgust or revulsion, as well as when punishment is dispensed for selfishness or greed. The insula is the part of the brain linked to social and moral behaviour.
	Both transparency of decision-making and equal treatment of others ensure that fairness is maintained.

FIGURE 11.7: David Rock's SCARF Model

In 1971, Philip Zimbardo, Professor Emeritus in Psychology at Stanford University, conducted an experiment that revealed how people conform to the roles they are expected to play.[22] This 'prison' experiment has now become one of the most controversial studies in the history of social psychology.

24 healthy and emotionally stable male college students were recruited to participate in the experiment for which they were paid $15 a day. On the flip of a coin, they were randomly divided into 'prisoners' and 'guards'.

The 'prisoners' were then arrested at their homes, blindfolded and taken to 'prison' (the psychology department of Stanford University) where they were stripped, deloused, given prison clothing and bedding and an identification number. Each 'prisoner' could only refer to himself and the other prisoners by this number.

The 'guards' were dressed in khaki uniforms, wore sunglasses and carried a whistle around their neck. They were told to do whatever was necessary to maintain law and order in the prison and to gain the respect of the prisoners. Physical violence was forbidden.

Within 24 hours each group adopted the behaviour of the group to which they had been assigned: the guards started to humiliate and insult the prisoners, and the prisoners became passive and resigned. The behaviour became so extreme that the experiment, which was due to run for two weeks, had to be terminated after six days.

The experiment highlighted that our behaviour can be shaped by the roles and labels we are given, as well as the environment we are exposed to. In other words, we behave as we are expected and set up to behave.

Although this experiment has since been heavily criticised for its set-up, the wording on the advertisement, the way the roles were manipulated, its visibility to an audience and its unpredictability, several facets of human nature emerged that have important implications for leadership today:

The situational impact on behaviour (the guards had not showed sadistic qualities before the experiment; the clothing and environment fostered their behaviour)
The positive aspects of a group (the prisoners united with each other)
The negative aspects of a group or deindividuation (the guards' group norms superseded individual accountability and led them to behave in ways that were far removed from their character and personal values; the prisoners referred to themselves by their prisoner number, not their name)
Learned helplessness, as described earlier in the book (the prisoners quickly learned to become passive)
The seductive feeling of power (some of the guards admitted to enjoying the authority they were given)

Temperature and noise affect our productivity

Our environment – temperature, colour and noise – affects our productivity.[23] Studies have shown that natural daylight makes us more alert and less stressed than artificial lighting.[24]

Different office temperatures have also been tested by Cornell University, with results showing that working at low room temperatures (20°C or 68°F) lead to 44% more mistakes than working at optimal room temperature (25°C or 77°F). Because our energy is being diverted to keeping warm, we are less likely to focus and pay attention to our work. Warm environments also make us happier.

Our brain cannot differentiate between physical and psychological sensations, so we interpret physical warmth and psychological warmth in the same way. We need to remember this when we are shaking someone's hand.

Participants were divided into two groups: one group was asked to test heating pads and the other group was asked to test ice packs.[25]

They were asked questions about either their actual employer or a hypothetical company.

Those whose hands were warm (heating pads) expressed higher job satisfaction than the other group.

The warm participants were also more likely to be generous with their colleagues, suggesting a relationship between trust and physical comfort.

The problem with traditional leadership

Douglas McGregor's two theories of motivation – *Theory X* and *Theory Y* – were first published back in the 1960s.[26]

Theory X	Assumes that people must be controlled, directed and motivated by the threat of punishment.
Theory Y	Proposes that people will direct their own effort, seek responsibility and be committed to their organisation when they are valued and respected.

In most leadership practices today, Theory X is still very much in evidence: we continue to assume that effort has to be directed through incentives and that mistakes often result in punitive measures.

The problem with systems that focus on reward or punishment is that people's attention is directed to precisely that, and not to generating new and creative ways to solve problems. As explained in Chapter 4, Our Brain and Attention, the attentional system is limited, and if it is aimed in one direction, by default it is aimed away from another. So if people are concerned with avoiding pitfalls and failure, their brain will not be able to entertain innovative approaches or solutions.

Even when leaders believe that they are adopting a more people-centred and empathetic approach by devoting time to listening and consultation, the carrot-and-stick approach is often used in the end. As discussed in Chapter 5, Our Brain and Language, the traditional performance appraisal is a case in point: it may be communicated as an opportunity to review progress and plan development, but, in reality, it is often viewed as a means of evaluating a shortfall of effort against objectives.

No matter how much the performance appraisal is dressed up to look positive, a negative message is frequently all that is registered. For example, even the use of words such as 'constructive' or 'developmental' carries a subtext that feels like fault-finding to the person on the receiving end.

Typical questions that are frequently used in business to direct people to the right answer include 'What effect do you think that had on the team?' and 'How do you think you should have done it?'

These are seemingly positive. But these questions fail to take into account the brain's negativity bias or the fact that people's previous experiences have often conditioned them to anticipate impending disapproval. Either way, the brain responds to these as an attack and immediately builds its necessary defences.

The still-pervasive influence of Theory X in leadership practices across many organisations means that leaders, however well intentioned, may never really get the best out of their people.

The 'Millennial' debate

As discussed earlier in the chapter, the use of labels can affect the way we see ourselves and others. Generational names have always been given to delineate age groups (for example, Baby Boomers and Generation X), but perhaps the focus on Generation Y, also labelled *Millennials*, is creating an *outgroup* that is accentuating normal inter-generational differences (see Chapter 7, Our Brain and Biases for *ingroup-outgroup bias*).

Born between 1980 and 1996, Millennials now represent the largest generation in the workplace, and yet debate is still ongoing about how best to manage and motivate them. It seems that this generation is causing confusion among older incumbents.

Numerous studies and surveys have been carried out in an attempt to understand the Millennial mindset. Gallup has produced guidelines on 'How Millennials Want to Work and Live' in which it concludes that Millennials are the least engaged generation in the workforce and that they change jobs more often than other generations, costing the US economy around $30.5 billion a year.[27]

Other studies have examined Millennial attitudes, aspirations, motivations and values:

A 2019 Deloitte study considered the views of 13,416 Millennials in 42 countries and 3,009 Generation Z (born between 1995–2002) respondents in 10 countries.[28] The report highlights the disconnect between Millennials' values and business purpose, with most Millennials believing that businesses are pursuing their own agenda and less than half of leaders are making a positive impact on the world. Over a quarter spoke about their lack of trust in the information they receive.

A Gartner report reveals how important technology is to Millennials and how much they value the use of personal devices at work.[29] Being in the office is less attractive to Millennials than it is to older generations. The Internet and social media are intrinsic to how Millennials live and solve problems.

ManpowerGroup research shows that money and security are Millennials' most important priorities, closely followed by good people to work with and flexible working arrangements.[30] The majority of those surveyed expect to move role within two years.

Trends are changing. We are all now accustomed to having everything instantly and the expectations of this younger workforce reflect our 'have it now' world. Convenience and speed fuel the way we live, from shopping to working, and organisations are having to rethink what they offer. Having lived through a tough recession and witnessed their parents cope with redundancy and job insecurity, it is not surprising that Millennials may not feel a strong sense of organisational allegiance.

Millennials have also been called 'entitled' and 'arrogant'. The May 2013 *Time* cover of 'The Me Me Me Generation' says it all.[31] But, are these inter-generational challenges really any different to the normal frustrations arising from the natural clash of age and experience with up-and-coming youth? And to some extent, are the Baby Boomers actually responsible for the problems they are now bemoaning?

Emerging from possibly stricter controls and a more disciplined framework, Boomer parents have compensated by wanting to provide freedom, grow confidence and build self-esteem among their young. Parental ties are harder to break and moving out of the family home is happening less. Rewards have been plentiful, yet too often devalued by their frequency and separation from achievement.

But some psychologists believe that this care has spilled over into fostering narcissism, and ultimately disappointment, when children discover that they cannot have it all – now.[32]

What is probably most fascinating is that, of all the generations criticising the Millennials, it seems that the Millennials themselves are most negative about themselves and have even called people in their age bracket 'self-absorbed', 'wasteful' and 'greedy'.[33] And many do not like the 'Millennial' label because it carries a tacit judgement.

As Simon Sinek said in a recent interview:

'What they don't see is the mountain. I don't care whether you go up the mountain quickly or slowly. But there is still a mountain.'

Wrapped up in the Millennial debate is the concern that social interactions today, though faster to initiate, are more fragile and short-term than before, and the immediacy of responses (especially 'likes', via social media) feeds impatience, anxiety and ever-worsening technological addiction. Peer pressure and the desire for peer approval are at an all-time high, and fear of missing out (FOMA) means that there is a need to be anywhere and everywhere. Authority does not hold the same sway, and there is no need to rebel because they do not see anything to rebel against.

Empathy is naturally affected: technological connection is precluding the need to be with people in person. And creativity is blocked because active exploration and deep reflection have been substituted for passive observation and endless distraction.[34]

Some organisations have introduced new initiatives, such as programmes titled 'Managing Millennials', which are aimed at merging generations together into a more workable solution.

> In some businesses, the Millennial turnover rate has prompted a recall of retired employees in order to retain a business' accumulated knowledge. This makes sense for those organisations wishing to hold on to their intellectual capital, acquired skills, corporate heritage and organisational culture. It seems to be a more logical step than investing in the younger generations that cannot commit to the longer term.

But perhaps trying to shoehorn Millennials into a traditional, hierarchical way of working is not the answer.

So, what can Millennials offer?

First of all, they are more tolerant and accepting of difference. Theirs is a world built less around 'them' and 'us' groupings, and more on a multifaceted, heterogenous and fluid set-up without constraints that merges work and life. Second, their self-esteem protects them against the angst that normally accompanies trial and error, and motivation is driven instead by a yearning for new experiences. And finally, they bring a social and environmental conscience that is forcing business leaders to sit up and take note.

Companies need to embrace and take advantage of what is now on offer. Millennials are a natural business disruption and a catalyst for change, and the questions they are raising about the employer-employee relationship and business in general are important for the progress of future work. And, as this chapter later proposes, perhaps we should stop using terminology that separates, and instead look for ways to integrate and unite.

Leadership is also about learning

The role of leadership should not be viewed as solely giving answers or setting direction, goals or objectives. Effective leaders are also learners who themselves facilitate learning in others.

We are far more engaged in a task when we are given the space and freedom to accomplish it for ourselves – and we are motivated on an intrinsic level. Learning to work with other people and solve problems collectively are skills that become hardwired in our brains.

The Toyota Production System involves all employees in the organisation – sales and marketing, administration, product development and management.

Toyota employees at every level have to learn the detail of each process in order to maintain the smooth operation of the company. This learning of detail is supported by the concept of the five Ss:

SEIRI – Sifting
SEITON – Sorting
SEISO – Sweeping and cleaning
SEIKETSU – Spick-and-span
SHITSUKE – Sustain

Daily meetings are held at each plant to give people the opportunity to discuss problems, improvements and decisions. Toyota employees are therefore constantly working and hardwiring these behaviours in the fabric of their brains.

Time is always the problem

Most leaders will claim that they know what to do in theory, but that they do not have the time to put new ideas into practice. It is often the case that tried-and-tested methods are familiar, comfortable, easy and quick, and therefore a lot more attractive than the prospect of trying something new.

And because we love feeling that we are solving problems quickly and efficiently, we keep doing it and our brain never has time to rest. The result is that, as pressures mount and change accelerates, we are stripped of the very same cognitive skills that are needed to meet these challenges.

If leaders are to create a working environment that gets the best out of their own brains and the brains of those they lead, it is more important than ever that a balance be found between activity and reflection. The faster we are expected to and want to work, the more imperative it is that we find some moments of peace and calm.

The irony is that the more we resist taking regular breaks, the more we actually need them.

Attitudes are contagious

Attitudes are contagious. Leaders should always question what kind of contagion their attitude brings to their environment and people. A leader's behaviour is constantly under scrutiny and being judged by those observing it.

A motivated workforce depends almost entirely on how motivated the leaders themselves appear.

However, because of the strong influence of our negativity bias, leaders need to keep reinforcing the positive in their communication, behaviour and practices. Positive emotions promote energy, counteract depression and anxiety, increase overall resilience and foster deeper connections with others.

The smallest act of kindness can make the biggest difference to other people.

Part 3: Stories and top tips

Manage Millennials? Get them to mentor YOU instead!

Rather than *manage* Millennials, some organisations have decided instead to harness the different skills Millennials bring to the working environment. Our digital age, with its associated demands, now requires new operational and learning paradigms.

Enter *reverse mentoring*. This is an initiative that originated in 1999, when the CEO of General Electric at the time, the late Jack Welch, instructed his senior leaders to find a junior mentor to teach them computer skills.

Today some Baby Boomer leaders are similarly using the Millennial generation to mentor their employees so that they can better understand rapid technological advances and social media opportunities.

Not surprisingly, the reverse-mentoring initiative is not widespread. For many senior executives, the prospect of learning from somebody younger and less experienced is anathema. However, the initiative is a great opportunity for people on either side of a generational gap to learn from each other, engage in a dialogue on an informal basis and view the world through the other's lens.

UnitedHealth Group, headquartered in Minneapolis, has implemented a reverse-mentoring programme pairing eight senior executives in its insurance division with eight Millennials – with an average age gap of 25 years.

The intention is that this programme will help executives look at the business differently and so help to prepare the working environment for the future.

PricewaterhouseCoopers, Cisco, Facebook, Microsoft and Procter & Gamble are among the companies that are following suit.

Perhaps the real answer here is in not labelling *Millennials* in the first place, thereby creating an outgroup (see Chapter 7, Our Brain and Biases). If we all see ourselves as belonging to the same group of working professionals, we may be able to work more effectively together.

Should we get rid of the performance appraisal?

Chapter 5, Our Brain and Language, discusses the format and content of the performance appraisal in detail, and offers some suggestions about how to construct more effective feedback conversations.

From a leadership perspective, the annual performance appraisal is a good example of a Theory X practice that may well have had its day.

Results from a recent Corporate Executive Board (CEB) survey highlight that 95% of managers are dissatisfied with their performance appraisal process, 90% of human resources heads claim they do not yield accurate information, and 80% of global organisations are considering major changes to their performance appraisal systems.[35]

There are a number of reasons why the conventional performance appraisal does not work:

The appraisal discussion is typically structured around the *feedback sandwich:* positive – negative – positive, which does not work well with our brain's natural negativity bias.
The appraisal discussion often uncovers the bias and the attitude of the appraiser rather than the person being appraised.
Leaders will often avoid difficult performance conversations until such time as the conversation can be positioned and protected by the formality of the annual discussion. They then shower the employee with feedback that can feel like an onslaught. Of course our brain will respond immediately to this and move into *fight or flight* mode.
Appraisers often focus on most recent performance and do not take into account a more overall view. The attention paid to past performance and not future potential does not really engender an appetite to learn and look ahead.
Many organisations are still using a rating system that was introduced in the 1970s to define human performance. This system ranks people on a 1–3 or 1–5 scale, with the lowest number or highest number denoting an outstanding performer and a problem employee being at the other end of the scale. The problem with this is that many leaders opt for the middle ground as it feels like the safest option: anything else needs to be justified or explained. In an attempt to distribute the scores more evenly, a forced ranking is often introduced.

General Electric became famous for its policy of having to rank certain individuals across the board and then let go of its bottom 10% (*rank and yank*). The problem with this forced ranking is that it feels exactly that: forced. And over time, it can backfire; when all the poor performers have been removed, the better performers are forced into the bottom percentile. So organisations may end up losing the people they actually do not want to lose.

Academics and business professionals alike have spoken out against any system that uses a numerical rating as a means of evaluating performance. The use of a scale that positions people relatively against others can make them feel dehumanised and disadvantaged: their *status* is compromised and they do not view the process as *fair* – two basic human needs, as explained earlier in Dr David Rock's SCARF model.

In 2013, a study looked at how different kinds of people react to negative feedback.[36]

Two hundred university employees were asked to rate how they felt about a recent performance evaluation; they were also asked questions about their personal goals. The researchers hypothesised that those who were more learning-oriented would benefit from a performance review.

The study found, however, that all employees, even those with stated learning goals and aspirations, disliked the performance reviews.

Consequently, the annual review is now being replaced in some organisations by a more realistic and accurate system, based on both the immediacy and the frequency of feedback.

Examples of organisations that have adopted new performance appraisal processes

In 2012, Adobe replaced its evaluations process on the basis that it was unpopular and ineffective. Under the old system, leaders focused on the past instead of directing people towards the future. Now Adobe has introduced a more informal process that works on the basis of continual and real-time feedback.

Microsoft redesigned its entire approach to appraising performance in 2013. It now focuses evaluation on results that people deliver together, leveraging and contributing to one another, emphasising continual learning and growth.

Accenture introduced a new process in 2015 that rejects forced ranking and is instead using an app to facilitate regular feedback.

Promote a culture of learning

At Google, employees have always set their own goals. Google leaders also focus on helping people learn – by encouraging them to learn from each other.

A programme called Googler to Googler enables employees to teach each other a wide variety of skills. Conceived by Chade-Meng Tan, an engineer at Google who started teaching mindfulness classes in the organisation, this initiative has enabled over 2,000 Google employees to teach over half of the company's education programmes across a workforce of 37,000 people.

Google's culture of learning means that Google employees also begin to promote the same philosophy themselves. Learning and helping others learn are disciplines that are now embedded in the way that Google people work together.

And so, if leaders promote a culture of collaborative learning, self-direction and self-discovery, people are more likely to strive for higher levels of success and achieve greater satisfaction and fulfilment.

> **'The real role of leadership is climate control, creating a climate of possibility.'**
>
> Sir Ken Robinson

A good culture brings out the best in all of us.

Top Tips
Remember: **TRUST**

Transform people's performance through regular, real time feedback and ongoing support. Show people that you are also learning and that you are open to receiving feedback. Try adopting new approaches that appreciate and reward desired behaviour.

Respect people's need for status, certainty, autonomy, relatedness and fairness. Create a positive working environment. As a leader, you can influence how people treat each other, communicate, work and learn together. Remember the importance of vulnerability and BRAVING connection.

Unite people behind a common purpose and language that connects rather than divides. Limit distractions and interruptions, especially in meetings. Focus is critical to building new neural networks and positive habits over time.

Set people breaks. Longer hours do not make us more productive. In fact, studies show that people who work long hours tend to be less effective.[37] Regular breaks increase productivity and encourage new thinking, and reflection and thought are critical to cognitive agility. Our brain needs time out and it always works best when it is relaxed and happy.

Touch people in an inspirational way. Be a positive contagion in your environment. This requires a high level of self-knowledge and self-reflection. Promote high standards of performance and behaviour. Your actions will speak louder than words ever will. Whatever you do as a leader will be noticed and replicated.

References for Chapter 11

1. The Global Workforce Leadership Survey. (2015). *Workplace Trends*. trends.com

2. Society for Human Resource Management. (2015). *Business and Human Capital Challenges Today and in the Future*, 9 December. shrm.org

3. Waltman, D.A. et al. (2011). 'Leadership and neuroscience: Can we revolutionize the way that inspirational leaders are identified and developed?' *Academy of Management*, February, 60–74.

4. Heisel, A.D., & Beatty, M.J. (2006). 'Are cognitive representations of friends' request refusals implemented in the orbitofrontal and dorsolateral prefrontal cortices? A cognitive neuroscience approach to "theory of mind" in relationships', *Journal of Social and Personal Relationships*, April, 249–65.

5. Salloway, S. et al. (2001). *The Frontal Lobes and Neuropsychiatric Illness*. Arlington, VA: American Psychiatric Association Publishing.

6. Goleman, D. (1996). *Emotional Intelligence*. London: Bloomsbury.

7. Baumeister, R.F. et al. (1998). 'Ego depletion: Is the active self a limited resource?' *Journal of Personality and Social Psychology*, 1252–65. https://doi.org/10.1037/0022-3514.74.5.1252

8. Vohs, K.D. et al. (2008). 'Making choices impairs subsequent self-control: A limited-resource account of decision making, self-regulation, and active initiative', *Journal of Personality and Social Psychology*, May, 883–98. http://doi: 10.1037/0022-3514.94.5.883

9. Rosenthal, R., & Jacobson, S.L. (1966). 'What you see is what you get. Teachers' expectancies: Determinates of pupils' IQ gains', *Psychological Reports*, August, 115–18.

10. Heitler, S. (2012). 'Psychological diagnosis: Dangerous, desirable, or both? How do labels hurt and how can they be helpful?' February Psychologytoday.com

11. Yeager, D.S. et al. (2014). 'The far-reaching effects of believing people can change: Implicit theories of personality shape stress, health, and achievement during adolescence', *Journal of Personality and Social Psychology*, 867–84. https://doi.org/10.1037/a0036335

12. Luft J., & Ingham, H. (1955). 'The Johari Window: A graphic model for interpersonal relations', *University of California Western Training Lab*.

13. Olivero, G. et al. (1997). 'Executive coaching as a transfer of training tool: Effects on productivity in a public agency', *Public Personnel Management*, Summer, 341–56.

14. Brown, B. (2018). *Dare to Lead*. New York: Random House.

15. Freeman, J. et al. (2015). 'Static and dynamic cues differentially affect the consistency of social evaluations', *Personality and Social Psychology Bulletin*. doi.org/10.1177/0146167215591495

16. Davila-Ross, M. et al. (2015). 'Chimpanzees (Pan troglodytes) produce the same types of "laugh faces" when they emit laughter and when they are silent', *PLOS ONE*. doi.org/10.1371/journal.pone.0127337

17. McNally, L. et al. (2012). 'Cooperation and the evolution of intelligence', *Proceedings of the Royal Society B: Biological Sciences*. doi.org/10.1098/rspb.2012.0206

18. Eisenberger, N. (2012). 'The neural bases of social pain: Evidence for shared representations with physical pain', *Psychosomatic Medicine*, February, 126–35.

19. Mischkowski, D. et al. (2019). 'A social analgesic? Acetaminophen (paracetamol) reduces positive empathy', *Frontiers in Psychology*. March. https://doi.org/10.3389/fpsyg.2019.005

20. Rock, D. (2009). *Your Brain at Work: Strategies for Overcoming Distraction, Regaining Focus, and Working Smarter All Day Long*. New York: HarperCollins.

21. Sapolsky, R. (2004). 'Social status and health in humans and other animals', *Annual Review of Anthropology*, June, 393–418.
22. Haney, C., Banks, W. C., & Zimbardo, P. G. (1973). 'A study of prisoners and guards in a simulated prison', *Naval Research Review*, 4–17.
23. *Business Insider*. (2013). 'The science of how temperature and lighting affect your productivity', 3 April. businessinsider.com
24. Münch, M. et al. (2012). 'Effects of prior light exposure on early evening performance, subjective sleepiness, and hormonal secretion', *Behavioral Neuroscience*, February, 196–203.
25. Williams, L.E., & Bargh, J.A. (2008). 'Experiencing physical warmth promotes interpersonal warmth', *Science*, October, 606–07.
26. McGregor, D. (2006). *The Human Side of Enterprise*. New York: McGraw-Hill.
27. 'How Millennials Want to Work and Live'. www.gallup.com
28. The Deloitte Global Millennial Survey. (2019). *Societal Discord and Technological Transformation Create a 'Generation Disrupted'*.
29. Gartner Research. (2018). '*Millennial Digital Workers Really Do Differ From Their Elders*', February.
30. ManpowerGroup. (2015). *Millennial Careers: 2020 Vision; Facts, Figures and Practical Advice from Workforce Experts*.
31. Stein, J. (2013). 'Millennials: The me me me generation', *Time*, May.
32. Twenge, J. (2009). *The Narcissism Epidemic. Living in the Age of Entitlement*. New York: Free Press.
33. Pew Research Centre. (2015). '*Most Millennials Resist the "Millennial" Label Generations in a Mirror: How They See Themselves*', September.
34. Hopkins, R. (2019). *From What Is to What If*. London: Chelsea Green Publishing.
35. Corporate Executive Board. (2013). *Human Resources Business Partner Survey*, 27 July. cebglobal.com
36. Culbertson, S. et al. (2013). 'Performance appraisal satisfaction', *Journal of Personnel Psychology*, 12(4). doi.org/10.1027/1866-5888/a000096
37. Staples Advantage. (2015). Workplace Index. *staplesadvantage.com*

"We are what we repeatedly do. Excellence, then, is not an act but a habit."

ARISTOTLE
Philosopher and scientist (384–322 BC)

Our Brain and Lifestyle

ABOUT THIS CHAPTER

The beginning of this book refers to the fact that we are hampered by our own biology, and many of us struggle with the pressures of keeping up with constant change and disruption.

As the digital world has sped up around us, we now spend most of our days sitting down!

The problems associated with our sedentary lifestyle are exacerbated by a lack of sleep and a poor diet. Many of us are compromising our long-term health, the negative effects of which are receiving increasing attention from scientists, researchers and business executives.

This final chapter explores our modern lifestyle and suggests ways in which we can maintain well-functioning brains and bodies. The three areas of lifestyle covered are sleep, physical exercise and nutrition.

Part 1: The science explained

Our brain and sleep

Why do we need to sleep?

We spend a third of our life asleep. Sleep plays a vital role in maintaining our health and wellbeing. During sleep, our brain is very active and works hard to maintain our physical and mental health.

Together with his research team, the neuroscientist and sleep expert Dr Matthew Walker has studied the impact of sleep on people's brains using functional magnetic resonance imaging (fMRI) to measure neural blood-flow activity, and electroencephalogram (EEG) tests to monitor neural electrical activity. The message is clear: every organ in the body is enriched through sleep.

A good night's sleep improves the way we learn and think. We also benefit from increased energy, a more robust immune system, sharper concentration, better decision-making and improved physical health.

From a neurological point of view, sleep consolidates our neural pathways by strengthening our memories and repairing our cells. For children, a deep sleep enables the release of growth hormone and promotes muscle development.

> Scientists have discovered a revolutionary new treatment that makes you live longer. It enhances your memory and makes you more creative. It makes you look more attractive. It keeps you slim and lowers food cravings. It protects you from cancer *and* dementia. It wards off colds and the flu. It lowers your risk of heart attacks and stroke, not to mention diabetes. You'll even feel happier, less depressed, and less anxious. Are you interested?
>
> Extract from '*Why We Sleep*' (page 107) by Matthew Walker.[1]

How do we go to sleep?

Our *neurotransmitters,* or brain chemicals, control whether we are asleep or awake. When we feel tired, two main neurotransmitters are involved in helping us go to sleep: *melatonin* and *adenosine*. Although research is still trying to uncover the precise role of these chemicals in sleep, our current understanding is that the build-up of both melatonin and adenosine in our body will make us feel drowsy.

Melatonin and adenosine normally peak together around 9pm, telling the body that we need to sleep.

Melatonin	Melatonin is released when our environment gets dark and switches off when it gets light again. The build-up of melatonin makes us want to go to sleep. This is why having a light switched on in the bedroom – even a light from an electronic device – may interfere with sleep.
Adenosine	Adenosine accumulates when we are awake. The more adenosine we have, the sleepier we feel. Sleep will lower our adenosine levels, but if we do not then get enough sleep, any residual adenosine in our body will make us tired. We may then need to sleep longer the following night to purge any excess adenosine. Caffeine interferes with the accumulation of adenosine and, as a result, gives us more energy.

The stages of sleep

We alternate between two types of sleep: *non-REM* and *REM* (rapid eye movement), as shown in Figure 12.1.

1) Non-REM sleep

We experience non-REM when we first go to sleep. There are four stages of non-REM sleep.

Stage One: **Light sleep**	We drift in and out of sleep and can be awakened easily. Our eyes move very slowly and muscle activity slows. As we enter sleep, our body may twitch involuntarily and experience a *hypnic* or *hypnagogic jerk*, which gives us a strange sense of falling. Scientists are divided as to why we do this: some claim that it is a final attempt by the brain to hold on to daytime motor control, while others say that this experience is a hangover reflex from more primitive days when we may have had to prevent ourselves from falling from a tree.
Stage Two: **Sleep spindles**	Our brainwaves now slow down, although there are still occasional bursts of rapid waves called *sleep spindles*. We spend the majority of our sleep in this stage. Sleep spindles refresh our brain, particularly in the hippocampus and the prefrontal cortex, areas that are essential for learning. The greater the number of sleep spindles we have, the better our cognitive functioning.[2]
Stage Three: **Deep sleep (1)**	Our brainwaves now become extremely slow. These are known as *delta waves* and they are interspersed with smaller, faster waves.
Stage Four: **Deep sleep (2)**	The brain now produces only delta waves, which is what we call deep sleep. During this stage, we have no eye movement or muscle activity. If we are awakened during deep sleep, we cannot adjust immediately and often feel disorientated for several minutes. Sleepwalking, whereby a person walks or may even perform complex behaviours while asleep, normally originates during deep sleep. Sleepwalking is more common in children than adults and is normally the result of sleep deprivation. It is very difficult to wake someone up during this stage of sleep.

2) REM sleep

We move into REM sleep approximately 90 minutes after falling asleep. REM sleep then occurs in cycles of between 90 and 120 minutes during the night.

This stage of sleep is when we dream and our brain speeds up and becomes very active. Our breathing also quickens and our eyes jerk rapidly in various directions (hence the name rapid eye movement).

During this stage, the muscles in our limbs become temporarily paralysed to prevent us from acting out our dreams. If we awaken during REM sleep, we often remember our dreams.

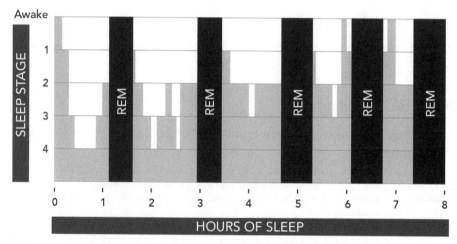

FIGURE 12.1: The alternating stages of non-REM and REM sleep

REM sleep may be reduced by antidepressants or smoking. Heavy smokers may find that nicotine withdrawal causes them to wake up every three or four hours during the night.

Alcohol may also affect our sleep quality and prevent us from accessing deep sleep.

Sleep cleans our brain

One of the most important functions of sleep is to clean our brain and remove the toxins that build up during the day.[3] Our brain's cleaning system is known as the *glymphatic system*. This system involves the flow of cerebrospinal fluid, which surrounds our brain and spinal cord, through our brain. The glymphatic system is similar to our *lymphatic network* of glands, which filters waste out of our body. In our brain, we have a specialised network that relies on *glial cells* (hence *glymphatic*), which support and supply nutrients to our neurons.

When we sleep, cerebrospinal fluid moves more quickly through our brain than when we are awake, thereby flushing out any toxins or waste more effectively. One of these toxins, *beta-amyloid,* is known to accumulate in the brains of patients suffering from Alzheimer's Disease. Sleep may therefore have an important role to play in the prevention or delay of dementia.

Our body clock

The biological changes that occur during the day are known as *circadian* (from the Latin meaning 'around a day') *rhythms* that constitute our 24-hour internal body clock.

These rhythms are controlled by a master clock, a structure of about 20,000 neurons situated in the hypothalamus, called the *suprachiasmatic nucleus* (SCN), as shown in Figure 12.2.

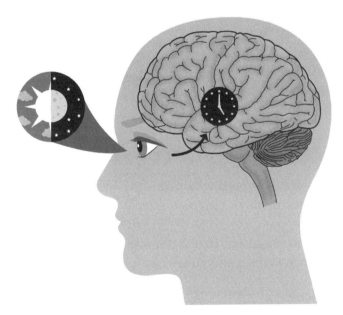

FIGURE 12.2: Our SCN or master clock

The **SCN** plays an important role in our sleep/wake cycle and governs our body temperature, hormonal release and blood pressure.[4]

When light enters the eye, signals travel along the optic nerve to the SCN and then on to several brain regions, including the pineal gland, which switches off the melatonin that makes us drowsy at night.

Our circadian rhythms normally follow the natural 24-hour clock and we feel more awake or sleepy at certain periods during the day (see Figure 12.3).

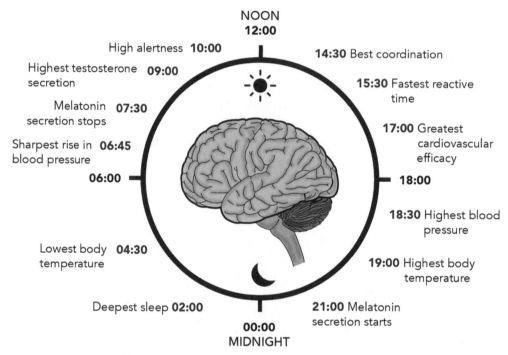

FIGURE 12.3: Our 24-hour circadian rhythm

These rhythms are disrupted when we travel across time zones, causing jet lag. It can take several days to reset our body clock and resume normal sleeping patterns.

A recent study has suggested that just a weekend camping is an effective way to reset our body clock since it encourages us to be more aligned with the natural light/dark cycle.[5]

How much sleep do we need?

Scientists continue to debate how much sleep we need and how this amount will vary throughout our lifetime.

A review of scientific literature across the world has recently been conducted to consider how the amount of sleep we get relates to performance, health and safety. Based on this review, we now have the first recommended age-specific sleep ranges for most age groups as detailed in Figure 12.4.[6]

Age	Sleep range (hours per day)
Newborns (0–3 months)	14–17
Infants (4–11 months)	12–15
Toddlers (1–2 years)	11–14
Pre-schoolers (3–5 years)	10–13
School-age children (6–13 years)	9–11
Teenagers (14–17 years)	8–10
Younger adults (18–25 years)	7–9
Adults (26–64 years)	7–9
Older adults (65+ years)	7–8

FIGURE 12.4: Recommended sleep ranges

Why do teenagers need more sleep than adults?

Teenagers may follow a slightly different circadian rhythm since adolescence causes a sleep phase delay. Teenagers' melatonin levels rise later at night than in other age groups, making it difficult for them to fall asleep before 11 pm.

This sleep phase delay can result in sleep deprivation because they are still expected to wake up for school. It is therefore important to keep the lights dim in the evening to encourage melatonin production at night and then to switch it off by bringing light into the room as soon as possible in the morning. And, of course, we should remove all electronics that detract from sleep.

The importance of alpha waves before sleep

When we are awake, our two dominant brainwaves are *beta* and *alpha waves:*

Beta waves are active when we are thinking, reading, working or talking.

Alpha waves help the brain to slow down and relax. They also occur during the early stages of meditation.

Our brain normally maintains a healthy balance between beta and alpha waves. If we have too many beta waves, we find it hard to relax, while too many alpha waves can slow us down too much.

Because our alpha waves are relaxing, they are often the gateway to sleep. The main benefits of alpha waves are that they help us to relax and they slow down our heart rate. This gives our body a chance to recover and helps to consolidate our learning and memory.

Different types of insomnia

Insomnia is a condition that prevents us either going to sleep or staying asleep. There are different types of insomnia.

Acute insomnia	Occurs for brief periods and is usually caused by short-term stress such as bad news, travel or a change in our life. Normally, acute insomnia resolves itself without any need for treatment.
Chronic insomnia	Longer-term issue where we find it difficult either to fall asleep or stay asleep for at least three nights a week over a period of three or more months. There are a number of causes of chronic insomnia, some of which are described later in this chapter.
Comorbid insomnia	Occurs with another condition, such as depression or any pain in the body that makes it hard for us to sleep.
Onset insomnia	We have difficulty falling asleep.
Maintenance insomnia	We cannot stay asleep and we often wake up during the night. This occurs typically when we cross time zones.

What causes insomnia?

There are various causes of insomnia. A number of medical conditions, such as nasal or sinus problems, indigestion, arthritis, back pain or Parkinson's Disease can all lead to insomnia.

Other disorders linked to insomnia	
Depression	Worsened by insomnia.
Anxiety	We worry about past and future events. One can worsen the other.
Restless legs syndrome	An uncomfortable urge to move the legs.
Sleep apnoea	The airways become obstructed and oxygen levels drop.

How to treat insomnia

If we are having problems sleeping, we need to address these. Poor sleep should not become a way of life!

It is always a good idea to examine our sleep habits and ensure that we are creating an environment conducive to a good night's sleep. Healthier sleep habits are critical to a healthy lifestyle.

For example, we should ensure that our bedroom is dark to stimulate the production of melatonin, and cool to compensate for our rise in body temperature during the night. We should also have no distractions around us, such as our mobile telephone or computer.

If we are really struggling to sleep, lying in bed worrying could make matters worse. It is better to get up and do something relaxing until we feel sleepy – and then go back to bed.

Why does lack of sleep make us hungry?

Sleep helps to keep our hormones in balance, and lack of sleep can upset this balance very quickly. *Ghrelin* is a hormone that makes us feel hungry, while *leptin* is a hormone that indicates we have had enough to eat and helps the body maintain its weight.

A lack of sleep causes increased levels of ghrelin and decreased levels of leptin, causing us to feel hungry (see Figure 12.5). This is why when we are jet-lagged, we crave high-energy foods such as carbohydrates.

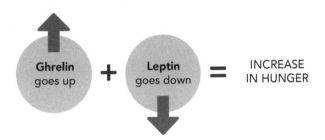

FIGURE 12.5: A lack of sleep makes us hungry

Why do we dream?

Dreams are effectively images that we experience when we are asleep. Our most vivid dreams occur during REM sleep, when our brain is most active. Some experts say we dream at least four to six times per night.

Dreaming is important to our health and wellbeing. Studies have found that when we are not allowed to dream, we experience more anxiety, depression, and concentration and coordination problems.[7] Alcohol and drugs affect the REM cycle and therefore our dreams.

Why do some of us regularly remember our dreams while others are unable to recall anything?

This question has been investigated by researchers who have discovered a specific brain region for encoding and remembering dreams.[8]

Using positron emission tomography (PET), researchers measured the brain activity of two groups of people during wakefulness and sleep:

Group 1: People who remember their dreams five days a week on average

Group 2: People who remember their dreams twice a month on average

In both wakefulness and sleep, the first group showed higher activity in two areas of the brain (*medial prefrontal cortex* and the *temporo-parietal junction*) that are responsible for paying attention to external stimuli – in particular, sound.

This study supports earlier brain research showing that damage to these regions can result in no dream recall whatsoever.

And so it seems that the more sensitive we are to what is going on around us when we are awake, the more likely we are to recall what happens to us when we are asleep.

Our brain and physical exercise

The brain is a muscle

Our brain is like every other muscle in our body in that we need to exercise it to keep it fit and healthy. While mental activities are good for our brain, physical exercise has an even more positive effect on brain function.

Exercise reduces our resistance to insulin, making it easier for us to break down sugars in our body. Exercise also reduces inflammation and stimulates the production of chemicals that maintain the health and survival of our brain cells.

Up until recently, scientists have claimed that exercising for 20 minutes is beneficial for our brain health.[9]

But, according to a 2018 study by Matthew Heath, Professor of Neuroscience at the University of Ontario, it now seems that even ten minutes of aerobic exercise improves our ability to concentrate.[10]

When we have to focus in detail on anything, a small region of the eye's retina, called the fovea, undergoes rapid rotations. These rotations are called *saccadic eye movements* and are directed by networks in the *frontal* and *parietal* lobes. Using specialised equipment to track these saccadic eye movements, the study showed that a ten-minute burst of moderate to vigorous physical activity (MVPA) on a stationary bicycle was enough to improve brain performance.

This suggests that any cognitive tasks benefit from some quick and vigorous physical activity beforehand.

A 2016 study found that schizophrenia patients who engaged in physical activity improved their cognitive function and quality of life.[11]

Exercise grows our brain . . .

Our brain uses 20% of all the oxygen in our body. When we exercise, we increase our heart rate, which, in turn, pumps more oxygen to our brain. In fact, it is regular aerobic exercise of moderate intensity, rather than low-impact alternatives, that enlarges the size of the hippocampus, which is specifically involved in memory and learning.[12]

This is an important finding because the hippocampus is also the area of the brain affected by dementia. Researchers say one new case of dementia is detected globally every four seconds. They estimate that by the year 2050 more than 115 million people worldwide will have dementia. Alzheimer's Disease is now the number one killer in the United Kingdom.

Physical exercise also leads to a higher concentration of growth factors in the brain, which makes it easier for our brain to grow new connections.[13] Studies are now pointing to other brain regions that show increased volume through exercise, such as the *prefrontal cortex* and *medial temporal cortex*. These areas are both important for the formation and consolidation of memories.[14]

. . . and even reverses signs of ageing

Although our brain growth slows as we age and our brain starts to shrink, exercise may nevertheless prevent or even reverse this trend. Six months of aerobic exercise has been found to increase brain volume and reduce age-related brain changes in a group of people aged between 60 and 79.[15]

Regular exercise by adults in this age group, even after as few as four weeks, has also been shown to cause an increase in cognitive ability.

Exercise alleviates symptoms of depression

Studies have shown that running has an antidepressant effect on our brain.[16] If patients suffering from depression exercise for five days a week over three months, they can reduce their symptoms by half.[17]

Regular exercise also releases endorphins (the word *endorphin* is derived from the words *endogenous morphine,* which is our internally produced painkiller) and increases our body's temperature. This has a calming effect and also reduces *cortisol,* the hormone we produce when we are stressed.

Exercise may not be the only treatment for depression, but it is certainly an effective means of reducing many of the symptoms people experience.

Exercise helps us to sleep

Because exercise reduces stress and makes us tired, it may help to regulate our body clock so that we sleep more effectively. Outdoor exercise during daytime is particularly beneficial because we absorb natural sunlight.

The time of day that we exercise will vary for each of us and will depend on our *chronotype,* which refers to our personal biological clock or natural preference for going to sleep or when we feel at our most alert and energetic. For example, some of us may prefer to exercise in the morning, while others prefer the evening.

We often refer to our chronotype when we say, 'I am/am not a morning person', which is discussed in Part 2 of this chapter.

Our brain and nutrition
What food is best for our brain?

We are frequently flooded with recommendations for food that we should/should not be eating for the sake of our health. In amongst all the advice and warnings, it seems that there are some foods that all scientists agree are good for our brain.

Our brain is about 70% fat and it needs omega-3, an *essential fatty acid* (EFA) to facilitate communication between neurons and repair any damage. The quality of our brain cells depends on the availability of EFAs and, since the body cannot produce EFAs on its own, we need to otain them through diet. Sources of EFAs include linseed (flaxseed), soya beans, pumpkin seeds, walnuts and their oils.

Omega-3 is particularly important in maintaining a healthy myelin sheath, the fatty substance that insulates our nerve fibres and enables proper functioning of our nervous system.

Omega-3 fats occur naturally in oily fish (salmon, trout, mackerel, herring, sardines, pilchards and kippers) in the form of EPA (*eicosapentaenoic acid*) and DHA (*docosahexaenoic acid*), which are the most important group of nutrients for our brain. Most modern diets do not provide sufficient omega-3 fats, and it is estimated that 70% of us do not get enough. Low DHA levels have been linked to an increased risk of Alzheimer's Disease and memory loss.

Other recommended foods include:

Blackcurrants (vitamin C)	increase cognitive agility.
Blueberries (vitamins K and C)	improve memory, reduce DNA damage and slow cognitive decline.
Broccoli (vitamin K, choline and folic acid)	strengthens cognitive abilities and memory consolidation.
Chicken, turkey, eggs and soya beans (vitamin B6)	enhance cognitive performance and raise mood.
Lamb, beef, feta and cottage cheese (vitamin B12)	protect against brain shrinkage (especially in the elderly).
Nuts (vitamin E and DHA)	support brain health, protect neurons and prevent cognitive decline.
Pumpkin seeds (zinc, magnesium and B vitamins)	boost memory, focus and cognitive function.
Tomatoes (carotenoids, calcium and vitamins A, C and K)	eliminate free radical damage that occurs in dementia.

The link between mood and food

Mood and food are definitely connected. Our *neurotransmitters* regulate our mood, while our food affects the regulation of our neurotransmitters. Proteins help us to manufacture *amino* acids – chemicals that are converted to neurotransmitters to help regulate our mood. A diet rich in omega-3 aids in easing depression and lowering suicide risk.[18]

Our food intake needs to maintain the right balance of neurotransmitters, as Figure 12.6 illustrates.

Related amino acid	Role	Some symptoms of deficiency	Food
Neurotransmitter: Serotonin			
Tryptophan	Inhibitory neurotransmitter. Plays an important role in regulating mood, happiness, relaxation, appetite, memory, bowel function, learning and hormonal release.	Depressed mood, anxiety, panic attacks, low energy, sleeping problems, feeling tense and irritable, impaired memory and concentration.	Fish, eggs, chicken, turkey and other meats. Iron, zinc. Vitamins B3, B6 and C.
Neurotransmitter: Dopamine			
Tyrosine	Both excitatory and inhibitory neurotransmitter. Responsible for movement, memory, pleasurable reward, attention, desire and drive to get things done. Known as our *motivation molecule*. Controls movement and posture.	Memory problems, poor concentration, difficulty initiating or completing tasks, lack of energy, lack of motivation, addictions, cravings, compulsions, a loss of satisfaction and libido. Too little dopamine is implicated in Parkinson's Disease.	Almonds, avocados, dairy products, pumpkin and sesame seeds. Folic acid, vitamin B6, magnesium and zinc.
Neurotransmitter: Glutamate			
Glutamate/ Glutamic acid	Major excitatory neurotransmitter in our brain. Involved in cognition, memory and learning.	Insomnia, problems concentrating, mental exhaustion and depleted energy.	Cured meats, aged cheese, soy sauce and soy protein, mushrooms, ripe tomatoes, broccoli, peas, walnuts, grape juice.
Neurotransmitter: GABA			
Glutamine Taurine Theanine	Inhibitory neurotransmitter. GABA (gamma-amino butyric acid) acts as a natural sedative and tranquilliser and calms nervous activity. Contributes to motor control and vision.	Anxiety disorders, racing thoughts, bipolar disorder, mania, poor impulse control, panic attacks, cold hands, shortness of breath.	Halibut, mackerel, legumes, brown rice, wheat, bran, bananas, spinach. Vitamins B3, B6 and B12.
Neurotransmitter: Acetylcholine			
Choline	Widely distributed excitatory neurotransmitter. Major impact on wakefulness, attentiveness and arousal. Needed to turn short-term memories into long-term ones. Released to activate muscles. (Botox is a neurotoxin that blocks the effect of acetylcholine, preventing the facial muscles from moving.)	Low energy levels, memory loss, learning problems, muscle aches, cognitive decline. People with Alzheimer's Disease have altered levels of acetylcholine. Also implicated in Parkinson's Disease.	Almonds, blueberries, cruciferous vegetables, cheese, eggs, fish, chicken. Vitamin B6.
Neurotransmitter: Noradrenaline			
Tyrosine	Excitatory neurotransmitter. Triggers changes in the body in response to stress (increased oxygen, heart rate and glucose) to raise our alertness and *fight or flight* capacity. Important for attentiveness, emotions, dreaming and learning.	Depression, loss of alertness, memory problems, lack of energy, focus and motivation.	Almonds, avocados, dairy products, pumpkin and sesame seeds. Folic acid, vitamin B6, magnesium and zinc.

FIGURE 12.6: Neurotransmitters, amino acids and food

What happens when we fast?

We fuel our bodies by eating food in the form of carbohydrates, fats and proteins which are broken down by the cells to release a high energy chemical called *adenosine triphosphate (ATP)*. **ATP** is essential for cellular function and muscular activity. This chemical reaction to produce energy is what we call *metabolism*.

Carbohydrates are broken down into *glucose*, our body's main energy source, and are most efficient at producing ATP, so they are first to be metabolised. Next, fats are broken down into *fatty acids*. Proteins can be used for energy, but their primary use is to be broken down into *amino acids*, our building blocks for hormones, muscles, hair and skin.

In order to survive, our body must be able to maintain glucose levels. The brain uses about 120 grams of glucose a day! Low glucose is known as *hypoglycaemia* and high glucose is known as *hyperglycaemia*, and both conditions are detrimental to our health.

Our glucose levels are balanced by *homeostasis* (our internal steady state, as explained in Chapter 1, Our Brain), which is regulated by two hormones, *insulin* and *glucagon*. When glucose levels are high, **insulin** is produced to drive levels down; when glucose levels are low, **glucagon** releases stored glucose into the blood stream.

During a period of fasting, we have fewer carbohydrates available and so our liver turns instead to our fatty acids, producing chemicals known as *ketone bodies* or *ketones*, as an important energy source. When glucose levels drop, **ketones** go up and vice versa. Because our bodies conserve energy during fasting, our metabolism becomes more efficient, lowering our heart rate and blood pressure.

As well as the obvious benefit of reducing body fat and weight, the release of ketones makes our brain more resilient by triggering the release of an important molecule called *brain-derived neurotropic factor (BDNF)*. **BDNF** helps the growth of neurons and strengthens neural connections in areas of the brain responsible for learning and memory.

Fasting has been linked to a number of health and brain benefits:

Increased longevity and improved protection against disease such as cancer[19, 20]
Lowered blood sugar levels and decreased insulin resistance, allowing glucose to be transported in the body more efficiently and stored body fat to be more accessible[21]
Increased levels of human growth hormone that aids fat loss and muscle gain[22]
Cellular repair through autophagy (from the Greek: *auto* meaning 'self', and *phagy* meaning 'to eat'), a process that removes old proteins that have built up in the cells[23]
Decreased levels of inflammation[24, 25]
Improved brain function[26]

Changing the timing of our meals may also make a difference. Early time-restricted feeding (eating only between 8am–2pm) has been shown to benefit the body's metabolism and cellular repair more effectively than fasting and then eating later in the day.[27]

But it is also important to acknowledge that fasting is not for everyone and should be considered carefully. Whilst intermittent fasting may be easier than continual fasting, for some people it may be more practical to focus on establishing healthier eating habits, such as avoiding sugars and processed food (following instead a plant-based diet), eating less at night and allowing the body to burn fat by not snacking between meals.

Clinical studies continue to highlight the range of benefits offered by fasting. Researchers are now suggesting that information about fasting should be included as part of medical school training and that physicians should be educated on the right way to provide advice and guidance to their patients.[28]

Part 2: Impact on our daily life

Our brain and sleep

We need to sleep

All of us need to sleep. The longer we have been awake, the stronger our desire to sleep. The longer we have been asleep, the more the pressure to sleep reduces.

But we are an arrogant species and we think we can override our body clock and beat sleep. Many of us are either not aware of the risks of sleep deficiency or we choose to ignore the signs. We believe that we can survive on a few hours of sleep a night and still function efficiently. In fact, we often do not even realise that we are suffering from lack of sleep.

Studies show that our ability to drive a car is as much affected by lack of sleep as if we were under the influence of alcohol. In addition, lack of sleep can cause an increase in hyperactivity and can affect our ability to focus on tasks – symptoms that are very similar to attention deficit hyperactivity disorder (ADHD).

What is the impact of sleep deficiency?

Sleep deficiency can be fatal. Even one night without sleep will have a significant impact on our brain and body. When we continually do not have enough sleep, we can suffer from both health and cognitive problems that may impact our decisions, behaviour and relationships. Severe sleep deficiency can contribute towards mental health issues such as stress, depression, extreme risk-taking and even perhaps suicide. Physical issues associated with lack of sleep may also be increased, such as risk of stroke, obesity and heart problems.

Sleep deficiency can cause our blood sugar levels to rise, making us more at risk of diabetes. Our neurons may also become depleted in energy, affecting our immune system and leaving us vulnerable to infection and illness.

Shift work can be dangerous

Shift workers who work erratic hours against their natural body clock are more likely to suffer from conditions such as cardiovascular disease, breast cancer and digestive problems. Shift work can also prematurely age the brain by over six years.[29]

> Research has shown that medical interns on the night shift are more likely to misinterpret hospital test records than the interns working during the day.

Scientists have examined methods of reducing shift-work tiredness, including bright lights, shorter schedules and intermittent naps.

Even though the brain is affected by night-shift work, it can recover and return to regular function – but this can take over five years.

In 1984, more than 40 tons of toxic gas leaked from a pesticide plant in Bhopal, India, killing thousands of people. More than 150 people were left severely disabled and 22,000 have since died of their injuries. This occurred during a night shift.

In 1986, the Chernobyl nuclear power plant went into meltdown, causing the deaths of thousands of people from radiation-related illnesses. The disaster was caused by a mistake during a night shift.

In 1989, the *Exxon Valdez* oil spill, during which 750,000 barrels of oil were spilt off the coast of Alaska, happened during a night shift.

Why are power naps good for us?

The *power nap* is increasingly being heralded as an effective way to boost our brain function. Power naps take us into Stages one and two of non-REM sleep and should ideally last for 20 to 30 minutes. Memory consolidation starts while we nap and this results in increased productivity, increased cognitive functioning, enhanced creativity and greater alertness.

However, if we nap too long, we enter Stage three sleep and may feel more sleepy and disorientated if we are awakened during this stage.

So power naps can make us more productive and energetic and reboot our system, improving our cognitive ability and sensitivity to sensory input.[30] They also decrease our risk of cardiovascular disease.[31]

Are we larks or owls?

There is much debate about whether morning people (*larks*) are more effective than evening people (*owls*). As mentioned earlier in this chapter, the term for whether we are morning or evening people is our *chronotype*.

About 10% of people are true larks and 20% are true owls, with the majority of us somewhere in the middle. Most people claim to be at their peak performance at a certain time during the day. For larks, this preference will be early morning, and for owls, it will be in the evening.

Evidence is contradictory about which **chronotype** is more successful. Some studies claim that larks report higher levels of happiness, productivity and fulfilment than owls. This may be explained by larks reporting that they feel they have greater choice and control over their mornings, while owls claim to suffer from lower wellbeing, higher stress and lower physical activity.[32] One study has claimed that owls are less reliable and less emotionally stable,[33] and more prone to depression and eating disorders, while another suggests that owls have higher IQs than larks.[34]

Whatever the research, it seems that culture plays a role in establishing our chronotype. For example, some cultures are constructed around evening activities, while others place more emphasis on daytime productivity. Of course, difficulties then arise when people cross over from one culture to another and need to fit in with differences in timekeeping as well as different time zones.

As we learn more about how our brains operate, perhaps we should be questioning working practices and adapting our schedules to fit in with our chronotypes, in order that we can give the best of ourselves.

Our brain and physical exercise

Is sitting the new smoking?

We sit for longer than we sleep! But scientists are now telling us that sitting for longer than six hours a day could be as bad for us as smoking a packet of cigarettes.

The human body is not designed to sit for long periods. We expend no or very little energy when we sit.

A number of studies highlight the risks of sitting all day:

Men who were sedentary for more than 23 hours a week had a 64% greater risk of dying from heart disease than those who were sedentary fewer than 11 hours a week.[35]

General risk of mortality is 1.54 times higher among people who spend most of their day sitting, compared to those who sit infrequently.[36]

Sitting at the computer or in front of the television leads to weight gain and obesity.[37]

Children who watch just one hour of television a day are 50 to 60% more likely to be overweight and 58 to 73% more likely to be obese, compared to children who watch less than an hour.[38]

To counteract the harmful effects of sitting, we need to stand up every 20–30 minutes, walk around and move our muscles. If we wait for longer than an hour, our fat-burning enzymes decline by 90%.

Can we walk and work at the same time?

The risks of excessive sitting are clear. As a result, studies have been looking at the benefits of the standing or treadmill desk.

Standing desks are gaining in popularity in offices all over the world. But it seems that standing is just the start. Standing burns 50 more calories per hour, but to gain optimal benefits it is important to walk around too.[39]

Although there is still some debate about their definitive benefits, treadmill desks are now being linked to improved attention and short-term recall.[40] Participants in studies of these desks' cognitive effects have reported paying better attention than the sedentary control group.

An electroencephalogram (EEG), a test that detects electrical activity in our brain using small electrodes attached to the scalp, has also revealed increased brain function in the region associated with memory and attention in those using the treadmill desk.

Our brain and nutrition

Stress either starves us or makes us fatter

Stress affects our appetite in various ways. Some of us eat less when we are stressed, while others eat more.

When we are stressed, we activate our fight or flight response and increase our levels of adrenaline (epinephrine), and suppress calming neurotransmitters such as serotonin, which regulates mood. Lack of serotonin increases anxiety and reduces feelings of hunger.

On the other hand, eating may become a coping mechanism and a strategy to deal with stress in our life. We may reach for high-sugar foods that give us instant energy, and then become conditioned to eat and crave the wrong food every time we feel stressed or anxious. We may feel unhappy that we are eating too much, but this does not reduce the craving to eat – in fact, we may want to eat even more!

The problem is that, if we gain weight through stress-induced eating, we are more likely to hyperventilate and suffer panic attacks. This in turn makes us crave the wrong food. So we need to break the cycle, ignore our instinctive response and understand that we have to work harder to maintain a healthy lifestyle when we are feeling stressed.

Qualified dieticians are a helpful resource when trying to establish the food that is best for your individual system and overall wellbeing.

Fat OR sugar – but not both!

There is no food in the natural world that combines both fat and sugar. In other words, our brain and body are not designed to eat cake or doughnuts! Research has shown that a combination of fat and sugar is so addictive that it could be one of the causes of today's obesity epidemic.

> In a study with rats, one group was given a sugar-rich diet and another group was given fat.[41] Neither group of rats gained much weight on either diet. However, when fat and sugar were combined (in cheesecake) the reaction of the animals was completely different. The rats did not just eat the food – they binged on it, even when they should have been full, and gained massive amounts of weight.
>
> Whilst a rat on a fat-only diet might take nearly two months to gain a small amount of weight, the cheesecake-eating rats gained significant

weight after just seven days. What was even more interesting was that, having eaten cheesecake, they showed absolutely no interest in healthy food afterwards, preferring to starve instead. They were even prepared to endure mild electric shocks to be able to eat the junk food, demonstrating that this had now become an addiction.

Is obesity linked to dementia?

For years, scientists have been reporting that being obese, at all ages, may be damaging the brain. In children as young as seven years old, studies have shown that obesity can lead to memory problems.[42]

A diet that is rich in sugar and fat causes inflammation of the hippocampus (the brain region used for memory and learning) and consequent memory impairment.[43] The hippocampus is particularly sensitive to diet. If the hippocampus is damaged prior to weight gain, through eating foods high in saturated fat and refined sugar, it may then cause the brain to crave the very foods that initially caused the dysfunction. Obesity is therefore often the result of a negative, repetitive cycle (see Figure 12.7).

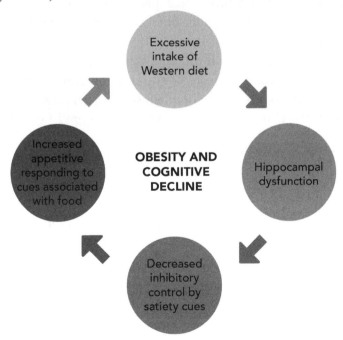

FIGURE 12.7: Obesity and cognitive decline – a vicious cycle

Adapted from Davidson et al.[44]

Can we get to the brain through the gut?

Our gut is teeming with trillions of organisms (including bacteria, yeasts and viruses) making up between 1% and 3% of our body weight. These organisms are collectively known as our *microbiome*. Our **microbiome** performs an essential role in digestion as well as protecting us against pathogens.

Many diseases, such as cancer, Alzheimer's Disease, Parkinson's Disease, obesity and depression, have been found to involve a disruption of the microbiome.

Although the exact relationships between obesity, inflammation, depression and the microbiome are still unclear, mounting evidence suggests that our microbiome plays a significant role in metabolism, the immune system, the regulation of inflammation in the body, as well as our overall brain health.[45]

Links continue to be made between the microbiome and mental health; one study has shown that obese people have a 38% higher chance of having depression.[46]

How are the gut and brain related?

Our gut and brain have a strong connection. Our gut communicates directly with our brain in a bidirectional relationship known as the *gut–brain axis* via the longest nerve in our autonomic nervous system, the *vagus nerve* (see Figure 12.8). A number of the neurotransmitters that play a key role in our mood, such as serotonin, dopamine and GABA (mentioned earlier in the chapter), are produced by our microbiome.

The blood-brain barrier, which protects the brain from unwanted molecules and cells in the bloodstream, is affected by our microbiome.[47] Our early years are a period of critical importance in the composition of our microbiome and an intact blood-brain barrier.[48] If the microbiome has been altered by childhood diet or

---

What is the link between the gut and depression?

Until very recently, most studies involving the microbiome have involved animals, but a 2019 Belgian study involving 1,054 people (173 of whom had been diagnosed with depression or claimed a poor-quality life) has found the absence of certain types of microbes, *coprococcus* and *dialister*, among those with depression.[49] The study also found the depressed people had an increase in bacteria implicated in Crohn's disease, an inflammatory condition, strengthening links between inflammation and depression.

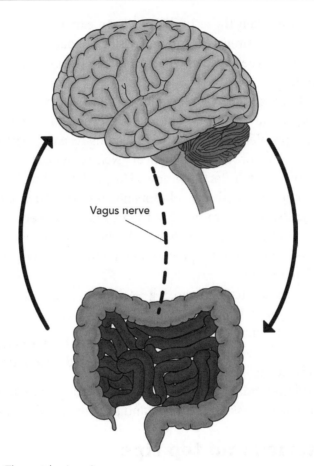

FIGURE 12.8: The gut-brain axis

medication, the blood-brain barrier may become more permeable, allowing in harmful bacteria, which may affect brain development, and even lead to serious illness.

A healthy microbiome is varied: the more diverse the range of foods, the more our gut strengthens. There are two groups of *probiotics* (beneficial live bacteria), known as *lactobacillus* and *bifidobacterium*, that produce GABA (gamma-aminobutyric acid), a neurotransmitter that is involved in reducing anxiety, as explained earlier in this chapter.

Lactobacillus	most commonly found in yogurt and other fermented foods. May ease symptoms of diarrhoea and lactose intolerance.
Bifidobacterium	also found in some dairy products. Helps to prevent constipation and give the immune system a boost.

People who have taken these probiotics have experienced improvements in feelings of wellbeing, less tiredness and better sleep quality.[50]

The association between food and mental health issues continues to be a topic of growing interest.

John Cryan, Professor of Neuroscience at the University College Cork and principal investigator at APC Microbiome, believes that today's epidemics of depression and gut problems are related. His leading research with the now retired Professor Ted Dinan, previously Clinical Neurosciences and Professor of Psychological Medicine at St Bartholomew's Hospital, London, has helped to raise awareness of the microbiome-brain relationship, referring to *probiotics* (explained previously) and *prebiotics* (fibre helping the desirable bacteria to flourish) that enhance mental health as *psychobiotics*.[51] The hope is that we will start to see a more integrated approach to prescribing medication, where diet is a key consideration of treatment.

The gut is our largest sensory organ, and understanding how it works is critical to our understanding of human behaviour and overall wellbeing. The more we know about our gut and our microbiome – and their relationship in our brain development and function – the better able we are to address our physical and psychological health.

As doctor and author, Giulia Enders, says:[52]

'Our 'self' is created in our head and our gut.'

Part 3: Stories and top tips

Sleep disorders are on the rise

With the proliferation of electronic devices across the world, we are now seeing an increase in sleep disorders in both children and adults.

Studies have highlighted the damaging effects of the blue light that emanates from laptops; it activates our SCN, or master clock, which in turn, decreases melatonin, resulting in a lack of sleep.[53]

Teenagers are most at risk of sleep disorders because of their obsession with social networking and video games; this disturbs their sleep patterns at night and makes them more tired during the day.

> Researchers suggest that over the last four decades the average total hours of sleep has decreased to less than seven hours per person per night.[54]

The impact of this sleep deprivation is being linked to increased insulin resistance and higher numbers of people suffering from obesity and diabetes.

Both deep sleep and REM sleep are particularly important for our brain growth and development, particularly in young children. These stages of sleep help the brain to hold on to important information and get rid of useless detail, preparing the brain for a new day of input.

When we learn something, we build a web of synaptic connections that are then reorganised during REM sleep. If we do not have enough REM sleep our brain is not refreshed, organised and ready to take in new information. As a consequence, we have problems focusing and learning the next day.

Sleep clinics are now looking at why children have trouble moving into deep delta sleep or REM sleep. Many teenagers are now sleep-deprived and get less than six hours' sleep at night. This lack of sleep, accompanied by higher levels of the hormone ghrelin, which makes us feel hungry, is also leading to more cases of obesity.

Teatime? Refuel in a sleep pod!

In response to growing research that extols the benefits of the power nap, a number of companies, including Google, Facebook, Procter & Gamble and NASA, are offering their workers sleep pods. These pods offer a break in the middle of the working day – and they are timed for a 20-minute nap. So when energy levels drop at around 3 pm, employees can refuel in a sleeping pod for 20 minutes. This power nap is reported as increasing alertness by around 30%.

Airports, including Abu Dhabi International, are now offering similar pods to people in transit, while many other companies are capitalising on this trend.

For example, Arianna Huffington's *Huffington Post*, based in New York City, now has two rooms designated for power naps after Ms Huffington collapsed from exhaustion at her desk one night. Arianna Huffington is now a strong advocate of health and wellness at work.

Running our way to happiness

For several years, a primary school in Stirling, Scotland, has made all its pupils walk or run a mile each day. The teachers at St Ninian's take their pupils out of lessons on to a specially built circuit around the school's playing field for their daily mile whenever it best suits that day's timetable. Only ice or very heavy rain results in a cancellation.

Not only are none of the children at the school overweight, despite the rise in childhood obesity across the United Kingdom, but their overall fitness, behaviour and concentration have also shown marked improvements. The children are also reported to be happy and productive in class.

The success of this scheme is so impressive that 500 other primary schools across the United Kingdom have adopted the *daily mile*. The interest that this scheme has generated has prompted Stirling University to set up a study to collect evidence of the daily mile's overall benefits to the children's physical, cognitive and emotional health.

> Two cities, Leeds and Amsterdam, have already seen a reduction in childhood obesity after implementing a programme for parents to refuse their children sugar and processed food. The Leeds study, supervised by Susan Jebb, a professor at Oxford University, reports that the biggest improvement may be observed among the most deprived children, particularly among the four-year-olds.[55]

Is clean eating a dangerous fad?

The pressures of social media, and, in particular, the *selfie*, have given rise to a growing obsession among teenagers with diets. *Clean eating* is a recent fad that has been linked to eating disorders, most particularly a fixation with strict rules about eating, which is becoming known as *orthorexia nervosa*. This is an eating disorder closely connected with *anorexia nervosa*, the mental illness with the highest mortality rate, and often starts as a desire to eat healthily and then becomes an obsession.

Cases of orthorexia are continuing to rise. The surge in *healthy food* bloggers, making links between weight loss and a desirable lifestyle, seems to have fuelled an obsession about dietary restrictions and limited food intake. This trend is not helped by the modern emphasis on self-publicity and lifestyle showcasing, with people comparing themselves unfavourably to the images that are promoted online.

But obsessive and restrictive eating habits lower energy and concentration levels, raise anxiety, and lead to an overall decline in physical health. A more beneficial approach is to eat with the right balance of nutrients, which enables us to live life to the full.

The 2016 documentary *Embrace* details the story of Taryn Brumfitt, who charts her own journey of self-discovery. Ms Brumfitt highlights the debilitating effects of poor body image. She explains why it is more important than ever to prioritise health over perceived beauty, and to be more accepting and appreciative of the body we have been given.

Life expectancy is falling

For the last few years, life expectancy has fallen steadily in the US[56] and UK[57] with growth slowing across Europe.[58] Health statistics point to drug addiction, liver disease, rising suicide rates and widening inequalities as major contributing factors. Other factors include alcohol abuse, poor diet, obesity, smoking and lack of exercise.

And even if we get to old age, we can expect to suffer a longer period in poor health.

The UK has started measuring the 'national rate of wellbeing' and is working towards a goal of increasing the lifespan by another five healthy years.[59, 60] New Zealand's government has structured its budget around 'wellbeing' priorities. Much of the business world is also moving towards more holistic goals that encompass organisational health.

Considerable investment is being made to boost global longevity, and 2018 saw a record high of funding in medicines to treat ageing and age-related diseases. But as we wait for medical and technological advances to come up with the answers, there are some lifestyle choices that we can all make regarding what we eat, how often we move and how much we sleep.

Are we drinking our way to death?

Much has been made over the years about the dangers of alcohol. Guidelines are published and updated regularly to encourage us to regulate our alcohol intake, and yet researchers have still not settled on one definitive rule. There are numerous studies that link moderate alcohol consumption with decreased risk of heart failure or stroke, and some studies even suggest that alcohol increases creativity.

There is no doubt that in many countries in the world, alcohol plays a strong role as a social lubricant. And we are all different, which means that the effects of alcohol depend on a number of individual factors, such as age, metabolism and genetics. Men and women are also affected differently, and the 'safe' limits vary around the world. The United Kingdom has recently suggested no more than 14 units a week (six pints of beer) to be consumed over several days.

A World Health Organization fact sheet (updated in 2018) states that alcohol is a causal factor in over 200 disease and injury conditions, causing over three million deaths worldwide per year, equating to 5.1% of all deaths. Alcohol consumption is now also linked to tuberculosis, pneumonia and more than seven types of cancer.

Alcohol currently sits alongside asbestos as a class 1 carcinogen. When our body breaks down alcohol it produces a chemical called acetaldehyde, which is strongly linked to cancer. Liver disease is another consequence of chronic alcohol consumption.

Interestingly, some people who drink in moderation exhibit lower cardiovascular risk than others who do not drink at all. This is probably due to the fact that moderate alcohol consumption, accompanied by regular exercise, sufficient sleep and a balanced diet, has a more beneficial effect than a sedentary lifestyle with no alcohol.

But this does not mean that exercise will nullify the effects of alcohol completely. While exercise may compensate for some of the damage associated with excessive alcohol consumption, a more worthy objective should be to maintain a healthy lifestyle overall.

The secret to a long and healthy life

Ikaria is a Greek island situated in the Aegean Sea, where the population of around 10,000 boasts a life expectancy about 10 years longer than Europe and the US. The inhabitants suffer much less illness and disease, and most remain physically active well into their 90s. Ikaria has been a source of fascination for writers and researchers striving to understand the secret to its people's longevity.

Diet seems to be a strong factor. A previous study has examined the Ikarian diet of herb tea, beans, green vegetables, potatoes, olive oil and goat's milk, and found that eating fish in particular significantly lowers the risk of depression among the elderly.[61] Cognitive agility is high because refined sugar and processed food are not readily available the brain does get not tired trying to resist it!

Sleeping in the afternoon is also customary on Ikaria.

A study across Greece has shown that regular afternoon naps reduce the risk of heart disease by almost 40%.[62]

But the secret to longevity is not to be found in one or two practices, but in an entire lifestyle that rests on a strong support system of relationships and a powerful sense of communal purpose. 40% of Ikarians are unemployed, and nearly everyone grows their own food and produces their own wine. Older generations are celebrated and integrated into family households where they can pass down traditions and customs. Food is shared, and crime is low, and exercise is taken by walking or gardening. Importantly, people do not wake up to alarms or rush to meet deadlines - in fact, there are few clocks on the island – but instead spend time appreciating their environment and the companionship of others.

Ikaria is not the only place to reap the benefits of a simple but meaningful lifestyle. According to explorer and National Geographic Fellow and journalist, Dan Buettner, Ikaria is one of the world's *Blue Zones* (a term introduced by Dr. Michel Poulain, an expert on longevity) – or geographic areas of the highest life expectancy and the highest number of centenarians.[63] Other **Blue Zones** have been identified in Okinawa, Sardinia and Costa Rica.

These Blue Zones share the same formula for life: a strong sense of community and a purpose for life that suffuses the way everyone lives.

In Okinawa, people live by *ikigai* — 'the reason for being'; in Costa Rica, it is known as *plan de vida* – 'the plan for life'.

For most of us who are caught up in the stresses and strains of modern life, it may be difficult to focus on an overall reason for being. The best approach is to identify what we love doing, what we are good at, what the world needs and what people will pay for.

As Dan Buettner says:

'A long healthy life is no accident. It begins with good genes, but it all depends on good habits.'

Our *ikigai* may be found at the intersection where all these converge.

Top Tips
Remember: HABIT

Heal yourself through sleep. Pay attention to your sleep habits and compensate for lack of sleep as soon as possible. Sleep deficiency builds up like an overdraft in the bank – and we need to pay it back! Avoid caffeine after 1pm and keep evening meals light. Remove technology from the bedroom and turn off all screens an hour before going to bed.

Avoid junk food and limit your intake of sugary and processed food that has little nutritional value. Instead, nourish your body with foods that are rich in protein, essential fats, vitamins and minerals. In stressful situations, increase your intake of magnesium and vitamin B12, which reduce anxiety and panic attacks.

Boost your heart rate on a regular basis. Standard recommendations advise half an hour of moderate physical activity most days of the week. Any exercise that increases our heart rate is beneficial, including household jobs or gardening. An oxygenated brain functions well.

Identify the stressors in your life. Stress is not good for us and can lead to lack of sleep and to eating the wrong foods. Find ways to develop healthy strategies to help deal with the pressures of life.

Think about your mood and state of mind. Make sure that you are developing strategies to create the right balance between motivation and relaxation. A balanced and nutritional diet will help promote greater calm and wellbeing. Focus on the positive aspects of your life and find your personal *ikagi*.

References for Chapter 12

1. Walker, M. (2017). *Why We Sleep*. New York: Penguin Random House.
2. Walker, M.P. et al. (2007). 'The human emotional brain without sleep – a prefrontal amygdala disconnect', *Current Biology*, October, 877–78.
3. Nedergaard, M. et al. (2012). 'A paravascular pathway facilitates CSF flow through the brain parenchyma and the clearance of interstitial solutes, including amyloid', *Science Translational Medicine*, August. doi.org/10.1126/scitranslmed.3003748
4. Gillette, M.U., & Tischkau, S.A. (1999). 'Suprachiasmatic nucleus: The brain's circadian clock', *Recent Progress in Hormone Research*, 33–58.
5. Stothard, E.R. et al. (2017). 'Circadian entrainment to the natural light–dark cycle across seasons and the weekend', *Current Biology*, February, 508–13.
6. Vitello et al. (2015). 'National Sleep Foundation's sleep quality recommendations', *Sleep Health: Journal of the National Sleep Foundation*, February, 6–19.
7. Naiman, R. (2017). 'Dreamless: The silent epidemic of REM sleep loss', *Annals of the New York Academy of Sciences*, August. https://doi.org/10.1111/nyas.13447
8. Ruby, P. et al. (2014). 'Resting brain activity varies with dream recall frequency between subjects', *Neuropsychopharmacology*, June, 1594–1602.
9. Tomporowski, P.D. (2003). 'Effects of acute bouts of exercise on cognition', *Acta Psychologica*, March, 297–324.
10. Samani, A., & Heath, M. (2018). 'Executive-related oculomotor control is improved following a 10-min single-bout of aerobic exercise: Evidence from the antisaccade task', *Neuropsychologia*, January, 73-81. https://doi.org/10.1016/j.neuropsychologia.2017.11.029
11. Dauwan et al. (2016). 'Exercise improves clinical symptoms, quality of life, global functioning, and depression in schizophrenia: A systematic review and meta-analysis', *Schizophrenia Bulletin*, May, 588–99.
12. Ten Brinke, L.S. et al. (2015). 'Aerobic exercise increases hippocampal volume in older women with probable mild cognitive impairment: A 6-month randomised controlled trial', *British Journal of Sports Medicine*, February, 248–54.
13. Molteni, R. et al. (2004). 'Voluntary exercise increases axonal regeneration from sensory neurons', *Proceedings of the National Academy of Sciences*, June, 8473–78.
14. McGinnis, S. (2016). 'Regular exercise changes the brain to improve memory, thinking skills', *Harvard Health Letter*, 29 November. health.harvard.edu
15. Colcombe, S.J. et al. (2006). 'Aerobic exercise training increases brain volume in aging humans' *The Journals of Gerontology*, November, 1166–70. https://doi.org/10.1093/gerona/61.11.1166
16. Bjørnebekk, A. et al. (2005). 'The antidepressant effect of running is associated with increased hippocampal cell proliferation', *International Journal of Neuropsychopharmacology*, September, 357–68.
17. Craft, L.L., & Perna, F.M. (2004). 'The benefits of exercise for the clinically depressed', *Journal of Clinical Psychiatry*, June, 104–11.
18. Hadzi-Pavlovic et al. (2006). 'Omega-3 fatty acids and mood disorders', *American Journal of Psychiatry*, June, 969–78.
19. Fontana, L. et al. (2010). 'Extending healthy life span–from yeast to humans', *Science*, April, 321–6. https://doi:10.1126/science.1172539

20. Zhu, Y. (2013). 'Metabolic regulation of Sirtuins upon fasting and the implication for cancer', *Current Opinion in Oncology*, November, 630–36. doi:10.1097/01.cco.0000432527.49984.a3

21. Arnason, T.A. et al. (2017). 'Effects of intermittent fasting on health markers in those with type 2 diabetes: A pilot study', *World Journal of Diabetes*, April, 154–64.

22. Ho, K.Y. et al. (1998). 'Fasting enhances growth hormone secretion and amplifies the complex rhythms of growth hormone secretion in man', *The Journal of Clinical Investigation*, April, 968–975. doi:10.1172/JCI113450

23. Alirezaei, M. et al. (2010). 'Short-term fasting induces profound neuronal autophagy', *Autophagy*, August, 702–10. doi:10.4161/auto.6.6.12376

24. Rajaie, S. et al. (2013). 'Comparative effects of carbohydrate versus fat restriction on serum levels of adipocytokines, markers of inflammation, and endothelial function among women with the metabolic syndrome: A randomized cross-over clinical trial', *Annals of Nutrition and Metabolism*, September, 159–67. doi:10.1159/000354868

25. Faris, M.A. et al. (2012). 'Intermittent fasting during Ramadan attenuates proinflammatory cytokines and immune cells in healthy subjects', *Nutrition Research*, December, 947–55. doi: 10.1016/j.nutres.2012.06.021

26. Lee, J. et al. (2000). 'Dietary restriction increases the number of newly generated neural cells, and induces BDNF expression, in the dentate gyrus of rats', *Journal of Molecular Neuroscience*, October, 990108. doi:10.1385/JMN:15:2:99

27. Sutton, E.F. et al. (2018). 'Early time-restricted feeding improves insulin sensitivity, blood pressure, and oxidative stress even without weight loss in men with prediabetes', *Cell Metabolism*, June, 1212–21. https://doi.org/10.1016/j.cmet.2018.04.010

28. de Cabo, R., & Mattson, M.P. (2019). 'Effects of intermittent fasting on health, aging, and disease', *New England Journal of Medicine*, December, 2541–51. https://doi:10.1056/NEJMra1905136

29. Marquié, T. et al. (2015). 'Chronic effects of shift work on cognition: Findings from the VISAT longitudinal study', *Journal of Occupational and Environmental Medicine*, March, 258–64.

30. Whitehurst, L.N. (2015). 'Autonomic activity during sleep predicts memory consolidation in humans', *Proceedings of the National Academy of Sciences*, June, 7272–77.

31. Kallistratos, M. (2015). 'Midday naps associated with reduced blood pressure and fewer medications', presented at the *European Society of Cardiology*, 29 August.

32. Rosenberg, J. et al. (2014). '"Early to bed, early to rise": Diffusion tensor imaging identifies chronotype-specificity', *NeuroImage*, January, 428–34.

33. Giampietro, M., & Cavallera, G.M. (2007). 'Morning and evening types and creative thinking', *Science Direct Personality and Individual Differences*, February, 453–63.

34. Roberts, R.D., & Kyllonan, P.C. (1999). 'Morningness–eveningness and intelligence: Early to bed, early to rise will likely make you anything but wise', *Personality and Individual Differences*, December, 1123–33.

35. Colberg, S.R. et al. (2010). 'Exercise and type 2 diabetes: American College of Sports Medicine and the American Diabetes Association: Joint position statement. Exercise and type-2 diabetes', *Medicine and Science in Sports and Exercise*, December, 2282–303.

36. Katzmarzyk, P.T. et al. (2009). 'Sitting time and mortality from all causes, cardiovascular disease, and cancer', *Medicine and Science in Sports and Exercise*, May, 998–1005.

37. Brown, W.J. et al. (2005). 'Identifying the energy gap: Magnitude and determinants of 5-year weight gain in middle age women', *Obesity Research*, August, 1431–41.

38. DeBoer, M. (2015). 'Children who watch just one hour of television a day are 50 to 60% more likely to be overweight and 58 to 73% more likely to be obese, compared to children who watch less than an hour', *Pediatric Academic*.

39. Levine, J.A. et al. (2006). 'Non-exercise activity thermogenesis: The crouching tiger hidden dragon of societal weight gain', *Arteriosclerosis, Thrombosis, and Vascular Biology*, April, 729–36.

40. Labonté-LeMoyne, E. et al. (2015). 'The delayed effect of treadmill desk usage on recall and attention', *Computers in Human Behavior*, May, 1–5.

41. Epstein, D.H., & Shaham, Y. (2010). 'Cheesecake-eating rats and the question of food addiction', *Nature Neuroscience*, May, 529–31.

42. Khan, N.A. et al. (2015). 'Central adiposity is negatively associated with hippocampal-dependent relational memory among overweight and obese children', *Journal of Pediatrics*, February, 302–08.

43. Beilharz, J.E. et al. (2015). 'Diet-induced cognitive deficits: The role of fat and sugar, potential mechanisms and nutritional interventions', *Nutrients*, August, 6719–38.

44. Davidson, T.L. et al. (2014). 'An application of Pavlovian principles to the problems of obesity and cognitive decline', *Neurobiology of Learning and Memory*, February, 172–84.

45. Kloosterhuis, N.J. et al. (2019). 'A proinflammatory gut microbiota increases systemic inflammation and accelerates atherosclerosis', *Circulation Research*, October, 94–100. https://doi.org/10.1161/CIRCRESAHA.118.313234

46. Mulugeta, A. et al. (2018). ' Obesity and depressive symptoms in mid-life: A population-based cohort study', *BMC Psychiatry*, September. https://doi.org/10.1186/s12888-018-1877-6.

47. Braniste, V. et al. (2014). 'The gut microbiota influences blood-brain barrier permeability in mice', *Science Translational Medicine*, November. https://doi:10.1126/scitranslmed.3009759.

48. Palmer, C. et al. (2007). 'Development of the human infant intestinal microbiota', *PLoS Biology* 2007;5:e177.

49. Valles-Colomer, M. et al. (2019). 'The neuroactive potential of the human gut microbiota in quality of life and depression', *Nature Microbiology*, February, 623. https://doi.org/10.1038/s41564-018-0337-x

50. Tillisch, K. et al. (2013). 'Consumption of fermented milk product with probiotic modulates brain activity', *Gastroenterology*, June, 1394–1401. https://doi.org/10.1053/j.gastro.2013.02.043

51. Anderson, S.C., Cryan, J.F., & Dinan, T. (2017). The Psychobiotic Revolution. *National Geographic*.

52. Enders, G. (2017). *Gut. The Inside Story of our Body's Most Under-Rated Organ*, London: Scribe Publications.

53. Holzman, D.C. (2015). 'Evening use of light-emitting eReaders negatively affects sleep, circadian timing, and next-morning alertness', *Proceedings for National American Studies*, January, 1232–37.

54. AlDabal, L., & BaHammam, A.S. (2011). 'Metabolic, endocrine, and immune consequences of sleep deprivation', *Open Respiratory Medicine Journal*, June, 31–43.

55. Rudolf, M. et al, (2019). 'Observational analysis of disparities in obesity in children in the UK: Has Leeds bucked the trend?' *Pediatric Obesity*, April. https://doi.org/10.1111/ijpo.12529

56. CDC/National Center for Health Statistics/Division of Analysis and Epidemiology.

57. 'Longer term influences driving lower life expectancy projections', *Institute and Faculty of Actuaries*, 7 March 2019.

58. 'Trends in life expectancy in EU and other OECD countries', *OECD Health Working Papers*, ISSN: 18152015 (online). https://doi.org/10.1787/18152015

59. https://www.ons.gov.uk/peoplepopulationandcommunity/wellbeing

60. Marteau, T.M. et al. (2019). 'Increasing healthy life expectancy equitably in England by 5 years by 2035: Could it be achieved?' *The Lancet*, June, 2571–73. https://doi.org/10.1016/S0140-6736(19)31510-7

61. Chrysohoou, C. et al. (2011). 'Fish consumption moderates depressive symptomatology in elderly men and women from the IKARIA study', *Cardiology Research and Practice*. https://doi.org/10.4061/2011/219578

62. Naska, A. et al. (2007). 'Siesta in healthy adults and coronary mortality in the general population', *Archives of Internal Medicine*, 296–301. doi:10.1001/archinte.167.3.296

63. Buettner, D. (2012). *The Blue Zones, Second Edition: 9 Lessons for Living Longer From the People Who've Lived the Longest*. Washington: The National Geographic Society.

"Joy does not simply happen to us. We have to choose joy and keep choosing it every day."

HENRI NOUWEN
Priest, professor, writer and theologian (1932–96)

And Finally . . .

The intention of this book is to provide an overview of just some of the work in neuroscience that has been carried out to date. I hope that it will spark an interest in how your brain works in order to help you get the best out of it – and the best out of others' brain around you – during your lifetime.

A great deal of emphasis has been placed on the importance of exercise in boosting memory and wellbeing. Our brain needs us to stay physically as well as cognitively active. We also need to work hard at keeping our brain open: open to other people, open to learning, open to new ideas. Conscious and concerted effort to remain positive will help us reduce the natural dominance of our negativity bias. And changing just a few habits may make a huge difference to how we feel and behave with the people around us.

We are all, to a greater or lesser extent, the authors of our own life's story. We continually make choices about how we live and act – what we eat, how we behave, where we spend our energy and whom we select to be part of our social network. We have the ability to make other people feel important and significant, and every day we choose how to respond to whatever challenges life throws at us.

These choices contribute to the world that we construct around us.

Our brain is a wonderful, changing, mysterious instrument that needs constant care and attention. The thoughts we have, the words we speak and the decisions we make all have an effect on our neural architecture.

We need to respect our brain's power as well as its limitations, and nurture it with healthy habits, good food, sufficient sleep, regular exercise, supportive and positive friends and, above all, with genuine laughter and joy.

As Dr David Eagleman says:

'The human brain is the most wondrous thing we have discovered in the universe. And it's us.'

A Note on Neurocomms

By Suzanne Ellis, Director

As a Director of leadership, change and employee engagement communications, it's my job to help organisations influence their customers', employees' and stakeholders' perceptions and behaviours. So, it's incumbent to be at the forefront of the latest tools and insights that make sure messages get heard, and acted upon, by the right people.

By applying neuroscience to communications, to what we are calling 'neurocomms', you can make sure that your message is persuasive and emotionally arousing enough for people to want to tune into – above the infinite sea of noise.

Together with Dr Helena Boschi, 'neurocomms' add another dimension to the work we offer at Lansons, looking at the science behind our own biology to affect real change and make a difference in influencing people and managing reputations.

We hope you enjoy learning more about the science behind Why We Do What We Do.

Index

Page numbers followed by *f* indicate figures.

brain injury effects 96
brain plasticity 208
brain shortcuts, vision 130
brain structures
    creativity 173
    memory types 56f
brainstorming 184–85
braking system, stress responses
        232–33, 232f
Bratton, Bill 212
BRAVING elements, trust 254
breaks from work 265, 270, 299
'Brexit' 43
Brignall, Harry 162
bring your own device (BYOD) initia-
        tive 212–13
Broca, Paul 25, 94
Broca's aphasia 96f
Broca's area 94
broken window theory 212
Brown, Brené 253–54
Brown, Roger 59
Brumfitt, Taryn 301
Buckingham, Marcus 109
Buettner, Dan 303
'but', use of word 106–07
Buy One Get One Free (BOGOF)
        offers 115
BYOD (bring your own device) initia-
        tive 212–13

Campbell, Joseph, *The Hero with a
        Thousand Faces* 117–18
cancer causes 302
Cannon-Bard theory 28f
Carr, Nicholas, *The Shallows* 61
Carrier, Willis 178

central nervous system (CNS)
        10–11, 11f
cerebrum 5–6
certainty, need for 257f
Chabris, Christopher 81
change 197–218
    challenges of 206
    facts and 213–14
    impact of 204–11
    necessity of 211–12
    pain of 197–99, 198f
    responses to 198–99
    rewiring brain 208–09
    science of 197–204
change blindness 82, 82f
chemicals of leadership 247–48
chequerboard illusion 133, 134f
child-like thinking 180f
children
    biases 161
    creativity 185–86
choice 150, 157–58
choice overload 158
choice paralysis 158
cholesterol medication 43–44
choline 288f
chronic insomnia 282
chronic stress 230
chronotype 286, 292
chunked words 53–54
Cialdini, Robert 210, 211f
circadian rhythms 69, 279–80, 280f
clarity in feedback 111–12
clean eating 300–301
Cleese, John 180
CNS *see* central nervous system
coaching 253

dementia 68–69, 228, 279, 285, 295
depression 283, 286, 296, 298
DHA (docosahexaenoic acid) 287
Diagnostic and Statistical Manual of
    Mental Disorders (DSM IV) 34
diffusion tensor imaging (DTI) 15
digital age 139
digital amnesia 61
disease–stress link 229–30
distal imagination 183–84
distraction 84, 86, 89, 90
divergent thinking 181–83, 183*f*,
    185–86, 188
diverse influences, bias 166
DLPFC (dorsolateral prefrontal
    cortex) 174
docosahexaenoic acid (DHA) 287
Dodson, John Dillingham
    231, 231*f*
'don't', use of word 107
dopamine 9*f*, 83–84, 208, 248, 288*f*
dorsal stream 124
dorsolateral prefrontal cortex
    (DLPFC) 174
Dr Seuss, *Green Eggs and Ham* 190–91
dreams 278, 284
Drew, Trafton 80–81
driver distraction 86
DSM IV (Diagnostic and Statistical
    Manual of Mental Disorders) 34
DTI (diffusion tensor imaging) 15
Dugmore, Dorian 237–38
Dweck, Carol 210, 251
Dyson, James 182
dysphasia 96

Eagleman, David 64, 151, 311
EAST framework 160

eating disorders 136, 300
Ebbinghaus's Forgetting Curve
    62–63, 62–63*f*
Ecker, Ullrich 116
Edison, Thomas 178
education and creativity 185
EEG (electroencephalography) 201, 293
EFAs (essential fatty acids) 287
eicosapentaenoic acid (EPA) 287
Einstein, Albert 19
Ekman, Paul 31
electroencephalography (EEG) 201, 293
email language 101–02
emotion 25–47
    braking system 232–33
    change leadership 204
    creativity relationship 174
    dark side of 42–43
    decision-making influence
        36–38
    identifying 32–34
    impact of 36–41
    language 113
    manipulating 41, 116–17
    positive emotions 44
    purposes of 26–28
    reading 29–32
    science of 25–35
    stress signs 228*f*, 240
    theories of 28*f*
emotional intelligence (EQ/EI)
    40–41, 40*f*, 247
emotional memories 38–39, 53*f*, 58–59
empathy 29, 30, 33, 44, 262
employee mobility 213
encoding information 51, 51*f*, 64
endorphins 29, 210, 286
entity theory of personality 251

myelin 11, 13
myelin sheath 13, 287
myelination 13, 18
MyKey system 18

names, importance of 103
nature/nurture debate 14, 16, 20, 21
negative feedback loop 4, 4f, 268
negative framing 159
negative language 105–07, 109–10, 119
negativity bias 151–52, 204
Neisser, Ulric 59
nervous system 8–9, 10, 10f, 226
'neurocomms' 313
neurogenesis 71
neurons 5, 7–8, 8f, 29–30, 126
neuroscience 245–47, 313
neurotransmitters 7, 8f, 9f
    balance of 21
    as chemicals of emotion 8
    food 287, 288f
    sleep 276–77
'new', use of word 104
New York subway 212
Newson, Martha 238
Newton's First Law of Motion 200, 202
Newton's Third Law of Motion 205
'no', use of word 105–06
nocebo effect 105, 110, 202
non-declarative memory
    54–55, 55f, 159
non-REM sleep 277, 278f
noradrenaline 9f, 239, 248, 288f
norepinephrine 239
nouns, response to 99
novelty bias 164
novelty/familiarity balance 104
nucleus accumbens 83–84

nudge theory 159–61, 162–63
nurture/nature debate 14, 16, 20, 21
nutrition 286–87, 294–98, 304
    see also food

obesity 294–95, 300
occipital lobe 96, 98, 124, 129
olfactory bulb 52
olfactory cortex 103
omega-3 287
onset insomnia 282
opt-in initiatives 160
opt-out initiatives 160
optimal inattention 180f
optimism bias 148
orbital frontal cortex 198, 257f
organisational change 204, 209,
    213, 214–15
originality study 173–74
Ornish, Dean 214
orthorexia nervosa 300
out-group bias 150–51, 161, 261
outcome-focused bias 164–65
overconfidence bias 147, 148–49
'owls' 292
oxytocin 9f, 34, 117, 248

pain perception 35
pain receptors 29, 256–57, 256f
pain treatment 44, 202–03, 257
Palmer, John 66
paracetamol 44
parallel thinking 189
parasympathetic nervous system
    12–13, 13f, 226, 226f
pareidolia 128
parietal lobe 19, 96, 172, 285
patterns, search for 132

shapes, words as 100–101
shift work 291
Shige, Yukio 238–39
short-term memory (STM) 53–54, 54f
sight and creativity 178
sign language 98
Silver, Spencer 175
similarity-attraction effect (SAE) 134
Simons, Daniel 81
sitting effects 293
Six Thinking Hats tool 189, 190f
sleep
    alpha waves importance 282
    as cleaning system 278–79
    constraint removal 190
    creativity and 190, 192
    exercise benefits 286
    habits 304
    hunger and 283, 283f
    'larks/owls' 292
    longevity and 302
    mechanisms of 276–77
    memory effects 60f, 63, 69, 71
    recommended amounts 281, 281f
    role of 275–76, 290
    stages of 277–78
sleep apnoea 283
sleep deficiency 291
sleep disorders 298–99
sleep phase delay 281
sleep spindles 277
sleeping pods 299
sleepwalking 277
smell 52, 53f, 178, 180
smiling 255–56
smoking 60f, 278
Snow, Shane 181
social media 139

social networks 206–07
social pain 256–57, 256f
social proof principle 211f
sociopaths 34
somatic nervous system 12
sound and creativity 178
Southwest Airlines 215
specificity in feedback 110–11
Spencer, Percy 175
Sperry, Roger 6
spinal cord 11
splenium 19
standing desks 293
status 257f, 267
Still-Face Experiment 32
STM see short-term memory
storytelling 117–18, 119
stress 221–42
    benefits 231–32
    causes 227
    definition 221–22
    effects of 223, 228–29, 230–35
    measuring 229
    memory effects 60f
    nutrition 294, 304
    origin in brain 224–27
    science of 221–30
    warning signs 228f
stress hormones 227f
stress pathways 225f
stressors 222
stroke patients 101
sugar 294–95
suggestibility 65f
suicide rates 238–39
sunk-cost fallacy 146
suprachiasmatic nucleus (SCN)
        279–80, 279f

sympathetic nervous system 12–13, 13*f*
sympathetic-adrenal-medullary (SAM) system 224, 225*f*
synaesthesia 108, 178
synapses 5
synaptic cleft 7
synaptic pruning 17–18, 173
System 1 thinking 37, 37*f*, 39, 45, 79
System 2 thinking 37, 37*f*, 41, 45
systemising brain type 33

taste 178
tau protein 68
team performance 152
technology
   attention effects 86–87
   memory effects 61–62
teenagers 281, 298–99
   see also adolescence
temperature and productivity 259
temporal lobe 67, 172, 247, 247*f*
temporo-parietal junction 284
testosterone 33–34, 248
thalamus 26, 27*f*, 77
Thaler, Richard 147
Theory X 260–61, 266
Theory Y 260
threats, response to 198, 230
Threshold Theory 179
time problems 264–65, 270
'together', use of word 105
top-down processing 76, 76*f*, 125–26, 125*f*
touch 178
Toyota Production System 264
transience 65*f*
transient global amnesia 58
treadmill desks 293

Tronick, Edward 32
Trump, Donald 113–14, 137, 163
trust/trustworthiness 134, 253–55
truth, subjectivity 135
tryptophan 288*f*
Twitter development 183
tyrosine 288*f*

uncertainty 197
unconscious bias 157, 163
Unilever solutions 182
United Kingdom, 'Brexit' 43
UnitedHealth Group 266

vagus nerve 296
Vanessa-Mae documentary 20
Velcro invention 175
ventral stream 124
verbs, response to 99
vesicles 7
visual cortex 124, 126
visual gaps, brain filling in 131–32
visual illusions 132–33, 140
visual imagery mnemonics 57
visual memory 50*f*, 51*f*, 52, 54
visual pathways 125*f*
visual perception 123–41
   complexity 126
   impact of 131–36
   preventing new thinking 134–35
   protection from 133–34
   science of 123–31
   words 98–99
visual–spatial memory 54
visual word form area (VWFA) 99, 100
vocalisation 45
Vohs, Kathleen 147
Von Restorff effect 57